D0876293

EQUAL
PARTNERS

EQUAL PARTNERS

Improving Gender
Equality at Home

KATE MANGINO

ST. MARTIN'S PRESS
NEW YORK

First published in the United States by St. Martin's Press, an imprint of St. Martin's Publishing Group.

www.stmartins.com

Designed by Nicola Ferguson

Library of Congress Cataloging-in-Publication Data

Names: Mangino, Kate, author.
Title: Equal partners : improving gender equality at home /
    Kate Mangino.
Description: First edition. | New York : St. Martin's Press, [2022] |
    Includes bibliographical references and index.
Identifiers: LCCN 2022002317 | ISBN 9781250276117 (hardcover) |
    ISBN 9781250276124 (ebook)
Subjects: LCSH: Sexism. | Sex role. | Sexual division of labor. | Equality. |
    Couples. | Homemakers. | Households.
Classification: LCC HQ1237 .M26 2022 | DDC 305.3—dc23/eng/
    20220310
LC record available at https://lccn.loc.gov/2022002317

First Edition: 2022

10   9   8   7   6   5   4   3   2   1

To Mom, Dad, and Dan

CONTENTS

INTRODUCTION

We are having more honest conversations about gender norms and roles than ever before. Topics once sequestered in university gender studies departments have made their way into the mainstream media, and the specific issue of household gender imbalance has become a topic of daily conversation.

We have reached this pivotal point for two reasons: the relentless work of researchers, writers, policy makers, and activists who were talking about household gender norms long before it was trendy; and the coronavirus pandemic. Of course, our household gender divide existed well before March 2020. But the COVID-19 pandemic exacerbated domestic disparity to the level of a national emergency.

It is no secret that women, particularly women of color, felt the pandemic's impact more than men. Nearly 1.8 million women left their jobs during the pandemic in order to care for family members.[1] Working moms and single parents who managed to maintain their jobs suffocated under the increased responsibilities of work, household management, and caregiving.[2] Because women had to cut back on hours, were laid off, didn't apply for that new job, were furloughed, and/or passed over for promotion during the pandemic, they will likely continue to earn less for decades to come. Assuming she can reenter the workforce in 2022, it is estimated that a woman who earned the median income of $47,299 before the pandemic will lose an accumulated $250,000 of potential earnings throughout her working life.[3]

We can no longer pretend these gender problems don't exist. We can't hide them in the closet and hope no one notices. It is too late for that. Our dirty laundry has been exposed for everyone to see.

Despite our understanding of feminist theory and the restrictions of traditional masculinity, household inequality persists. It is now commonly acknowledged that, on average, women do far more in the household than men, and this "second shift" has negative impacts on women's careers and emotional health.[4] Although less commonly recognized, there is a growing public understanding that traditional gender norms can also be detrimental to the emotional health of men and boys.

However, these conversations typically end here, leading one to wonder: What now? Having defined the problem, how are we going to solve it?

Much of our household gender inequality problems are structural, so we turn to experts to make the policy changes we all long to see: paid parental leave, mandatory sick leave, and subsidized childcare. But our household gender inequality issues are not only structural—these issues are also social. I wrote this book to remind us that cultural norms and traditions are just as influential to our gender behavior as law and policy.[5] While we work to bring about structural change that benefits all Americans, what can we do on a personal level to work toward gender equality in our homes and communities?

I didn't want to just *write* about our gender problem; I wanted to *do* something about our gender problem. I wrote this book because

I believe other people feel the same way. I am grateful to everyone who has helped diagnose this problem and bring the issue into the mainstream. I want to move the discussion forward by focusing on practical solutions.

This book is filled with ideas, stories, interviews, and suggestions about what you can do to address household gender inequality with your partner, your kids, your grandkids, your friends, and your community. My hope is that every reader can find a handful of actionable ideas that feel doable. Ideas that might make you think, *That makes sense. I can give that a try.* I believe that if we all make a few small changes here and there, relationship by relationship, we can move the needle on household inequality.

Skeptical? Sure, I'm a skeptic, too. A little skepticism is healthy. But the information in this book is evidence based. I have worked in gender equality and social change for more than twenty years, and this book's methodology comes from decades of best practices. To better explain what social change looks like, let me tell you a story from my work in Indonesia.

Several years ago, I partnered with a local women's empowerment organization in East Java to see if we could engage the husbands of the female members to boost family support for the program. As part of this process, I found myself facilitating a meeting of twenty men, all of whom were married to a member of the local women's empowerment group.

The meeting took place in the town hall of a small village. We arranged plastic chairs in a circle and took our places. All the men wore their best clothes: freshly ironed khaki pants and batik shirts in a range of bright colors. It was hot and humid. Everyone used scraps of cardboard to fan away the sweat and the flies. I could sense that the men had come reluctantly. Although they were all respectful and kind to me, none of them appeared particularly interested in "women's issues." There was a lot of smoking and side conversations. But to be honest, I was grateful that anyone even bothered to show up.

I was desperate to get the conversation started. I needed genuine participation or else the day would be a failure. So, after introductions, I asked everyone, "Please give me an example of how your family has benefited from your wife's involvement with the empowerment group." There was awkward silence at first. Most men looked down at their feet; many lit another cigarette. It was painful to sit in silence, but I waited, keeping a hopeful smile on my face. Finally, thankfully, after what felt like ages, someone spoke up.

The man appeared unenthusiastic, but slowly he began to tell his story about how, before the empowerment group, annual school fees were a problem for his family. He was a farmer who did not own his own land. After paying his monthly expenses, there wasn't much left over. He never managed to save all the money needed for annual school fees. So, each year, the family had to take out a small loan to pay for school. Education was important. Neither he nor his wife attended school past sixth grade, and he promised himself that both his boys would graduate from high school.

But the interest rate was high and took months to repay. Money he could have saved during harvest was used to repay last year's interest, so he never managed to save for the following year. This cycle of debt had continued for nearly a decade. He explained that he had always been frustrated that the school fees ended up costing two or three times as much this way, but he never found another solution. He just couldn't get ahead of those school fee payments.

He paused and seemed to gain a bit of confidence. He sat up straighter and made eye contact with me for the first time. When he continued, he explained that, in her empowerment group, his wife and some friends thought up the idea of starting a small business selling homemade snacks. The women would gather in someone's home a few days a week to slice, fry, and package sweet potatoes. They would portion them out in small bags and sell the snacks to local kiosk owners. They tasted good and sold quickly.

The money was not much at first, but it started adding up. The first week she saved 1,000 rupiah (about 70 cents US). Then it was 2,000 rupiah. Then 10,000. After several months, it had become clear that the family would have enough saved up to pay for school fees when they came due. This was life changing for this family. They would not have to get a bank loan, and they would not have to pay interest— which would save them even more money. They would be able to use their earnings from this year's crop to invest in new farming tools, or a new variety of seed. They could save some money in case of an unforeseen health emergency. All of this was because of the work of the women's empowerment group.

When the man finished, he shyly smiled, and the group murmured approval. I offered words of thanks and asked if there were other stories.

Another man chimed in and shared his story. His wife and her group wrote a proposal to the local government to fix the village road, and it was accepted. That new road meant a world of difference when the man took his crops to the city to sell. A third man added that his wife was more confident and happier, often singing in the house, which gave the home a more joyful feeling. He now looked forward to coming home from his fields and would try to get home early when he could. Eventually—one by one—every single man in our circle shared a detailed story about how he and his family benefitted from the women's empowerment program.

Although the individual stories were all powerful, the true change came from that discussion about the empowerment program. During that conversation the whole mood changed. The men were sitting forward on the edge of their chairs, eager to give their opinion and listen to others. That conversation led to a full day's work around gender norms and roles, and ended with the men making a greater commitment to their wives' work. When they left, each man came forward to shake my hand and thank me for initiating that conversation. When I returned six months later, the women couldn't wait to tell me about all the changes in their home—all borne from that first men's meeting.

I have witnessed similar results from other projects: from preventing early childhood marriage in Malawi, to household decision-making in Guatemala, to HIV prevention in Zambia. My colleagues and I have produced and shared data that proves that social change works. (We have also been part of projects that failed, and we learned some painful lessons. That data helps, too.)

If I have learned anything during my career thus far, it is that gender inequality does not only happen to other people, in other places, far away from where you live. Gender inequality happens everywhere. I have seen just as much gendered behavior in the United States and Canada as I have in Zambia or Indonesia. True, gender inequality looks different from place to place, and it changes over time. But it never goes away. This means there is probably gender inequality going on in your neighborhood, in your office, in your school, and maybe even in your home. We cannot pretend this is someone else's problem. This is our collective problem, and we all must be part of a collective solution.

I'll be honest up front—there is no magic formula and no quick fix. Real social change takes time, and this slow process involves hard work: learning, self-reflection, discussion, and plenty of uncomfortable moments. But it is possible.

A few decades ago, a trend took off—the idea was to combat gender-based violence by teaching women self-defense. These classes became popular, and I am sure many women learned a beneficial skill. But self-defense classes were a Band-Aid, not a solution to a problem. Eventually someone realized, *Oh right, women are not assaulting themselves. Maybe, to get at the source of the problem, we should focus our energy on those people perpetuating violence.*

Then came the idea that, in order to address the gender pay gap, we needed to teach women negotiation skills. Because that is what is missing, right? The problem is that women just don't have good enough negotiation skills. Once again, we set out to improve women. And again, I am sure many women learned something that was helpful to their career. But we eventually realized, *Oh right, negotiation skills don't matter if the workplace policies and hiring committees are perpetuating misogyny.*

Now we know better. We don't need to fix or improve women. To break the cycle of violence, we need to work with men and boys. To address the pay gap, we need to reinvent hiring procedures.

Taking these history lessons to heart, I will not address household gender balance with a book targeted to working women with children. Focusing the message solely on women suggests this is a women's problem, and it implies that women need to fix it. But the truth is that household imbalance can restrict people of all genders, and it can be perpetuated by people of all genders. Focusing the message solely on mothers suggests this problem exists only when children are part of the equation. But we know that household imbalance happens in many households without kids.

And let's just openly acknowledge the elephant in the room. Working parents with small kids are already functioning at maximum capacity. Balancing kids, aging parents, and a full-time job (or many jobs that piece together enough income to cover expenses) is hard, relentless work. I hear you, and I get it. The last thing any working parent needs to do is add "solve gender inequality" to their to-do list.

Our society shouldn't delegate this task to already stretched parents. Household gender inequality is a broad social problem that is passed from generation to generation, and the ramifications are harmful for everyone. Household gender inequality is not an individual's problem or even an individual family's problem. Everyone in our extended family and community has a role to play, so we must recruit everyone to initiate change.

I believe readers of *Equal Partners* fit into at least one of the following categories. I specifically tried to address these three perspectives throughout the chapters of this book.

1. Future Partners, New Partners, New Parents, and Young Parents. These are the people who will be directly impacted because they are (or will be) part of a couple trying to make parity work.

2. Parents, Grandparents, and Supports to Category 1. These are the people who will be indirectly impacted. They may not be concerned about finding equality in their own relationship, but they are very close to someone who is interested.

3. Friends, Family, and the Greater Community. Everyone interested in supporting gender equality.

I know it is a cliché, but it can't be avoided: it takes a village to support an equal partnership. The thing I heard loud and clear from everyone I interviewed for this book was that community matters. There are very few people that exist in their own nuclear bubble; most humans are part of a larger network of communities. Sometimes communities are biological, ethnic, or cultural. Sometimes we adopt communities composed of people with whom we share common values: neighbors, political groups, colleagues, faith communities, and close friends. All of these people in the greater network can be supporters of gender equality. No matter your role—whether you are part of a young family, or whether you see a young family every month—you can have an impact. Whatever your partnership status or your gender identity, you have work to do.

Families come in many shapes and sizes, and the two-person structure does not work for everyone. I am not at all advocating for a two-person, dual-earning, nuclear family. But I do acknowledge that dual-earning partnership is the most common family configuration in North America right now. Even if you don't participate in one yourself—many people around you likely do.

Have you noticed who I am excluding? No one. No one gets a pass from participating. We are all part of communities, organizations, companies, neighborhoods, and families that perpetuate gender inequality. This gives us all the opportunity to be part of a solution.

If you have gotten this far and are thinking, *I'm already a feminist. I'm progressive. I'm good. This isn't for me,* I ask you to reconsider. Those of us who took gender studies classes in college will know the theory, but it is often hard to turn theory into everyday practice. We all (and I include myself) accidentally lean back on gender stereotypes, sometimes without even realizing it. Additional self-reflection is never a bad idea. I ask that you be open to the possibility that you could do *even more* for gender equality than you already are.

This is especially important for those readers who identify as *cisgender*, heterosexual males—in other words, straight guys. Please know that I am not targeting you, and I am not trying to demonize you—not at all. I am talking directly to you because you make up a large percentage of our communities, and as a group you hold a lot of influence and power. I am asking you to be open to the fact that you may not always "see" gender inequality around you. To move forward as a culture, that needs to change.

For all readers, take a moment to consider where you are in your life. Which category do you find yourself in at this time? Jot down a few notes about the roles you currently fill in each box, so as you continue through the book, you can better recognize the stories and anecdotes relevant to your situation. Maybe you are in two groups—or even all three.

WHERE DO YOU FIT?		
Category 1 (Future Partners, New Partners, and New Parents)	Category 2 (People Directly Supporting Category 1: Parents, Grandparents, and Supports)	Category 3 (Friends, Family, and the Greater Community)

* Please note that I use the word *parent* broadly; it in not confined to a biological relationship. The word *parent* refers to anyone who is parenting: stepparents, guardians, in-laws, etc.

A NOTE ABOUT PRONOUNS

I do not believe in the gender binary, and I prefer to use language that includes all gender identities, including *male-identifying, female-identifying, nonbinary, transgender, queer,* and *gender nonconforming.*

I admit this is hard to do with the English language. Have you ever realized that there is no gender-neutral word for the child of your sibling? We have *niece,* and we have *nephew.* The same goes for the sibling of your parent; there is only *aunt* and *uncle.* There are not enough words for us to describe people that do not identify as male or female. This makes English quite frustrating when one writes about gender. It often means that being gender inclusive requires clunky writing that can detract from the content. I hope, in the future, the English language evolves to meet our needs. For now, we work with what we have.

My goal is to recognize that our cultural past has greatly impacted the way we see the world, the way we act today, and the way we continue to raise our children. I try to do this without perpetuating cis, *heteronormative* assumptions. It is important to acknowledge the past while speaking to our present.

I agree with other writers who have pulled back from using a simple male/female descriptor to talk about gender roles more broadly. Anne-Marie Slaughter uses the terms *breadwinners* and *caregivers* in her 2015 book, *Unfinished Business,* and Kate Manne speaks of *human beings* and *human givers.* When I quote research that presents results in terms of men and women, I use that language. But as much as possible, I refrain from talking about what women do and what men do, and I choose to use the terms *Female Role* and *Male Role.* I believe these terms acknowledge the tremendous influence gender has had on our domestic patterns, while avoiding the assumption that all people taking on female roles are women, or that all people taking on male roles are men. For ease of language, I often use *he* when discussing the Male Role and *she* when discussing the Female Role. But I am fully aware that a person of any gender could take on either of these behaviors.

When I use pronouns, *she/her* reflect female-identifying people, and *he/him* reflect male-identifying people. Please know I do not assume that these two pronouns collectively describe all people, nor that our adult gender identity is the same gender we are assigned at birth. Therefore, when I reference all humans, I often write *people of all genders* and not *men and women.* When I write about parents, I try to avoid *mom/dad,* and instead use *birthing parent/non-birthing parent.*

If any of these words are new to you, feel free to refer to the gender glossary at the back of this book for clarification.

INTRODUCTION

WHAT YOU CAN EXPECT

I divided this book into three sections. Part 1 begins with some background information that diagnoses our household gender problem, and then explains how social change methods can help us make a change. Part 1 also includes a deeper look at the two life events that often cause the greater gender shifts: partnership and the birth of a first child.

Part 2 is solely focused on a group I affectionately call the EP40. These forty men are, by my definition, equal partners in their households; they intentionally take on half the physical and emotional load of their household. Part 2 digs down into this group of positive deviants, using their personal stories to answer some core questions about this group of men: Where did they come from? What is their motivation? How do they do it? What advice do they have for raising the next generation of boys? This section also includes the interviews I did with the partners of the EP40.

Part 3 is the personal action piece of the book. After reading eight chapters full of stories, anecdotes, statistics, and data points—now what? Part 3 is about which specific changes you want to make in your own life.

One last note before you begin: you do not have to wait until you read part 3 to look for solutions. I never intended for readers to have to get all the way to the end of the book to start thinking about how to initiate social change. Solutions and practical tips can be found throughout all chapters of this book, and I encourage you to track the ones that resonate with you. For this reason, I have provided a notes section at the end of parts 1 and 2 for you to jot down particular statistics, stories, and anecdotes that you want to remember.

VIOLENCE AND FEAR

This book is for individuals who feel safe in their relationships and in their homes. These chapters are not for people who are currently experiencing violence, or who fear potential violence from their partner. If you have experienced domestic violence, or if you are concerned that violence is a possibility, then I strongly recommend that you put this book down and talk to a professional. Initiating intimate conversations about gender in a violent home could lead to further assault, which is to be avoided at all costs. Please remember that whatever is happening, it is not your fault, and there are many people out there who can help. I suggest you look into resources in your community that specialize in survivor support: a therapist, the YWCA, and/or a shelter that specializes in domestic and intimate partner violence. You can always contact the National Domestic Violence Hotline at 1-800-799-7233 or thehotline.org.

PART ONE

ACKNOWLEDGING INEQUALITY

1

OUR MODERN HOUSEHOLD REALITY

Melissa* and I have been friends for many years. Melissa identifies as white and lives in Maryland. Although we haven't worked for the same organization in over a decade, we manage to check in with each other several times a year. We work in the same field, and now we both have partners and kids. So, our conversations drift back and forth between work, kids, and figuring out life with work and kids. In one memorable conversation during the first wave of pandemic lockdowns, Melissa updated me on her household situation. She was working from home; her husband's job required him to physically go into work. Their older child was doing pre-K distance learning from the living room. His little brother needed constant attention. I asked how much her husband was helping on the days he was home.

"He helps a lot when he is home. I can get up and get online right away, knowing he'll do breakfast. That sort of thing is nice. But honestly, I'm still the one thinking about what we have in the fridge for lunch and dinner, if there are enough clean clothes or if I need to throw a load in. I'm the one that realized deliveries are

---

* Everyone interviewed for this book was given a pseudonym.

17

weeks delayed, so I knew to order extra Pull-Ups in time. That stuff isn't on his radar."

I asked about facilitating distance learning. Does he act as teacher on the days he is at home?

"Yes, but I always remind him when Jasper has a video meeting for school. Last week, he had a science experiment to do. And yes, [my husband] sat next to him during the video call and helped him with it. That was great. But I was the one that gathered all the supplies together and made sure they remembered to log in to the computer on time. And another thing—all the school emails go to my in-box, and I am the one who gets these updates ALL DAY. Those definitely distract me from work because I have to read them all, decide which ones are important, and be the education coordinator."

Melissa was on a roll.

"And I'm the one trying to do the fun stuff—make life enjoyable and happy. Take Jasper's birthday. I was the one who planned, in advance, to make sure he had gifts, cupcake mix, balloons, etc. I know that isn't life-and-death stuff—but still, right now especially, the kids need fun things to look forward to. That's more strain on me—it's work, keeping everyone alive and keeping things fun, making it special. All of that lands on me. It's a lot to carry."

Melissa unknowingly summarized one of the reasons why I am writing this book. Our modern reality is that yes, on average, men are doing more in the home than before. In this example, her husband was getting up to make breakfast, and he helped the kids with distance learning. He is undoubtedly doing more than his father or grandfather ever did. But Melissa is still doing a disproportionate amount of work in the home, simply because she is a woman. And she is not happy about it.

WHAT EXACTLY ARE WE TALKING ABOUT?

There have been fantastic advancements in gender equality since the baby boomers were kids. But research has shown that improvements outside the home have not translated into comparable improvements inside the home. The Pew Research Center reports that dual-income households have been on the rise for the past several decades. In 1970, only 25 percent of households earned two salaries, but by 2012 that number rose to 60 percent.[1] In 2020, the United States Census Bureau confirmed this statistic by reporting that 60 percent of married couples with kids aged eighteen or younger earn a dual income.[2]

Even though the majority of families split income responsibilities, they do not split household responsibilities. In dual-income families, women perform the vast majority of unpaid tasks required to run a home, which perpetuates a traditional sexual division of labor.[3] Academics have come to use the term *neo-traditional* to describe the most common modern household dynamic in North America. A neo-traditional home simply means both people participate in the economy, but the Female Role is the one responsible for the bulk of the household chores, household management, and caregiving.

Many researchers generalize the current dynamic as a 65/35 split. In broad terms, in different-sex relationships, 65 percent of physical household work is done by women and 35 percent is done by men.[4]

Our collective mothers and grandmothers might think this is wonderful—a huge improvement compared to the years they were raising kids. At least, they say, men are now doing *something*. But a closer look at those numbers shows how inadequate a 65/35 split can be.

In 2020, the Organisation for Economic Co-operation and Development (OECD) posted the statistic that American heterosexual women between the ages of fifteen and sixty-four did about 66 percent more housework than their male partners.[5] Let's translate this into terms familiar to us and consider a typical workweek. For every forty hours of work a man does at home, his female partner does sixty-six hours. OECD reports that Canadian women have it slightly better at sixty hours, and women in the United Kingdom do a bit more at seventy-one hours.

Imagine all the extra hours men in this study can invest in other activities. While his female partner continues to do housework for twenty, twenty-six, or thirty-one more hours—he can devote this time to hobbies, relaxation, exercise, hanging out with friends, sleep, work, and/or continued education. Essentially, he has the opportunity to do so much more with his life than she does.

Aside from the hours spent doing household tasks, we also need to consider the kind of tasks that are coded for men and for women. Academics have long divided household work into two categories: routine and intermittent.[6] Routine work must be done on a regular basis—perhaps daily or even multiple times a day. These tasks include, but are not limited to, cooking and meal preparation, washing dishes, bathing children, doing laundry, cleaning, grocery shopping, taking children to and from school, and caring for pets. If any of these tasks are skipped even once, it is noticed. Imagine how disgusting the kitchen gets after twenty-four hours of ignoring dishes, or what the kids would do if you just decided not to feed them one day. These tasks tend to be female coded, and are traditionally thought to be women's work.

Intermittent tasks, however, are those that are done once in a while. These tasks include, but are not limited to, cutting the grass, fixing the shelves in the kitchen, managing family finances, reorganizing closets, raking leaves, and changing the oil in the car. Although these tasks are important and contribute to the well-being of the household, if they are skipped once or twice—or put off for a week—it rarely has a negative impact. These tasks tend to be male coded, and are traditionally thought to be men's work.

It will not surprise you that, according to data gathered from recent chore diaries, women still tend to take primary responsibility for routine tasks, and men tend to take primary responsibility for intermittent tasks.[7]

This means that the average Female Role's unpaid to-do list is relentless. One may be able to take a night off through a combination of pizza delivery and procrastination, but in a day or two the pileup will become unbearable for the household. Routine work requires regular attention. This means the Female Role must find a way to make the time to complete these responsibilities day in, day out; they have no choice and little flexibility. This, in turn, means less free time. And let's remember that plenty of intermittent tasks are also female coded: sewing on a button, packing away the winter clothes, planning holiday dinners with family. These add even more responsibility and more time.

However, the average Male Role's unpaid workload is more manageable. If this person decides to put off lawn care until next weekend—no problem. The family can also live with a few burned-out light bulbs or a creaky door for another month. The Male Role does not have day-to-day responsibilities. The Male Role has more choice with time and more flexibility, which, in turn, offers more free time.

Some researchers categorize chores as inside versus outside. Inside chores tend to be female coded: cooking, cleaning, doing laundry. Outside chores tend to be male coded: lawn maintenance, snow removal, small home repairs. By this rationale, one might expect men in urban areas to shift and do more inside work than men living in rural areas because, when one lives in an urban apartment or small home, there is far less work to do outdoors. On the contrary, the same chore diaries show no significant difference in the number of indoor chores of urban men compared to rural men. Broadly speaking, men in urban areas have more free time than men in rural areas.

THE EMOTIONAL BURDEN

In the 1970s, researchers began differentiating between physical and emotional labor. Physical tasks are easier to pin down: cooking, shopping, paying bills. Emotional labor is defined as the hidden, often unnoticed tasks necessary to run a home. In *The Cost of Living,* novelist and essayist Deborah Levy eloquently describes this concept as "an act of immense generosity to be the architect of everyone else's well-being."

Over the years, we have all come to understand the emotional burden as the management of a home. It is about looking at the school calendar for the whole semester to see when the kids are off, and figuring out who is going to watch them. It is about monitoring the refrigerator every time you open the door, mentally keeping track of when shopping needs to be done and what needs to be purchased. It is about knowing who has birthdays and anniversaries coming up, and making sure you have cards and gifts ready. It is about monitoring a parent or grandparent in a care facility. It is about knowing when the dog needs his checkups, where to buy his favorite treats, and when to schedule a grooming appointment. It is about going through the kids' closets to find a new home for the clothes that they outgrew, and determining how to pay for new clothes.

Allison Daminger is a sociologist who does research on the concept of the emotional burden. Daminger, however, prefers the term *cognitive labor,* and she describes those who carry the household load as *cognitive laborers*. Through her own research, Daminger has reached the conclusion that cognitive labor can be divided into four categories: anticipating needs, identifying options, making decisions, and monitoring the outcomes.[8] She believes that all "invisible" tasks related to the home can be found in one of these four steps. Anyone who monitors processes in their home or at work understands that doing an actual task is only a fraction of the work. The bulk of time is spent worrying, planning, strategizing, feeling anxious, deciding, and problem solving before and after the task is complete. It is the sum total of these invisible mental tasks that constitutes the emotional burden. Some tasks have a short timeline. Other cognitive tasks are stretched over weeks, months, or years.

Several years ago, my daughter started to show an interest in music. She was in kindergarten, which seemed about the right time to begin music lessons. I anticipated the need for instruction, initiated conversations with her once in a while to gauge which instrument she was interested in, and made sure to talk to her about the responsibility that came with taking lessons. In the summer before first grade, I began identifying different ways to take lessons. I looked into music schools and private teachers in the neighborhood. I called her school to see if they had recommendations. I compared prices, sent some emails, and figured out which options were the best fit for our family's weekly timetable. Then I made a decision about which situation was best, signed a contract, and sent in a check. Throughout the year, I took her to lessons about 80 percent of the time, always evaluating the relationship between her and her teacher. I made sure to know which weeks were canceled for whatever reason, and I constantly checked with my daughter and her teacher on their progress, asking how we could better support her music education at home.

These steps are important because they describe duties that might not surface in a chore diary. I do a lot of anticipating when I am showering, commuting to work, or sitting in a waiting room. But if I were recording my time in a chore diary, none of these activities would qualify as housework.

Daminger's research also unearthed a gender dynamic within cognitive labor. She found that in cis, different-sex couples, women did more cognitive labor than men. Although there was a degree of equity when it came to the identifying and decision-making steps, women overwhelmingly took responsibility for anticipating and evaluating steps.

From the moment one wakes up in the morning, to the moment one drifts off to sleep, the cognitive laborers are constantly going through the to-do list—endlessly checking their mental cycle and keeping up with a variety of tasks that are somewhere on that four-step cycle. People who do this professionally are project managers, directors, and CEOs. They have advanced degrees and are financially rewarded for their ability to multitask and oversee many subprocesses in order to keep a company or organization going.

The household cognitive laborer earns no money and is rarely rewarded. In fact, other members of the household might even deny that the work happens at all. In the worst cases, they poke fun of the cognitive laborer for being a nag.

Let's look back at that 65/35 split and remind ourselves that this statistic comes from chore diaries that recorded time doing *physical tasks*. Based on collective data, we know that the average Male Role's 35 percent is spent doing intermittent tasks that carry little of the home's cognitive labor, whereas the Female Role's 65 percent includes routine tasks *as well as* the majority of the household's cognitive labor.

This is essentially the difference between having a part-time retail job and being a regional manager for a chain of shops. The part-time employee shows up for shifts, completes whatever tasks their manager asks for that day, punches out when their shift ends, and always has the option of calling in sick. The manager, however, has to account for coverage, sales, losses, security, infrastructure, marketing, and management of all staff. There is no punching out at the end of the shift—the regional manager works until they have done enough to go home.

No one would ever argue that a part-time employee does one third of the work in a retail chain. But we routinely fool ourselves into thinking the average man does 35 percent of work in the home—and that 35 percent is somehow enough.

WHY ARE WE TALKING ABOUT THIS?

Even after hearing these statistics, some people still give me a big shrug. I've heard plenty of excuses as to why household imbalance isn't a problem: *That's just how it is. Women and men are just different. Women are better at home stuff. Men don't really know how to be parents. I have more important things to think about. My work is more demanding than hers. My husband likes to play with the kids, but he isn't good with the everyday stuff. My wife is a control freak; she LIKES to be in charge. Women expect too much.*

But household imbalance is a problem. Gender inequality is direct and personal, and we see its limitations and restrictions play out every day. Gender norms are impacting our lives today, and they will impact our children in the future. Here's why.

1. GENDER NORMS CAUSE PSYCHOLOGICAL HARM TO WOMEN

Carrying the cognitive load of a home while participating in the workforce is physically draining and emotionally exhausting. Researchers have found that carrying the emotional household burden makes women feel empty and contributes to mental health problems,[9] and the perception of inequality in the home is associated with poorer psychological well-being and lower levels of marital satisfaction.[10] This can lead to an unhappy partnership, a separation, and even a divorce. Stephanie Coontz writes in *Marriage: A History* that an unequal division of labor in the home is a solid predictor of conflict.

Somehow those statistics do not do this topic justice. Terms like *feeling empty* or *psychological distress* do not adequately articulate the day-to-day sadness that comes with the heavy burden of cognitive labor. Emotional hurt is very real and very personal. It is not about a statistic of a nameless human—it is about your friend or sister or co-worker.

I reached out to women in my personal network and asked: When the emotional burden of your house is your responsibility, how does this make you feel? This is how they responded:

- "I feel resentful that my partner gets to check out—that he doesn't lie down at night thinking of the things he might forget. I resent that he doesn't co-bear this burden. It makes his life less stressful and [my life] exhausting."
- "I feel lonely. Really, really lonely. Not only that I am the only one carrying the emotional load—but that I am the only one who cares. I feel like—when he doesn't care enough to take part of the emotional load—that he doesn't care about me. Or worse, that he doesn't care about the kids."

- "I feel limited. Because it takes so much energy to get through our days, to anticipate the challenges of the coming weeks, and to plan all the extracurricular busyness of our lives, I don't feel I have energy left to take on a bigger job—even though that does potentially interest me."
- "I feel angry that I'm the director, secretary, and coordinator of our life, and that he only has to keep track of *his* stuff."
- "I feel actual fear. [I am] terrified of how things would unfold if I [suddenly died]. I worry—could he keep track of all the things? Would he keep track of all the kids' stuff in some way that stays normal for them? Does he know where all the Christmas decorations are? Would he wrap their birthday presents? Would he fold the laundry? I literally lie in bed worried about this sometimes."
- "I feel like a failure. Decades of women fighting for my rights. And I talk about feminism and I talk about equality—and then I just keep the cycle going by taking on the household load."

I have to remind myself that these quotes are not about adversaries. These are quotes from women who generally characterize their partnerships as healthy, women who love and care about their partners.

Perhaps you have your own story to tell—or a friend's or a sister's. If you have carried the emotional burden of a household, how did it make you feel?

2. GENDER NORMS PREVENT MEN FROM EMOTIONAL CONNECTION

I am not advocating for revised gender norms only to support women. I am advocating for revised gender norms to support people of all genders, because traditional gender norms are limiting for men, too. Sure, many gender norms reward men with more time and fewer responsibilities. But gender norms can also saddle men with financial expectations, prevent men from making strong emotional connections, and—arguably the most harmful of all—exclude men from caregiving experiences.

There is plenty of research and data to suggest that caregiving is beneficial to men. The most recent *State of the World's Fathers* report, produced by the MenCare network, states that caregiving improves men's physical, mental, and sexual health. Experience in caregiving is linked to limiting unhealthy behaviors, such as smoking and drinking. Caregiving leads to better romantic relationships among couples, and lower rates of domestic violence.[11]

In part 2 of this book, I will introduce you to the forty men living as equal partners in their relationships—working against gender norms to take on half of the physical and emotional tasks in their home. But I want to present a few quotes now to personalize this information. It is one thing to read that caregiving improves men's mental health—but what does that look like? This is what some of the men I interviewed had to say about their experiences as caregivers:

- "Being a caregiver made me realize so much of my own potential. It gave me a motivation for my own greatness. I appreciate the level of maturity [caregiving] gave me. I am a better person because of that experience."—Edward, Maryland (Black)
- "There's nothing I've done in my life as satisfying as being a competent caregiver to my children. Through that experience, I have gained deeply meaningful interactions; they really mean everything to me."—Logan, Hawaii (white)

- "I love being a nurturer. I love being in touch with this side of myself. For example, my mom always sang to me when I was little. And now I sing my girls to sleep. The other day, I watched my oldest sing to her baby doll—the same song I sing to her—and she sang and she tucked her doll into bed. Knowing she learned that from me, that was honestly one of the best moments of my life."—Martin, Texas (Latino)
- "My definition of a peaceful home is one where we take care of each other equally. I didn't get married to be served. There is so much comfort and joy in this balance. And I appreciate everything she does for me, but I also appreciate the opportunity to be the one who can also take care of her."—Adam, Washington (Chinese American/white)

Yes, caregiving can be exhausting, painful, and tedious. But caregiving can also be one of life's most beautiful and rewarding experiences. Caregiving for various people in my life has taught me patience, love, appreciation for a range of gifts and abilities, and the understanding that finances are not the only indicator of success. Caregiving triggers a sense of selflessness and humility that, I believe, make us better people. I would not be the person I am today had I not been a caregiver in my life, and I am sad that our culture discourages men from having these experiences.

3. GENDER NORMS CAUSE ECONOMIC HARM FOR THE FAMILY

In homes with greater household balance, women find that they can take full advantage of economic, educational, and professional opportunities. Data compared across thirty-three countries shows that there is a significant correlation between women in the economy and a fairer division of labor in the home. Household balance was linked to the percentage of women in government, percentage of female managers, and percentage of household income earned by women.[12]

Experts widely agree that there is a direct correlation between household burden and economic success. The Female Role, because of a heavier household burden, is less likely to volunteer for a work trip or a new project or put in overtime hours to impress the boss. They are less likely to nominate themselves for a raise or promotion. Those in the Female Role are drawn to work that is flexible because they know how valuable flexibility is when balancing family responsibilities. But the high-paying jobs reward hours; employers that offer flexibility know they can get away with paying a lower salary. And the cycle continues.

A group of economists recently published that this disadvantage is greater than many realize. This research suggests that college-educated women make about 90 percent as much as men at the age of twenty-five. This 10 percent gap is bad enough. But by age forty-five, that wage gap has grown to 45 percent. This means the average college-educated man improves his salary by 77 percent between the ages of twenty-five and forty-five. His female partner, however, only improves her salary by 45 percent.[13] By breaking out the wage disparity during childbearing years, one can clearly see that women (literally) pay a higher price for being moms than men do for being dads.

This is an objectively massive pay gap, indicative of the fact that the "Can women have it all?" conversation is, sadly, still relevant. Generally speaking, men have the ability to move ahead professionally and financially AND have a family. Whereas women typically sacrifice professional ambition and higher wages for a family.

I would also like to consider *when* the Female Role puts in those hours at home, which can be just as limiting as the number of hours. For example, on a typical day, I have the responsibility of picking up my kids from school. My partner, Evan, comes home a few hours later. Even though this might only add up to ten hours per week, the responsibility of stopping work at 3:00 P.M. every day has a big impact on my work. I don't have the luxury of working just fifteen more minutes to complete a task or finish a meeting that is running late. Sure, I can go back and make up hours later on, which I most often do. But some opportunities don't wait. There are jobs I can't take and meetings I can't attend, simply because my cutoff is 3:00 P.M.

I posit that, because the average Male Role's household tasks are fewer and intermittent, this person has more flexibility at work, which allows this person to take work-related risks that could propel them to higher titles and wages. Because the average Female Role's household tasks are greater and routine, this person has less flexibility and is unable to take as many work-related risks that could propel them to higher titles and wages.

Everything inside the home is connected to everything outside the home.

Making less money, not rising to the highest ranks at work, not reaching their full professional or economic ability—this is certainly a problem for a family, who might be giving up earning potential. And it might be a problem for an individual, who has to live with their own untapped capacity. But this is a bigger problem for our society. Household load is a major obstacle to women's full professional participation across all sectors and industries. What big-picture impact does that have?

- There are fewer female CEOs in the United States than there are CEOs named John.[14]

31

- The 117th U.S. Congress includes a record number of elected women, but it is still only 33 percent female.
- Only about 20 percent of corporate board seats in the United States are held by women.[15] (Less than 5 percent are held by women of color.[16])
- Only 20 percent of the top two hundred universities have a female president.[17]

Scholars regularly cite two reasons for this gendered imbalance in the public sphere: unconscious bias against female leaders and . . . wait for it . . . household burden.

THIS IS ALSO OUR MODERN HOUSEHOLD REALITY

Chase identifies as white. He was born in the mid-1980s and grew up in rural New England with a mother and an alcoholic father. His parents divorced when he was young. His mom had custody of Chase and his sister, but the kids saw their dad most weekends. Chase rarely wanted to go to his dad's, but he had no choice. "Sober dad was affectionate and wise. He would take me fishing, and we would build snow forts together. But drunk dad was clumsy and embarrassing. Drunk dad was a jerk. Abusive, actually. He wasn't a role model. I always knew, growing up, that I didn't want to end up like my dad."

Chase graduated from high school and started taking college classes, but in his first year he and his girlfriend realized they were pregnant. Kids were coming before he had planned, but Chase wasn't upset about the baby. He knew he wanted to be a dad, and he was eager to be a better dad than his own. Chase married his girlfriend, dropped out of school, and got a construction job to support his family. Chase's wife did not contribute to the family's income. His own salary wasn't huge, but it was enough for the young family. When his first daughter was eighteen months old, the couple found out they were expecting a second girl. Chase was happy again—being a family man was his dream. He wanted to create the stable, loving family that he never had himself.

But fatherhood wasn't what he expected. Chase wanted to be involved, but all that seemed to be expected from him was his salary. His wife, his mother, and their friends all sent him a clear message—whether direct or indirect—that his job was to make money and nothing else. "[My wife] had very strong opinions about how to raise kids and what to feed them and how to discipline. When I tried to give my opinions, I was just pushed away; she made it very clear that she knew best because she was the mom, and I knew nothing because I was just the dad."

So, Chase did what was expected of him; he worked. "The kids always seemed to need stuff, and stuff costs money. So, I kept picking up more and more hours to bring home a bigger paycheck. And I did feel good about that, but I also felt like I was pushed out of my daughters' lives. I remember my wife sending me a video of my little girl's first steps. That was so hard to watch, it just about broke my heart. I wanted to be there, too. I didn't want to see that on a video. I missed my kids and my wife. I felt completely pushed out of their life. I admit it; I was depressed."

Chase had succeeded in one sense—he was not like his father. He did not have a substance abuse problem, and he was not abusive toward his wife or his kids. But due to gender norms, he was suffering emotional harm; he wasn't anything close to the husband and father that he wanted to be.

We need to address household gender inequity as much for Chase as for Melissa.

WHAT IS THE RISK OF NOT TALKING ABOUT THIS?

Three data points illustrate the change in men's share of household contribution in different-sex relationships over the past several decades. Research based on time diaries reported that in 1965 men did about 15 percent of household work, in 1985 men's contributions had more than doubled to about 33 percent,[18] and currently, men's contribution still hovers around 35 percent.[19]

This means that we can give credit to those baby boomer men and those older Gen X men who increased their household imprint. But since the mid-1980s, we have not seen much of an increase. This means that collectively, younger Gen X men and millennial men have not made any significant gains in household participation.

GENERATIONAL TIMELINE

Baby Boomers: Born 1946–1964

Generation X: Born 1965–1980

Millennials: Born 1981–1996

Generation Z: Born 1997–2012

Generation Alpha: Born 2013–Present

Disagree? Doesn't sound quite right to you? Darcy Lockman's book *All the Rage: Mothers, Fathers, and the Myth of Equal Partnership* explains how our gender imbalance came to be and why our perception of gender equality is not our reality. In her book, Lockman explains that the "culture of fatherhood" has changed, even if men's actual behavior has not. Because men today do more in the home than generations past, there is a shared (if not quite correct) perception of greater equality. We see reminders in our everyday life: men wandering the aisles of the grocery store, the young dad with his baby strapped to his chest, and dads volunteering at school functions. All of these signs lead us to believe that we must have reached equality, since these men are all doing so much more than the men of the past.

Lockman posits that this false perception has led many people to buy into this culture of fatherhood myth, thereby preserving mediocrity for another generation. After all, who would try to become better and do more if the collective perception is that you are doing enough?

If you need further proof, we have data showing that millennial men are more likely than Gen X men to report that their wife/partner expects them to do too many household chores. Fifty-four percent of millennial men report doing more household work than they get credit for, while 45 percent of millennial women think their husband/partner gets more credit than he deserves.[20] This suggests that millennial women expect more equality, and millennial men expect less. And how about a 2020 Gallup poll that reported that, among different-sex couples, those aged eighteen to thirty-four were no more likely than older couples to divide household chores equitably.

So, millennials didn't make much headway. What about younger men? Is Gen Z naturally falling into patterns of equality in their relationships?

Pilar McDonald and Lola McAllister founded an organization

called Project Matriarchs during the first wave of the pandemic. Their goal was to meet the immediate need of helping women stay in the workforce by providing college-aged online tutors for kids. I talked to them about their Gen Z perspective and whether or not the issue of household balance was on their radar, since their work specifically centers on caregiving dynamics in the home.

McAllister agrees that traditional gender norms can still have a powerful influence, even with a generation that often rejects gender conformity. She explained, "I think we need to learn to anticipate, and to be intentional. We need to understand how we can improve, so we don't also fall into these same gendered patterns."

McDonald had a personal experience that exemplified the need for this conversation among a younger generation. For one summer during college, she shared an apartment with her boyfriend. "We had been dating for three years and I really did not expect that there would be an immediate gravitation toward gendered roles, but I felt it come out in cooking, cleaning, and planning in the few months we were living together. It made me very frustrated, maybe because I was hyperaware of the possibilities of these dynamics, and also because it felt a bit hopeless. I thought we wouldn't fall directly into these roles. I thought we knew more than that."

I wondered if other Gen Z women would agree. To find out, I spoke to a group of unmarried women between the ages of nineteen and twenty-four. All thirteen participants said they were open to marriage at some point in their lives, and all of them expressed their specific intention to work and contribute to the family's income. I asked what their expectations were for partnership: what they wanted, what they thought was realistic, what they thought was unrealistic.

Zoe from Pennsylvania said, "My mom stayed home and my dad was the breadwinner. And he worked a lot. So, it was my mom's job to take care of us and take care of the house. But I want to work. And yeah, I think sharing household chores is realistic." Several other women expressed a similar perspective. There was an assumption that, if both partners were working outside the home, both partners would automatically help manage the home. There was a shared agreement among the group that equality just happened naturally. I asked, "Have you ever specifically discussed this in relationships—past or present?"

One woman noted that a previous boyfriend was not interested in an equal partnership—that he wanted his future wife to stay home, like his mother did. She said it was a big reason why the relationship ended. This did not surprise me; many women feel that their partners' contributions in the home are a direct signal of their worth. Studies show that heterosexual women believe there is a direct correlation between what a male partner does for her and how much he cares about her.[21]

Clearly, these young women had thought about equity at some level, but I suspected none of them had thought deeply about gender roles in the home. I don't blame them; I certainly didn't understand the complexity of the household balance when I was their age. So, I shared some statistics to illustrate how an equal split is not happening naturally in dual-working families. I explained the concept of the neo-traditional household and raised the concept of the emotional burden. And then I asked them how those statistics made them feel.

Natalie from New Jersey was the only one who was engaged to be married, and she had the most to share. Her wedding was not for another fourteen months, and the couple was not yet cohabitating. They had talked about both of them working. But had they talked about the emotional burden? Or how to achieve equality in the home? "No, not as in-depth. We haven't looked at it on a deeper level. I find myself bringing it up in conversations—what will this look like when we live together. For him, he is thinking that the schedule is fine right now. But I see how busy he is and how long his days are, and I want time for me. I always thought of that as a female's perspective . . . it's just not resonating with him yet."

It sounded to me that Natalie was explaining some "anticipating" work. She is not just looking at her relationship right now; she is looking ahead and trying to avoid problems before they happen. I can see how a woman in Natalie's situation could easily slip into the cognitive laborer role.

Perhaps because of our age difference, or perhaps because I genuinely liked Natalie, I found myself wanting to warn her. I wanted to explain to her that we have data to tell us that when he says, *Your career is important,* this will not necessarily translate into his actions.

It seems I am not the only one with these mother hen instincts. I heard the following story from a friend of a friend, about a woman named Marta who attended Williams College. In 2013, Williams held an event to celebrate the thirtieth anniversary of its Women's, Gender, and Sexuality Studies program. At this event, Marta and her classmates found themselves chatting with a lineup of distinguished professors past and present. In Marta's description, they were all powerful, wise women: women Marta looked up to.

At one point in the conversation, another student asked the professors, "For those of us graduating, what wisdom can you offer us?" Marta waited to hear the reply with anticipation. She was not sure what she expected to hear, but she was certainly disappointed by the answer. "It sounded outdated, to be honest. I mean, I don't ever want to get married; that wasn't anything I was even thinking about. But the most important advice they had for us was that, if we chose to marry, to set household boundaries and rules at the beginning of the relationship. They told us that once our house is out of balance, it is very hard to get that back."

I can understand why Marta was surprised. Thirty years of academic experience in gender studies—and these women focused on an issue that felt very outdated. This conversation does not at all sync with what feminism is tackling today. I suspect those female leaders at Williams College knew how important this topic was; they likely knew the statistics, and perhaps they had lived the reality. Like me, they might have felt the need to warn younger women.

Marta isn't the only person I have spoken to who is surprised by this conversation. Feminists, academics, and advocates moved on from heterosexual household relationships years ago, with good reason. I am thankful that today's feminist-thought leaders are talking about gender identity in an inclusive way, and thankful that fourth-wave feminism is grounded in an intersectional lens and a focus on traditionally marginalized groups.

I believe we can support progressive feminist theory *and* continue this conversation about household balance. Frankly, we must. Despite women's continued participation in the professional space, our household situation is not changing. The Canadian Research Institute for the Advancement of Women estimates that, at the current rate, despite women's continued participation in the professional space, we will not achieve gender equality for 164 years. The

World Economic Forum believes it is closer to 108 years. MenCare, a global network devoted to men becoming equitable partners and caregivers, has the most optimistic prediction—gender equality in 75 years.

Before you keep reading, stop and consider that for a moment. Even the rosiest of predictions means that the great-grandchildren of babies born this year will be the first generation to see household gender equality. Not addressing this issue means another 75–164 years of the status quo.

The flip side, of course, paints a brighter future. In balanced homes, people of all genders report having happier marriages. Women report that they feel more confident and more appreciated when they are treated as true equals, and not regarded as hired help. Men report that they feel satisfied knowing that they are doing their fair share.

We cannot get lulled into the culture of fatherhood, burying our head in the sand and telling ourselves things are better than they are. We need to admit that there is a problem, and that we can do better. And most of all we need to keep talking about it, to make sure this topic stays on everyone's radar.

Have you ever been with friends or family, and a subject comes up, but you find it hard to defend your view because you don't have the details on the tip of your tongue? It is at these precise moments that we need to remember a few facts and figures to articulate our case. Who has the brain space for that—on top of everything else we have to do in daily life?

I chose the following five facts as the most compelling to illustrate the ramifications of inequality. If you can remember only five things, then, taken together, these five will help you articulate this problem when you find yourself in this conversation—with work colleagues, neighbors, or the parents of your kids' friends. If you need to cheat a little, snap a photo of this box with your phone for easy reference at a later date.

5 FACTS TO HAVE IN YOUR BACK POCKET

1. The general consensus among academics and researchers is that, in North American dual-working homes, women do twice as much housework as their male partners. (Bonus points if you remember that women do most of the routine chores, and men do most of the intermittent chores.)

2. The household gender balance is not fixing itself with time. The 65/35 split has remained steady for the past 30+ years.

3. At age twenty-five, college-educated women make about 90 percent the salary of college-educated men. (Not too bad, perhaps.) By age forty-five, college-educated women make only 55 percent the salary of college-educated men.

4. A 2018 study found that single mothers, on average, completed fewer hours of housework per week than women married to men.[22] (And it is not because single women have dirty homes. This study found that, when women are married to men, they tend to "perform gender" and spend hours doing household chores that they feel they are expected to do.)

5. Working mothers today spend as many hours taking care of their children as stay-at-home mothers did in the 1970s.[23] (The expectations of motherhood in the 1970s and 1980s were very different than expectations today. So, when a woman thinks back to her own mother and wonders, *How come she wasn't as frazzled as*

I am now? Or a man thinks, My mom seemed to do it fine, so why is my wife struggling? This is why.)

What other statistics have resonated with you? Use this space to jot down additional data points you may want to remember.

_____

_____

_____

_____

AN INCLUSIVE CONVERSATION

Most of the data I have offered thus far is from cis, heterosexual couples. Like it or not, our current social norms are built upon generations of *heteronormativity*. However, partnerships today do not face the same restrictions of the past. Equal partnership is not a concept unique to married heterosexual couples with kids. The concept of equality is universal to all couples: cohabitating, sharing resources, and/or married; kids, no kids, or co-parenting; different-sex or same-sex; cisgender, trans, or queer. When two people come together, whoever they are, they need to figure out the household-work balance to make the relationship work for both people.

Of course, like all relationships, how much (or how little) gender norms impact a relationship rests with each couple. But looking at data, there is evidence of two typical paths in same-sex relationships.

Sometimes, in same-sex relationships, traditional gender norms do not have a strong influence. Dozens of studies have found that many gay, lesbian, and queer couples practice greater equality in the home. This isn't to say all same-sex couples manage fifty-fifty equality, but on average, these partnerships divide household labor more equally than different-sex couples.[24]

There are many theories that aim to explain why. Some researchers find that same-sex couples value the concept of equality more than different-sex couples. Some posit that this stems from a time before equal marriage legislation, when both partners had to work and own property to protect their own financial future. When same-sex couples did not have the same legal protections as different-sex couples, one partner taking on household specialization was economically risky.

Other experts suggest that gay and queer couples are simply better equipped for equal partnership than heterosexual couples. Whereas different-sex couples can subconsciously fall back on gender roles, same-sex and queer couples tend to be more adept at navigating a gendered social system and setting their own social norms. The most equitable relationships documented are in lesbian unions in which both parents take turns birthing children, thereby equally dividing the physical strain of pregnancy and birth, and the time away from work during maternity leave.[25]

However, other resources show that traditional gender assumptions can heavily affect same-sex relationships. Because the American social structure has, for so long, assumed one working parent (Male Role) and one stay-at-home parent (Female Role), institutions have grown to reinforce this divide. Consider, for example, pediatricians, schools, camps, veterinarians, and eldercare homes. Many ask for one primary contact person and assume this primary contact is always available for drop-offs, pickups, special events, lessons, meetings, conferences, and appointments.

This situation is exacerbated in the United States, where health insurance is affiliated with one's job. Regardless of gender, this structure often forces at least one person to take a full-time job that comes with a benefits package. Full-time jobs are demanding and often take up more than the forty-hour workweek: overtime, on-call hours, commuting, weekend shifts, answering email at night from home. This often requires the other partner to have a part-time, or at least flexible job, to tend to the home, kids, pets, extended family, etc.

Alyssa Schneebaum researches the economics of same-sex couple households. One of her findings was that some same-sex couples decide that one person should specialize in paid work, and the other in unpaid work. She found that in both male and female same-sex couples, the lower-wage earner spends more time on housework and childcare.[26] This can be verified in other data; a Family Process Institute study found that, between 1975 and 2000, same-sex couples became less equal in terms of household work.[27]

I discussed these statistics with Christopher Carrington, the author of *No Place Like Home: Relationships and Family Life Among Lesbians and Gay Men*. He wasn't surprised by this statistic, explaining that he has seen an increase in gender inequality in the relationships he studied after California's anti-marriage equality ballot measure passed in 2008. He said, "Whereas lack of legal protections forced same-sex partnerships to remain economically independent before 2008, the presence of legal protections has meant that many couples could choose to devote one person to specialize in work, and one to specialize in household affairs."

The point here is that yes, same-sex couples do, on average, have a more equal balance in the home than different-sex couples. But, because we constructed our systems and institutions around our cultural gender norms, those systems and institutions are now perpetuating those gender norms, even in queer relationships. The fact remains that having an equal partnership is hard no matter the gender identity of the people in that union, and this book aims to help all people transcend those barriers and find greater parity in their homes.

It is also crucial that the concept of partnership and household balance is not oversimplified as only a gender issue. There are many identities that factor into our relationships and our communities. Modern partnership deserves an intersectional approach—a lens that takes a variety of power sources into consideration. Aside from gender, we also need to include identities around race, country of origin, ability, religion, economic class, and all other structural issues that influence our relationships and our communities.

Some published data about gender is disaggregated by race and/ or economic class, which tells a more complex story. For example, three American studies completed in the 1990s found that, on average, Black men do more housework than white men, but Black women still do far more in the home than Black men. Research on Latinx households concluded that the male participation is about the same as in white households.[28]

Some data, however, is not disaggregated. In these cases, we must be careful not to make assumptions about all people when only looking at numbers from an urban, white, cisgender, heterosexual, college-educated subset. And we must avoid the trap of assuming the white household is our independent variable.

Data is taken for what it is—pieces of information that give us a starting place for a conversation. In that conversation, we can talk in greater detail about our complex identities. We know that racism, homophobia, and xenophobia lead to structural obstacles that prevent people from accessing education, employment, health care, and housing. But do we know if and how those structural issues affect a relationship at home? It is important to discuss how those external factors play into partnership.

Many of the Gen Z women I interviewed made specific comments about how their identity affects their view of partnership, which affects their expectations for the future. One woman raised the intersection of gender and culture. "Both for my mom and I think overall in the Indian culture, they value [the] mom staying home longer than maternity leave. . . . I watched my mom doing what she thought she had to do. I then watched her take several years off . . . and then struggle to get back into the workforce."

Another woman raised the intersection of gender and immigration. Nisha's family moved to Canada from Bangladesh when she was a child, and she grew up in a tight-knit Bangladeshi community. "From the immigrant perspective . . . what happens if mom and dad both have to work, is that mom works in more precarious jobs, with lower wages, and they experience sexist discrimination on top of racist discrimination. For them to come home and take on extra chores, there are a lot of dimensions to these things." There is a strong connection between ethnicity, immigrant status, and gender norms in Nisha's identity. Separating them would not make sense to her; they would not tell an accurate story about who she is and who she wants to be.

The stories in this book are not solely stories of white, college-educated, cis, heterosexual, Judeo-Christian urbanites. Those opinions are included, but so are the opinions of people who identify as Black, Latinx, Cajun, rural, first-generation American, working class, Muslim, gay, and Appalachian. When people spoke about the connection between gender and other identities, I was careful to weave those perspectives into their story. Structural patterns absolutely shape our experiences and our behavior; our behavior is heavily influenced by our lived experiences. This is why it is important to highlight the particular challenges raised by individuals facing multiple forms of oppression. But we also have to be careful and remember that structural patterns do not always regulate our behavior, and humans possess the self-agency to change.

With this in mind—knowing that our shared definition of partnership is inclusive and our approach is intersectional—the most important objective I have for this book is not to prescribe any specific goal. Everyone is on their own path. We all live in our own unique situation, with our own history, our own comfort level, and our own end goal. Granted, if you're reading this book, I assume you already value gender equality and have some level of interest in living that value. But what you want for yourself may be very different from what I want for myself. There is no right or wrong.

For this reason, I do not intend this book to be an instruction manual. Please think of it as a menu. I hope many ideas resonate with you, but I am sure some will not. Take what applies and leave the rest. This book is not about achieving someone else's definition of perfect; this book is about discussing social norms, questioning our own beliefs, listening to other views, and making purposeful decisions for ourselves and our relationships. We are simply trying to move forward with purpose and intention.

2

SOCIALIZED INEQUALITY

In 1989, researchers came to the conclusion that gender is the biggest predictor of the household-labor split. Income, free time, employment, ideology—nothing mattered nearly as much as gender.[1] Experts have not changed their opinion in the last three decades. It is widely accepted that our collective attitudes about gender roles are the number one cause of an unequal division of housework in the home.[2] Before we can begin to discuss solutions to household imbalances, we have to get at the root of the underlying issues around gender roles.

Just to make sure we're all on the same page, let me share one quick reminder about the words *sex* and *gender.* Academics tend to use the word *sex* to describe a biological difference. If a baby is born with a penis, the baby's sex is assumed to be male. If a baby is born with a vagina, the baby's sex is assumed to be female. When a pregnant person goes for a prenatal checkup, it is more accurate to inquire about the *sex* of the baby, not the gender.

There are, of course, physical differences between people based on sex, but these are very limited. Most of the characteristics we assign to males and females are socially constructed, and not biological. The word *gender* refers to the way people act according to their society's expectations for men and women. Gender norms are assumptions to which women and men are expected to conform; they define what a given society considers appropriate male and female behavior. Gender norms are subjective. They differ from place to place, and they change over time.

In the busyness of everyday life, we often blur sex and gender. Gender norms become very real to us; we see them as intrinsic truths that govern our social lives. For example, I often hear people state that women are better equipped at handling cognitive labor than men. This statement is rarely posited as an opinion or a suggestion, but as a fact—as if it had something to do with sex, a biological truth. But a few questions quickly clear up what is sex and what is gender.

- Is there any scientific data to validate this statement? *No.*
- Is there anything about a woman's biology that makes her better at anticipating needs, accepting responsibility, and multitasking? *No.*
- Is there anything about a man's biology that is an obstacle to him anticipating needs, accepting responsibility, and multitasking? *No.*
- Do we subconsciously conclude that women are better at handling cognitive labor because most of the people in our lives who carry the emotional burden are women, and we associate women with an emotional burden? *Yes.*

Gender norms run deep. Even those of us who claim to genuinely believe in gender parity still make subconscious assumptions that lead to inequity. Some of my friends who work in gender waver on the nurture-versus-nature point. "But," some say, with an uneasy hesitation, "sometimes boys and girls are still just *different.*" Most people have a handful of anecdotes that support notions of biological difference. These stories come from their own childhood or from observations of other kids. And I've heard hundreds of them.

Most stories tend to paint boys as higher energy, more aggressive, less interested in people, and more interested in sports. *Boys can make a gun out of anything—a stick, a Barbie leg, a carrot!* Girls are described as calmer, more emotional, more mature, more natural nurturers. *Girls are just so emotional when they're teenagers. And they can be so mean.* I firmly believe that this anecdotal evidence stems from social differences.

Gender socialization is the process of learning the "correct" gender behavior in a culture. This pattern repeats itself through generations of replicating behavior and practice. We use these assumptions to condition children to fit into social molds; we raise boys to fill the Male Role, and we raise girls to fill the Female Role. This is why gender socialization tends to work like self-fulfilling prophecies. If we assume women and girls are better at being cognitive laborers, then girls will be raised to anticipate the needs around them. Girls are taught to value things like having a clean and tidy home. Women get lots of practice doing household management because from a young age, girls are asked to help their mothers and sisters.[3] The result is that now there is a legitimate argument in saying that women are better than men at handling cognitive labor. But this is learned behavior, not biology.

Gender norms are often shrugged off, dismissed as "jokes" that do not have any real impact. Throughout my personal and professional life, I have repeatedly had people roll their eyes at me and tell me I am "taking things too seriously."

But gender norms are serious—norms impact our decisions and actions, and in turn, impacts people's lives. Gender norms can prevent a gifted male educator from taking his dream job as an elementary school teacher, a pregnant woman from getting a job promotion, or a father from showing affection for a child. Gender norms can be most harmful to those who do not identify as either male or female. Because traditional gender norms only acknowledge two gender identities, nonbinary, trans, intersex, or gender-nonconforming people can become invisible.

AN IDEAL MAN?

Gender inequality is not a women's issue. It is a human rights issue that is a social construct: an historic imbalance of power between men and women. From the early 1980s, a growing number of academic researchers and nonprofit organizations have contributed to the notion that to address gender inequality, we must work with men and boys. Promundo International, Sonke Gender Network, A Call to Men, and MenCare are all organizations that have been working with men and boys for decades. They collectively cover a range of issues, including anti-violence, reproductive health, and fatherhood.

I regularly borrow tools from these organizations in my own work, and I credit A Call to Men's work on the *Man Box* for this particular exercise.[4] During gender-themed workshops, I often ask participants to split into small groups and brainstorm the characteristics of an "ideal man."

When I ask participants to identify what makes an ideal man, I am often met with silence and blank stares. I remind participants that there are no right or wrong answers; I'm interested in their thoughts about what an ideal man is considered to be in their culture. If society could collectively manufacture the ideal man, what would he look like? How would he act? Slowly, people pick up their markers and begin to make a list.

Before you continue reading, complete the Quick Answer activity in the box below. I'll soon share common results from my work, and you can compare those answers with your own ideas.

QUICK ANSWER 1

List five characteristics that you feel are commonly used to describe an ideal man.

_____

_____

_____

_____

_____

The results vary, but generally the lists provided by groups— from the Americas, to Africa, to Asia—are similar. Groups describe the ideal male physique: tall, strong, muscular, athletic, and handsome. Some cultures also add the necessity of facial hair. Ideal attributes tend to be described as in control, a leader, not emotional, street-smart, commanding, wise, focused, economically secure, popular with women. Some cultures also add pious, well educated, and/ or funny.

How does your list compare? Did any of those ideas overlap with your own?

Next, I ask my groups, "How many men do you know that fit this description?" This is when most people laugh and admit very few, if any. Participants might mention a movie character or TV persona as a good example. No one knows many ideal men in their day-to-day lives because these collections of adjectives do not describe real people. So, if it is not real, why does the description of an ideal person matter?

I asked this last question to a group of college students in Tokyo. After a few minutes of thought, one brave guy raised his hand and said, "I guess because boys spend their lives trying to measure up to that ideal, but most of us don't come close. So, we sort of feel like we're failing every day."

Women are not the only ones tasked with the impossible. Boys grow up conditioned to fit an ideal they cannot possibly meet. Many boys will not grow tall enough, develop muscles big enough, or be handsome enough. Many boys are born into poverty or into a minority group that prevents them from achieving the prevailing social ideal. And in the rare case in which a boy is born into a body and an economic class that aligns with the ideal, even they face extreme pressure to obtain degrees from elite institutions, assume leadership positions, and maintain appropriate emotional distance.

The root causes of gender inequality are not simple, and thus the solutions are not going to be simple. In order to create an equitable life for everyone, we need to understand the pressures faced by people of all genders. Everyone labors under stereotypes and expectations. It is therefore necessary to understand all stereotypes in order to adjust our expectations of the ideal.

The following table highlights some frequent responses I get when I ask groups to think more deeply about the everyday consequences that stem from the notion of an ideal man. Feel free to add a few of your own in the space provided.

EXPECTED CHARACTERISTICS FOR MEN

CHARACTERISTIC	HOW IS THIS LIMITING TO MEN?
1. Provider	Men are still considered the sole source of income for their families, and being the sole breadwinner for a family is stressful. His family's financial needs might prevent a man from seeking higher education or participating in a training program. A man might do a job he dislikes because he feels he has no choice. Men of color are also routinely paid less than white men for similar work, which makes it even more difficult for men of color to earn enough money to support themselves or their families. Harmful to Equity: Because men are raised to focus their attention on earning for a family, they may dismiss the importance of a woman's career, or of sharing household responsibilities.
2. Stoic	Boys are not encouraged to acknowledge their emotions or talk about their feelings, which can prevent them from forming meaningful and supportive relationships. Men can feel pressure to bury their emotions, and are often forced to handle trauma and loss alone, without help. This causes stress and, in extreme cases, can lead to depression, addiction, or suicide. Harmful to Equity: The inability to connect emotionally can take a toll on partners, leading to superficial relationships, unhappy marriages, separations, and divorces.
3. In Control and Decisive	Men are often assumed to be in control of their surroundings, both work spaces and home spaces. (Although he might not do the everyday work of maintaining the home, he is still considered the king of his castle.) Mistakes are not tolerated. Asking for help is a symptom of weakness; even when help is offered, they think a real man would handle the issue on their own. This puts an enormous amount of pressure on men to take care of everyone, alone, without help, or ever making a mistake. Harmful to Equity: If men are in control of professional and domestic spaces, where do women fit in? Or people who do not identify as male or female? How can one assert themselves professionally when they are deemed a weaker sex?

4. Unlike a Girl

Boys and men prove their masculinity by doing the opposite of what is perceived as feminine, with the assumption that anything "girl-like" is wrong, weak, lesser, and embarrassing. Young boys hear, *You throw like a girl.* When they are older, they are told, *You're such a pussy* or *Don't be a bitch.* There are also plenty of derogatory words comparing boys to homosexual men. A boy or man whose authentic self includes female-coded characteristics is banned from participation. This exclusion can lead to extreme physical and emotional harm. Harmful to Equity: This is blatant misogyny. There can be no equality at home or at work when there are underlying assumptions about boys being the superior sex and women (and homosexual men) being the weaker sex. If a man should not be like a woman, and women clean the house, then clearly a man isn't going to contemplate cleaning the house.

5.

GENDER DEFAULT

Gender norms, like all socialized norms, are passed from one generation to the next through role modeling and reinforcement. This means that, as children, we learn what men and women are supposed to do in the world, not by sitting in a classroom and reading a textbook, but by observing and mimicking the behavior of our family members and the people in our community.

We certainly do not do this consciously. Most of the time we are only passively aware of the gender role modeling around us. From the time of infancy (or even before birth), we treat boys and girls differently. We buy them different clothes, decorate their rooms differently, give them different toys to play with. We use different words to describe them: she is sweet, and he is strong. We tend to be tender and gentle with girl babies, and rougher and more playful with boy babies. These gendered practices continue for toddlers, children, teenagers, and adults. As we age, many people just assume this is how things are.

We also assume children fit into the gender binary as either male or female. We accept as truth that genitals correlate with that child's gender identity. We assume all children fit into one set of norms or the other, thereby excluding the perspective of nonbinary, trans, and intersex identities.

Acting in this way, we are living in a state of unawareness—blind to the differences between facts and social constructs. It is somewhat like gender cruise control or gender autopilot. I refer to this pattern of behavior as *gender-default mode*. Living in this mode allows us to mix up sex and gender, accept and perpetuate gender norms without consciously thinking about it, and see the world according to presumed guidelines about what men and women do—and do not do.

Turning off our gender default is not immediate; one cannot flip a switch and become gender aware overnight. The reality is that, even those of us who believe in gender equity, still switch between gender default and gender awareness all the time. We might be in gender default at home but gender aware at the office—or the other way around. We may be gender aware in class but fall back into gender default in the voting booth. We may see clearly in job interviews, but with fogged vision when dealing with our own kids at home.

I've experienced many of these disconnected situations. I once had a playground conversation with a mother who, in the course of five minutes, ranted about how frustrated she was about the pay gap between men and women, and then admitted she is harder on her daughter than her son "because girls are just more responsible than boys." I used to work with a man who passionately supported women's equality programs in the office, and then, with a laugh and a wink, said to me at a reception, "This gender equality is fine for women like you. But I prefer that my wife stay home. Who else will do my laundry?"

I admit that I catch myself slipping into gender default, even after years of working in this field. Even more embarrassing is when someone else catches me in a gender default moment. While writing this book, I made the incorrect assumption that a toddler was a girl because he had long, flowing hair—and I was mortified when corrected. It is hard to shed a lifetime's worth of gendered assumptions. "Seeing" our gender norms takes work and practice for all of us. But it is possible.

I am going to pause for a quick activity here and encourage you to identify some of the most harmful norms in your life—and then start to think about what change would look like. My colleague, Lori Rollieri, who is also a professional gender facilitator, gave me the idea for this activity.

REWRITING GENDER NORMS

Identify three negative gender norms that bother you. These can be norms in your home, community, work, or family. I'll give you a few examples and leave room for you to add your own.

- (Example) Women should always prioritize family over career.
- (Example) All women, deep down, want to be mothers.

- _____
- _____
- _____

Now, using the theme from what you wrote above, rewrite each of those negative norms to be positive gender norms—norms you wish were pervasive in your family or community.

- (Example) Men should put equal time into their relationships and their careers.
- (Example) Some people want to be a parent. Some people do not want to be a parent. Both options are socially acceptable.

- _____
- _____
- _____

When you complete the chart above, I suggest you reread your three revised norms and take a few minutes to think: *How would my life change if these were the actual norms my community embraced?*

Recognizing harmful norms, and recognizing that they are socially constructed, is the first step.

Then what? How do we actually exit gender default? The answer is simpler than you might think. We change the same way we learned in the first place: through role modeling, reinforcement, and norm perception.

ROLE MODELING

Role modeling is about demonstrating behavior. There are those who are role models, and there are those who are watching—who then begin to mimic that observed behavior to others. Role modeling can be purposeful, but most of the time it happens subconsciously. Sometimes behavior only needs to be role modeled once, and sometimes it takes years of role modeling to make behaviors stick.

No one ever sat me down and specifically explained how to be a girl, nor did I read a book about appropriate femininity when I was young. But over the years, I subconsciously learned how women acted and how men acted by watching those around me. Even the most innocuous of occasions help teach children how to act according to their assigned gender. Let's take Thanksgiving as an example.

Every year your family gathers at your grandparents' house for the holiday. It is a time that you look forward to. Early Thanksgiving morning you (passively) observe a sexual division of labor. Your mother, aunts, older female cousins, and grandmother meet in the kitchen to tackle meal prep. While the women chat, they also chop, dice, mix, fry, bake, and clean. The women stay sequestered in the kitchen until they set the table and serve the meal. At that time, everyone sits together and eats as a family. As soon as dinner is finished, the women clear the plates from the table, and the small army of female workers attack the dishes and pack away the leftovers.

During this same time, your father, uncles, male cousins, and grandfather venture into the garage. Grandpa likes to ask for help with small household maintenance projects. By noon, the men grab a few bags of chips and head inside to watch football. There they stay, swapping football trivia and comparing fantasy scores. Eventually, when the women serve the meal, the men emerge and everyone eats as a family. As soon as the meal is complete, the men quickly retreat back to the game. There they remain until it is time to go home.

Year after year you have watched this routine. Up until now you have played in the basement with your younger cousins, but here you are, twelve years old, and you have become bored with Chutes and Ladders. So, you head upstairs to claim your spot with the adults. Where do you go?

Likely, if you are a girl, you join the women in the kitchen. If you are a boy, you join the men in the TV room. Either way, you find yourself joining one group or the other based on your sex (or, at least, based on the gender assigned to you at birth). If you identify as nonbinary or trans, this situation could be confusing and painful. No one told you what to do—you just did it because you were going through the motions and subconsciously following social cues. You were in gender-default mode, following the path others set before you. The decision of where to spend your Thanksgiving Day *was made for you.*

Role modeling gendered behavior does not just happen on Thanksgiving Day. People role model gendered behavior every day of the year. We learn how to dress, how to sit, how to manage friendships, how to navigate school, how to initiate sex, how to apply for a job, how to dress, how to act in an interview—and yes, how to approach the unpaid work we do in the home—based on role-modeled behavior from others.

We often don't stop to think about what we role model from generation to generation. Living in gender default, we continue to act the way others act around us. But there is great value in taking a moment to think more intentionally about the behavior you role model to others.

This is an exercise inspired by an activity frequently used in Promundo International programming.[5] I find that this works well in groups—and I have found it to be personally helpful as well.

Sometimes, older generations role model positive traits—such as a strong work ethic, love for family, or belief in education—values we want to continue to pass along to our children and grandchildren. But sometimes, older generations role model traits that we do not necessarily want to pass along to future generations. These traits could include the inability to share emotions, prejudice toward others, or traditional expectations around gender.

INTROSPECTION EXERCISE: ROLE MODELING

1. Take a few moments to think of two values role modeled to you that you want to pass along to younger generations. (Younger generations could mean your own children, stepchildren, nieces or nephews, grandchildren or great-grandchildren, etc.)
2. Now take a few moments to think of two values role modeled to you that you do NOT want to pass along to younger generations.

If we learn gender norms through role modeling, then we can *unlearn* gender norms by changing the behavior we role model.

What if, growing up, you did not see a gender division on Thanksgiving Day? You instead saw a division based on interest. Family members who prefer to cook congregated in the kitchen to prep for dinner. And family members who prefer to lounge on the couch and watch football congregated around the TV, or some people drifted back and forth. In such an environment, when you leave the playroom and venture upstairs at age twelve, you would not feel pressured to join one group or the other. You would simply gravitate toward the group that shares your interests. You would make the decision, instead of the decision being made for you.

I understand that our real lives are more nuanced and complicated than this example, but the concept that we can reteach and relearn gender norms through revised role modeling is applicable to nearly all situations.

REINFORCEMENT

Both positive and negative reinforcement can be effective. When people praise our actions, we are more likely to repeat them. When people criticize our actions, we are more likely to stop.

Throughout life we test our boundaries and receive feedback from others on a range of behaviors, including gender: the way we dress, the words we use, the tone of our voice, how assertive/passive we are, what groups and clubs we join. Every day we give gendered feedback to others. We reward or condemn the behavior exhibited to us. In return, we react and recalibrate based on the way people reinforce our behavior. We live in, and perpetuate, this cycle of gender default.

Sometimes the feedback comes directly, and someone says out loud, "Dude, don't do that." Other times the feedback is passive, and you mysteriously stop getting invited to happy hour.

Sometimes we use reinforcement to make us feel better about our own experience. When I was on maternity leave after the birth of my second child, I started hanging around a group of other new moms at a local playground. We all had babies as well as older kids, and the adult conversations (at first) were my salvation; they broke up the monotony of very long days. But I found that group to be somewhat of a reinforcement circle: always complaining about their husbands, and always reinforcing stereotypes about what men were incapable of. This reinforcement circle didn't change anything at the core, but it did seem to bring a bit of levity into the lives of these tired, stressed-out women—because everyone told each other, *This is just how it is. We're not doing anything wrong. And there's nothing we can do to change our lot in life.* (Eventually, I found these endless conversations more exhausting than my own toddler, and I started going to a different playground. But I do see how those relationships can be critical for people going through a hard time.)

Observed reinforcement can be powerful, too. This is when an individual is witness to another person being rewarded or penalized. Kids find out how to stay out of trouble by observing older siblings; new staff learn the workplace culture when they see what kind of person is made Employee of the Month.

Here are some more examples of how people reinforce day-to-day behavior that specifically perpetuates gender stereotypes. As you read these, think about how the person in the example may be affected by the feedback. What might they continue to do? What might they shy away from in the future?

Here are examples of how people reinforce gendered behavior:

* When a mom is late to work because of the kids, everyone rolls their eyes. When a dad is late to work because of the kids, he is praised for being such a wonderful, involved father.
* A bunch of men are heading to the bar after work. They invite the new guy. He says, "I should really go home and help my wife with the kids." This is met with gales of laughter.

63

- A dad finds a condom in his teenage son's wallet. He winks at the boy and puts it back.
- A young girl is playing with a doll. Her mother praises her for playing so quietly, and tells her what a good mother she will make some day.
- A young boy is pushing a toy baby stroller down the sidewalk. People frown and shake their head at him. One person outwardly laughs.
- A female college student updates her family on what she is studying in college. They reply, "Oh, that's a great choice; you can easily go part time when the babies come."
- A male college student updates his family on what he is studying in college. They reply, "Oh, that's a great choice; you'll make a good income for your family someday."
- A human resources director, trying to be inclusive of all employees, wrote new policy using the blended pronoun s/he. The director never stopped to think how this might make a person who prefers they/them feel excluded.
- A young woman heads out to a bar with her friends. She is the only one not wearing revealing clothes. She is also the only one not getting any attention from men.
- A boy builds a large block tower. His grandmother turns to his grandfather and says, "Look at that great tower! Boys are such natural engineers."

In her 2019 book, *Down Girl*, author Kate Manne explains that sexism is the judicial system that sets the rules for what men do and what women do. Misogyny, however, is the policing force that ensures men and women follow the rules. Role modeling and reinforcement are the misogynistic way we police gender. Sexist rules persist because we collectively reward men and women for "correct" gender behavior and punish those who exhibit "incorrect" gender behavior. This enforcement often happens subconsciously, accidentally, and unintentionally, but it still happens. The harm occurs, regardless of intentions.

If we can unlearn gender norms by changing the behavior we role model, we can also unlearn gender norms by the way we reinforce behavior. Instead of reinforcing gender norms, like in the previous examples, we need to change the words we use to send messages about equity. When we experience someone trying to reinforce gender norms, we need say something. (We'll talk more about this in chapters 9 and 10.)

Your age may affect the way you think about this next exercise. Those who grew up fifty or sixty years ago likely had a very different upbringing than someone who is just coming of age now. So, regardless of age, I ask that everyone focus on incidents during the past ten years.

INTROSPECTION EXERCISE: REINFORCEMENT

1. Read the previous list of behaviors. Circle all of them that you have personally experienced or witnessed in the past ten years.
2. Try to think of three additional examples of negative gender reinforcement from your own recent experience that you could add to this list.
3. Think about how you could flip those three examples from negative to positive. What could have been done differently to reinforce equality instead of misogyny?

NORM PERCEPTION

In the introduction, I told a story about a workshop in Indonesia during which I talked to men about how much they appreciated their wives' empowerment program. In that situation, the men I worked with already knew each other, since they came from the same village. They saw each other day in, day out, walking to and from their plots of land, gathering in the mosque, visiting each other's homes. My work didn't introduce them to new people or even new ideas. The discussion did not actually change anyone's mind. What was exciting about that meeting was that, for the first time ever, those men were given the opportunity to articulate ideas that they hadn't previously discussed before—and to do so in a public setting.

During that meeting, the men realized that they all agreed about how valuable the women's empowerment project really was. By having this one public conversation, they all became acutely aware of how much all of their families benefitted from the women's group. All of a sudden, women's empowerment went from being an undiscussed topic to a community treasure.

The realization was fairly easy to translate into action. Later in the afternoon I asked, "What can you all do to support your women to be even more successful in their empowerment group?" By that point, the men were eager to brainstorm ideas: some began volunteering for their wives' group; some men allocated more family income to invest in the empowerment group; one man agreed to drive the group's snacks to market once a week.

This same phenomenon can be seen here at home. The most far-reaching impact of the social media posts about #MeToo was in building solidarity—survivors coming forward and having an open conversation about sexual assault. What was staggering to many people was how many women had been sexually assaulted in their lifetimes. Many people were shocked and saddened to hear close friends and family members openly talk about their experiences. #MeToo was not just about changing minds. Like the experiences of the Indonesian men, it was also about becoming aware of a truth that we had never publicly processed. Academics refer to this as a *social norms approach,* or *norm perception.* It occurs when a group of people publicly acknowledge a previously held, but unspoken, belief in public. This is done in order to debunk false assumptions and find comfort in a (newly discovered) shared belief.

But public acknowledgment is only the beginning. The actual change comes afterward. Experts agree that *using* the newly agreed-upon information is what allows groups to initiate change.[6] The end result of the men's group in Indonesia was that they began to invest more time and money in women's empowerment. The end result of #MeToo is that society can no longer make excuses for sexual assault.

Let us return to the earlier scenario to demonstrate how norm perception could work in the Thanksgiving situation.

Maybe your family has always had a sexual division of labor at Thanksgiving, but what you did not know is that everyone secretly hates it. Maybe there are many men who do not like football, and some women who are fans. Maybe there are men who want to try a new recipe, and plenty of women that loathe cooking and cleaning. In this case, just asking a simple question could bring this to light and make the family cognizant of a shared belief. *Hey, chefs—mind if I bail on football this year and join you? I want to learn how to make perfect gravy.* If it is too weird to ask everyone in person, try a group text or email, or ask that cousin to speak up—the one who doesn't mind being the inappropriate social assassin. (There's one in every family.)

Of course, there is also risk in asking these questions. You could be outvoted, and your family could stick to traditional roles on Thanksgiving Day. But at least you have introduced the topic, you have gained information, and you likely found a few allies who agree with you. Perhaps this exercise takes you out of gender-default mode and gets you thinking about how you might make your own changes in the future. Maybe you do not have much control over Thanksgiving, but when New Year's is hosted at your house, you will do things differently.

There is greater risk in silence than in asking the question. If we never held that meeting in Indonesia, those men would likely have continued going through life not thinking of women's empowerment much, or even realizing the extent to which women's empowerment improved their individual lives. Staying silent confirms the status quo.

GENDER CHECKUP

Statements can be threatening. Statements can put up walls and end dialogue. A question, however, creates the space for us to hear other opinions. A question can help us consider another perspective or help us articulate our own viewpoint. Listening to another person answer a question can initiate debate and discourse.

As a professional facilitator, I love a good question. A good question focuses our attention and forces us to acknowledge what behavior was role modeled to us, and what we role model to others. A good question helps us identify positive and negative reinforcement in our lives, and opens the door to changing that reinforcement in the future. A good question can prompt us to be more gender aware.

The following Gender Checkup is a series of questions that help you think through your current gender situation. Maybe everything is wonderful, and no change is needed. Maybe something has been on your mind, and this is a great place to begin addressing your concern. Maybe you have not consciously articulated a problem before, but when asked, it gets you thinking.

This checkup is designed to be used over and over—every six months, every year—whatever suits you. Simply answer the questions that apply, and skip those that do not. As your life and circumstances change, you may find yourself answering different questions. It can be helpful to review past answers to see how your roles and perceptions evolve over time.

As you complete this checkup, and as you proceed through the rest of this book, I ask each reader to do two things:

1. BE HONEST. We all put on shows for various reasons. We may act extra-competent in front of our co-workers. We may act übermaternal/paternal in front of the other parents in the park. This is all normal. It is also normal to put on a bit of a show for yourself. I routinely tell myself, *Everything is fine* when I have so much going on between home and work that I am five minutes away from a meltdown.

However, as you read this book and answer these questions, please take a moment to be honest with yourself. Catch yourself if you say, *I don't mind working full time AND cooking dinner every night* or *It doesn't bother me at all that I pick up the kids from day care every day while my spouse goes to the gym.* Stop and ask, *Is this how I truly feel? Or is this the way I have come to feel because it suits my partner, or my kids, or my boss?* Ask yourself, *Am I trying to live up to an idea of perfection that has been role modeled to me? Or am I trying to live up to my own ideal?* Be honest with yourself.

2. BE PURPOSEFUL. We live in gender default for much of our lives, meaning that we have been shaped by social cues without con-

EQUAL PARTNERS

sciously thinking about it. So, while reading this book, try to be gender aware. See things in a new light. Do not answer these questions based on what you have observed, or on what "everyone knows is right." Do not assume the consensus is correct, or accept things the way they are because of silent confirmation. Answer based on what you think and what you feel.

GENDER CHECKUP

1. How would you rate your overall awareness of gender socialization in your life?

   1 = Novice. This is totally new for me.
   2 = Beginner. I notice one or two things a week.
   3 = Getting better. I notice about three to six things a week.
   4 = Expert. I am already gender aware. I notice gender socialization all the time.
   (This is to gauge how much gender is on your mind and whether you are "seeing" gender norms.)

2. Are you currently performing duties that were assigned to you because of your gender identity that you *do not mind*? These could be work related or personal.

   (Sometimes people are happy to do a job, even if it is gendered, because they genuinely enjoy it. But it is still good to be aware of it. For example, I am in charge of all gift wrapping for my family, which I admit is a female-coded task. But I don't care—I genuinely love wrapping a pretty gift.)

3. Are you currently performing duties that were assigned to you because of your gender identity that you *do mind,* and you wish you could change? These could be work related or personal. (For

example, I often fall into the social-planner role for my family, even though I don't want the responsibility for this role. I know it falls on my shoulders only because I am female, and I don't like it.)

4. Is there any role you fill at work that you believe was assigned to you specifically because of your gender identity? Is this something you can live with, or something you would like to change? (For example, a woman is asked to pass around a birthday card, or a man is asked to move heavy furniture.)

5. Do your household chores fall along gendered lines (Female Role = routine and inside; Male Role = intermittent and outside.) Are you content with the division of cognitive labor in your home? Do you think your partner is content with the division of cognitive labor in your home? Do either of you want a change? If so, are both of you open to a change? (This question focuses on all household chores that do not relate to kids. Remember the difference between routine tasks and intermittent tasks that were discussed in chapter 1.)

6. Is there something that you value greatly, perhaps because of your own gender socialization, but your partner does not? Is there any-thing your partner values, but you do not? Is there any desire to better support each other? (For example, one of you thinks taking the time to decorate for the holidays is important, and the other thinks it is a waste of time. Or perhaps you disagree on the definition of clean.)

7. If you had fewer household responsibilities, would you (and do you want to) do more professionally? Would fewer household responsi-bilities mean you could get promoted, take on more responsibility, work different hours for higher wages, etc.? (Often, both people in the relationship will answer yes, and that is normal. But are you both giving up the same amount? Is it balanced? Or does one partner bear the majority of the burden?)

8. Think about the kids in your life. Do you think you are role modeling and/or reinforcing gender equality? Or are you perpetuating negative gender norms? Are there any small changes you can make to role model gender equality? (Consider the questions you ask, or the greetings you use. Do you often tell girls they are pretty and that you like their dress? Or do you ask girls what books they have read lately, or if they like to play any sports in school? Those questions send messages to kids about what society does and does not value.)

If you do not have kids in your home, stop here. If you do, please continue.

9. When it comes to kid-related activities, do you think you do more than your fair share, less than your fair share, or the right amount? Who is the cognitive laborer? Are you content with the amount of time your partner spends on childcare? Do you think your partner is content with the division of childcare? Do either of you WANT a change? Are either of you open to a change? (Remember the phases of cognitive labor when you answer this: anticipating, researching, decision-making, and monitoring.)

10. If you had fewer child-rearing responsibilities, would you (and do you want to) do more professionally? Would fewer responsibilities/hours with kids mean you could get promoted, take on more responsibility, work different hours for higher wages, etc.? (Answering yes to this question does not mean you will act on it—and it could be that your partner also feels as though fewer childcare hours would improve professional outcomes. This question is simply documenting your current perception. It helps when both partners discuss this with each other.)

3

INEQUALITY WITHOUT KIDS

When two people make a commitment and move in together, some shift in routine is inevitable. Theoretically, both partners could continue to do their own laundry, shopping, cooking, cleaning, etc. But in reality, most couples partake in some form of specialization, dividing up household responsibilities. Gender norms, as we have seen, still play a big role in determining who does what.

Jennifer Petriglieri, author of *Couples That Work,* writes that dual-working partners generally fit into three categories:

1. The couple who strives for parity, ensuring that they both have equal time for work and home.
2. The couple who takes turns. One person devotes more time to work and cuts back at home, while the other cuts back at work to focus on home. (They begin this with the understanding that at some point the dynamic will change, and the roles will switch.)
3. The couple who allows one person to take on the household burden for the life of their partnership while trying to maintain a full work schedule.

Experts agree that categories 2 and 3 frequently result in gendered behavior.[1] In category 2, the Female Role is much more likely to step back, and do so more often than the Male Role. In category 3, the person who is burdened with that second shift is almost always in the Female Role, even when that person earns a higher salary. (More on that later in this chapter.)

As detailed in chapter 1, the most common chore divides in North American culture are indoor/outdoor and routine/intermittent. This means that the person filling the Female Role assumes responsibility for the inside tasks and the routine tasks: cooking, cleaning, laundry, and social management. The Male Role assumes responsibility for the outside tasks and the intermittent tasks: mowing the lawn, taking out the garbage and recycling, cleaning the gutters, and managing finances.

According to Medium writer Anja Boynton, the Female Role also tends to be the "Noticer" in the home. I like this label because it captures all the little touches that help make a home cozier, and life a little more enjoyable. The Noticer makes more ice when the tray is low, stocks favorite snacks for a long weekend, switches out warmer blankets in the winter, cracks the windows to clear out a musty smell, and prints out favorite photos for frames in the living room. I find myself in this role all the time. When my first grader's school closed for spring break, he was sent home with his entire desk contents to allow for a classroom cleaning. I noticed the pencils in his case were dull, so I sharpened them all and put on new erasers. I noticed his folders were torn and spruced them up with some duct tape and stickers.

Non-Noticers may read the paragraphs above and think—this is choice, not necessity. No one *needs* ice cubes or picture frames. Kids can sharpen their own pencils at school. But to the Noticer, it is not a choice. Being the Noticer is part of the Female Role's duty. The Noticer feels that this work is expected of them; and if this work goes undone, they will be judged.

I realize that often the Noticer's acts are done willingly and with love. It gave me genuine pleasure to pack up that little pencil case. But being the Noticer does take time and energy, and requires both thoughtfulness as well as active forethought. Perhaps these individual acts do not make or break a household, and one could dismiss them individually. But collectively, they make the home friendlier, more inviting. Noticing adds comfort to everyday life. I venture to guess that non-Noticers appreciate these warm touches more than they care to admit.

But we can't stop at the fact that the Female Role just *does more* in the home. Sometimes the tasks associated with the Female Role are simply more time-consuming than we realize.

Christopher Carrington, whom I referenced in chapter 1, writes about how simple roles such as "feeding work" do not get the credit they deserve. (I'll simplify by calling the person doing "feeding work" the Feeder.) He found, in his research of same-sex couples in Northern California, that the person who identified as doing the feeding work of the home did far more than simply prepare and plate dinner; the Feeder also did all meal planning and shopping, maintained staples in the house, and remembered to bring home specialty items when needed. The Feeder had a deep and detailed knowledge of the tastes and preferences of their partner. When Carrington asked the Feeder what their partner liked to eat, they would launch into a long explanation about allergies and preferences, noting minute specifics such as a fondness of pasta shapes over noodles. This bank of information demonstrated a high level of devotion to and caretaking of the other person; the Feeder not only thought it was important to know what the other liked, but took the time to commit this knowledge to memory and prepare meals accordingly.

On the flip side, when Carrington asked the non-Feeder what their partner liked to eat, they would reply with statements like, *Oh, you know—she likes just about everything.*

Understanding the high level of time and attention it takes to be the house Feeder is essential in understanding how gendered household roles can be so unequal. If the Female Role cooks dinner seven nights a week, and the Male Role washes the dishes, that can appear to be an equal division of labor. But when one fully appreciates the time and attention required of the Feeder, we can easily see this division is not equitable in the least. To balance out this relationship, either the couple needs to trade off and on as Feeder, or make sure the dishwasher is also handling some other cognitive tasks in order to better balance their overall responsibilities.

FRIDA AND MIRIAM

Throughout this chapter, I am going to rely on a couple I have named Frida and Miriam to demonstrate several concepts. Frida and Miriam are a composite of many couples I have met throughout the writing of this book. I have personified Frida and Miriam as women. They could just as easily be two men, a different-sex couple, or a queer couple. The sex of these two characters is less important than the roles they play in their relationship.

Frida and Miriam have been together for several years, and they were recently married. Frida is a public school teacher, and Miriam has a management position at a software company. Miriam earns more money than Frida. Ever since they moved in together, Miriam has taken on the Male Role, and Frida has taken on the

Female Role. They never discussed it—the division just happened naturally.

Frida often stops at the grocery store after school. She decides what to buy and is tasked with all meal prep. She usually gets home about 5:00 P.M. She enjoys cooking, but she wishes it didn't fall on her shoulders every day. Miriam comes home about 7:00 P.M. every night, just about time to help set the table. Most nights they do the dishes together while they continue to chat about their day.

As a teacher, Frida has more days off during the year. She has two weeks off around New Year's, a week off for spring break, and then ten weeks off during the summer. She tutors during these breaks to earn extra money, but these breaks also allow plenty of time for big house projects, such as cleaning out closets, painting, and decorating. Miriam is always appreciative of this kind of household work. She hugs her wife and tells her, "I could never do everything you do—you are amazing! What would I do without you?"

Miriam rarely works on the weekend, but Frida averages five hours every Saturday during the school year. While Frida grades papers and writes lesson plans, Miriam relaxes; she might go for a run, curl up with a book, or meet a friend for coffee. Weekends are also a time to get caught up with housework. Frida tends to track what needs doing; she takes the lead on weekly laundry, cleans the cat box, and scrubs the bathrooms. Frida also has a lower threshold for an untidy home; dishes piled up in the sink or dust bunnies lurking under the couch are triggers for her. Frida feels stressed when her space is a mess, so she takes the extra time to clean her classroom at school—and her house at home.

Miriam isn't lazy. When she notices her wife doing chores, she always asks what she can do to help. But Miriam has a higher threshold for an untidy home. She can turn a blind eye to clutter on the kitchen table or mineral stains in the shower. These things don't bother her very much, so she often dismisses their importance. When Frida uses part of her Sunday to clean the back porch, Miriam will shrug that off. She'll think, *That's just Frida's thing. She brings this work on herself.*

On weekend nights, they tend to spend a lot of time with friends. When she meets new people, Frida has started introducing her partner by saying, "This is my husband, Miriam." Miriam knows this is not a compliment, but she is aware she does less around the house, so she usually laughs and lets it go. On one recent occasion, however, Miriam felt annoyed with this jab. Last weekend, she countered the comment by saying, "Don't believe it for a second. Frida is such a control freak; she makes all the rules. I'm not even allowed in the kitchen!"

The biggest argument they have had since the wedding occurred on the weekend Miriam's parents visited. Frida still didn't feel at ease in front of her in-laws. They lived several hours away and didn't see each other often. Frida saw this weekend as a time to impress, and she searched recipes online for a week leading up to the visit. She wanted everything to be perfect. So, she ran out of school as soon as the bell rang on Friday, did a big grocery shop, and picked up fresh flowers. When she got home, she cleaned the guest room, changed the sheets, and set the table with the platter her in-laws gave them as an engagement gift. The women briefly ate dinner together, and then Frida returned to the kitchen to make a tiramisu for Saturday's dessert. (She knew it was her father-in-law's favorite.)

Miriam sulked around the house for a few hours. She thought Frida was going overboard (after all, it's just her *parents*) and didn't understand her partner's anxiety and fervor. This caused palatable tension in the home. At 10:00 P.M., when Miriam announced she was going to bed, things erupted.

Frida was furious. Knowing she had hours of work ahead of her that night, she couldn't believe Miriam was abandoning her. They argued, both saying things they regretted, and each got so angry they ended up rehashing old arguments about things that happened long ago. Miriam eventually went to sleep when there was nothing left to say. Frida fell into bed hours later. She was exhausted, but she felt good that the house was immaculate and the tiramisu was made.

The women made up in the morning. They both apologized for losing their temper and headed off to the airport to pick up their guests. Miriam's mom immediately complimented Frida on the house when she walked in the door, and Miriam's father raved about the dessert. Frida was thrilled. When Miriam's mom made a snide comment about her daughter, suggesting that Frida was doing too much work in the home, Frida was the one to defend her wife. "Oh, I don't mind. I like cooking. And Miriam is so busy with work—she deserves to relax on a Friday night after a big week."

WHY (AND HOW) ARE WE PERPETUATING DOMESTIC INEQUALITY?

The Pew Research Center reports that 80 percent of Americans agree with the statement "women are deserving of the same rights as men." This seems to be a value that transcends class, race, and political party.[2]

So, why do household imbalances continue? Why do we still expect the Female Role to do so much and the Male Role to do so little?

Why is it that people who value equality still find a way to perpetuate sexism in their own homes?

One reason relates to the culture of fatherhood that we discussed in chapter 1. Like it or not, many people think male participation in domestic spaces has improved so much in the past fifty years that, surely, this is as good as it gets.

When I was first married, I was frequently annoyed about the fact that Evan never rinsed the sink clean after he did the dishes. This resulted in bits of food drying on the side of the sink, which then made the mess harder to clean the next morning. I asked him about it a few times, but that didn't change his behavior. In the end, I decided that either I had to suck it up and rinse out the sink before going to bed, or put up with dry yucky stuff the next morning.

One afternoon I found myself complaining to my mother. I expected a bit of sympathy, but surprisingly, I received a very different message. "I hate to break it to you, honey, but you are expecting too much. You should just be glad he's doing the dishes at all. You've got to be realistic about what men are capable of doing. I suggest you just wash out the sink and let this go."

For the first time in my life, my mother was telling me to lower my expectations. Not once through school, friendships, travel, or jobs had my mom ever encouraged me to settle. But here she was, essentially telling me, *Kate, don't fight this. This is as good as it gets.*

My mother said these words to me from a good place. She was trying to be loving, helping me understand the realities of relationships. She truly believed that it was best not to expect too much from a male partner, and she encouraged me to focus on the good parts so I didn't drive myself crazy over the sink.

But this response can also come from an angry place. I've also heard these "as good as it gets" assertions stemming from self-affirmation.

People who validate other situations are doing so to validate the gender imbalance in their own homes, shielding themselves from criticism. By declaring that "this is as good as it gets," we forgive ourselves as well as each other. This perceived truth holds us back. As long as we collectively assume this is as good as it gets, and we instruct others to believe the same, we will perpetuate the status quo.

The other reason gender inequality persists in our homes is because couples find ways to cover up their gendered behavior by disguising their actions. This happens when people who value gender equality in theory find themselves not living up to gender equality in reality. This is normal and happens with a variety of issues—not just gender. For example, we might *value* environmental awareness, but hope no one notices our long showers or the fact that we put the air conditioner on high all summer long. Connecting our values to our actions is hard, and can require sacrifice.

Allison Daminger, the cognitive-labor researcher introduced in chapter 1, applied an older theory about social dissonance to household labor.[3] She explained to me that when a person's values do not match their actions, they have three options: they can change their values, they can change their actions, or they can *reframe* the perception of the situation so they do not have to change their values or their behavior.

Changing one's values is an unlikely solution. And changing one's behavior is difficult work that requires time, patience, and communication. Not surprisingly, Daminger has found that when it comes to gender roles, couples in her research group often go for the third choice, and reframe their situation. Reframing happens when a couple shifts the focus away from gender, and onto something else, in order to disguise their gendered behavior.[4]

Daminger's work was a big inspiration for me; it gave me the context I needed to make sense of the myriad excuses I hear couples use to cover up their gendered behavior. The six following reframing tactics emerged while I was conducting interviews for this book. I found that these most often explained the various ways our culture tends to hide or cover up harmful gender norms. These are the excuses we tell ourselves and each other—the way we rationalize behavior that clearly isn't living up to our values. I think most people use these subconsciously. We use them because they are easy, because we are tired; we rely on them because they are comfortable shortcuts that gets us through the day.

If you have found yourself using one or more of the following reframing tactics to de-gender your relationship, or de-gender other relationships, don't be hard on yourself. We all do it. These methods of reframing relationships to cover up gendered behavior are so pervasive and so accepted in our culture that they are often hard to detect. Recognizing which tactic(s) you use to reframe your gendered behavior is a great start to making a change. Once you can more easily recognize these tactics, you can better react when they are used.

REFRAMING TACTIC #1: ECONOMICS

Economics is a common way to explain away a gender imbalance in the home. Many people in the Female Role claim that they take on more at home because their partner brings more income to the family. Or, vice versa, people in the Male Role excuse their lack of household attention because of their financial responsibility. But data shows that doesn't stick when the roles are reversed.

Research by Sanjiv Gupta[5] at the University of Massachusetts demonstrates that in different-sex couples in which the female makes a higher income, she still does more work in the home than her male partner. Men whose partners earn more do not, according to Gupta's work, step up at home. The only statistically significant correlation here is that the more money a woman earns, the more she can afford to outsource work. High-earning women do not seem to expect more from their male partners, rather, they expect more from lower-earning laborers who are paid to do household work: nannies, cooks, and cleaners.

Frida and Miriam used this reframing tactic. Even with part-time tutoring work, Frida couldn't earn what Miriam does. Frida feels, if even subconsciously, that because she earns less money, her job is of less value to the family. On the flip side, earning more makes Miriam feel as if she has the power to stay late, which by default leaves her lower-earning partner with more work.

I can't end this section without mentioning the nasty cycle this produces. Women tend to earn less in the economy, so when partnered with a man who earns more, they step up at home to compensate. These additional responsibilities often prevent women from going after more money in the future: applying for a promotion or new job, taking on a special project, going back to school, etc. While she continues to do the bulk of the housework, however, her male partner has the time to do everything necessary to move up the salary ladder. The couple's income gap widens as he receives a promotion, and she does not. Thus the cycle continues.

REFRAMING TACTIC #2: PERSONALITY

How often do you hear the following phrases?

- *She's so much better at organizing.*
- *I am better at managing the kids schedule than he is.*

- *It is really just her personality.*
- *I'm just not as good at multitasking.*

People of all genders use these excuses to cover up the fact that the Female Role is doing more in the home than the Male Role. The prevailing theme is that the Female Role's "personality" lends itself to characteristics required to manage a home. I have heard countless men use this tactic to excuse themselves from housework, suggesting their wife's personality is the reason why she does more in the home than he does. (I find it ironic when the men who use this tactic turn around and demonstrate these same skills in a work environment: leadership, organization, multitasking, and order. No one can convince me that men who set goals, manage teams, and monitor projects at work cannot apply those traits to their homelife.) But I have also heard countless women use this tactic to explain away their own household imbalance.

Frida and Miriam demonstrated this when they met with friends over the weekend. Miriam, likely bruised from being called Frida's husband, tried to cover up the unequal distribution of work. She didn't take ownership of her behavior. Instead she reframed her own shortcomings in terms of Frida's personality, and referred to her wife as a "control freak." No doubt, the traits that allow Miriam to be successful at her management job would nicely translate to the home, if she chose to apply her skills to a domestic situation. But instead of tackling that hard conversation, she chose to deflect at the expense of her partner.

Let's be clear: no one's personality makes them more equipped to handle domestic work. Yes, of course, there are type A personalities that like things a certain way. But the data clearly shows that across North America, in different-sex partnerships, we see a decades-long pattern of women consistently doing at least twice as much work as men in the home. No one can explain that data point with personality; the correlation between work and gender is far too strong.

Here is the more likely explanation: Knowing that she is responsible for, and will be judged on, the state of her home, a woman cultivates a skill set to help her succeed. List making, multitasking, and organizational skills are not biological traits—they are learned coping strategies to help women survive the extraordinary social demands of the Female Role.

Closely related to personality is skill. Many couples might also divvy up the household work based on skill sets: Who is better at what? Who can do the job faster? But similar to the personality argument, gender can also determine skill simply because many of our skill sets stem from our gendered upbringings. Would you be surprised if she is better at deep cleaning a bathroom, and he is better at mowing the lawn? No, because the two people in that relationship bring the skills they were taught as children to their new home.

I find that the reliance on skills is most harmful when discussing matters concerning caregiving. Even in homes without children, there are many things to care for: pets, parents, plants, neighbors, friends—and of course, each other. Caregiving is a female-coded job, and because girls have more opportunity to practice caregiving growing up, the Female Role is assigned caregiving roles as an adult. This is unfair, as caregiving duties are often laborious, but I also find this unfair to the Male Role, as caregiving duties are highly rewarding. Assigning the Female Role all the caregiving duties of the house simultaneously creates far more work for one person, and limits important emotional bonds for the other.

However, there are times when relying on skill sets can be an equitable exercise that ends with a fair result. In fact, in part 2, several people I interviewed actually recommend this strategy for bringing greater parity to the home. I warn you to be careful when depending on skill sets to assign chores. Also make sure to discuss enjoyment level, and take the time to look behind the skill and see if there is a gendered upbringing that enabled that skill to take root in the first place.

REFRAMING TACTIC #3: DIFFERENT PRIORITIES

Priorities are a very convincing tactic because they reframe our household actions as choices. On the surface, who can argue with that? If I choose to do this, and he chooses to do that, who is anyone to say we have a gender problem? But it is worth our time to think a bit more deeply about what lies beneath choice.

Everyone is busy, and no one has the time to do everything they want, all the time. We are forced to prioritize; we start with the No. 1 most important task, and work our way down the list. So, how do we decide what is a priority and what is not? This is when we are influenced by gender norms.

A quick note to Male Role readers: As you read through this section, please remember that I am not trying to justify any and all Female Role behaviors. Try not to fixate on the most eccentric projects, but think through the more routine tasks that take up the bulk of the Female Role's time. Ask yourself, *What does your partner do to help maintain family harmony, communication, and traditions? What would my life be like if my partner stopped doing all these small things that make our home comfortable?*

In chapter 2, we talked about how the messages we hear as children can greatly affect how we act as adults, consciously and subconsciously. When we live in gender default, our priorities often coincide with the tasks that society expects us to do. For example, the gender norm associating boys with income generation can lead to men prioritizing work over the home. The gender norm associating girls with caregiving can lead to women prioritizing home over work.

Western society assigns the Male Role the responsibility of earning enough to provide for his family. If, for whatever reason, he fails to do so, our culture tends to judge him for it. This puts enormous pressure on all men to find a job that pays enough to sustain his family. When an individual or family struggles to make ends meet, it is often the man who is blamed.

Knowing he is the one who is judged when he can't pay the bills makes income generation a priority in this person's life. Therefore, he is less likely to be take notice of things in his home. He is less likely to be concerned about the quality of the couch, or think it is worth the time to put photographs around the room.

Our cultural expectation is that the Female Role should be the homemaker. It is now perfectly acceptable for women to participate in the economy, but the unspoken expectation is that she can work if she earns income along with taking care of the home, which remains her cultural responsibility. When the home is unkempt (physically or emotionally), she is the one held accountable and judged for her failure. This makes "taking care of the home" a huge priority in her life.

Just like paid work, we prioritize domestic work based on responsibility and judgement. If we feel solely responsible for something, and we know that we will be judged if it doesn't get done, we make it a priority. If not, we let that task slide down our to-do list. One can't accept shame for something we do not feel we are supposed to do.

When the Male Role uses the "priorities" tactic to validate the lack of work he does in the home, he essentially dismisses the experience of being raised as a woman in our culture, and mandates that his list of priorities is the list of priorities that everyone should adopt for themselves. This is easy for him to do because he isn't held accountable for any of those to-do list items that are left undone.

Frida and Miriam demonstrate this the night before Miriam's parents arrive for a visit. Miriam sees Frida as "choosing" to go overboard with preparations. Miriam thinks that the house is clean enough and figures they can all go out for dinner on Saturday night. Because she assumes the Male Role, Miriam does not feel responsible for the home. If the house was dirty or unkempt, she wouldn't accept judgement and would likely dismiss criticism. Miriam believes that Frida is simply "choosing" to put on a show for her parents. Believing this is a choice excuses her from all responsibility. She not only gets out of helping Frida, but also manages to avoid any shame for uncompleted tasks.

Frida does not feel like her weekend work is a choice at all. In her mind, the way she was socialized to behave, this must be done—not for the sake of clean sheets or fancy dessert, but because this is how love is shown. This weekend sends a message to Miriam's parents: *We care about you. We are willing to go the extra mile for you. We want you in our lives.* This weekend is an important step to becoming closer as a family. All those special touches are an important and necessary part of strengthening family bonds.

REFRAMING TACTIC #4: THE BOSSY WIFE DECOY

Another effective reframing tactic is to use a decoy to make it look like your house is the opposite of the stereotypical gender divide—

that the Female Role is actually the one in charge: setting the rules, making the decisions, and calling household shots. If there's a bossy wife in the home, how could the Male Role possibly be slacking off? After all, he isn't setting the rules—he is just following them. Do these retorts sound familiar?

- *She wears the pants in our family.*
- *Don't ask me—go ask "The Boss."*
- *I don't make the rules, I just live here.*
- *Happy wife, happy life.*

These tropes perpetuate the notion of the bossy, overbearing wife. We've all heard these phrases; they usually come with a roll of the eyes and a shrug of the shoulders, reminiscent of the old comedic line about a ball and chain. In this light, the Male Role is the one we tend to sympathize with: the "sweet guy" who just tries to keep his partner happy at all costs; the man who repeats "yes, dear" ad nauseam and works to keep the peace in his home. This trope is not only perpetuated by men—people of all genders buy in to this role. I once saw a couple wearing matching T-shirts in a hotel lobby. His read VACATION FINANCER, and hers read VACATION BOSS.

This dynamic may speak to how a couple communicates, to their collective sense of humor, or to how they prefer to project themselves to others. But it certainly doesn't correlate to the gender balance in their home. In fact, it is quite the opposite. In my mind, those who pivot to the bossy wife decoy are very likely participating in a traditional household balance. If it is the Female Role making rules, she is also likely doing all the work to operationalize and enforce those decisions.

Miriam leans into this tactic during their story as well. To deflect attention from her own lack of work in the home, she makes a comment (meant to be funny, of course) about how Frida does not allow Miriam in the kitchen. We know from the description that they are not living an equal lifestyle; far from it. Frida's decision-making in their home in no way correlates with Miriam's input in household work.

It is also worth noting here that this reframing tactic is often used along with humor, and often in public spaces, which makes it uncomfortable to counter. Women who push back are often gaslighted. Their words are either "proof" of their control, or they are dismissed as being too sensitive. These are common ways that structural misogyny polices our actions, putting noncompliant women back in their place.

Closely related to the concept of being bossy is the concept of nagging. I personally hate the word *nag,* and I fought with myself whether or not I should use it in these pages. But many people in the Female Role are called a *nag* when they attempt to keep their partner on task. How often have you heard this type of exchange?

FEMALE ROLE: Have you texted your sister yet? It's her birthday.

MALE ROLE: Not yet, but I will.

FEMALE ROLE: I have been reminding you all morning. Why can't you just do it? It will take ten seconds.

MALE ROLE: I'll get to it when I get to it. I'm an adult. Don't nag me.

FEMALE ROLE: I wouldn't have to nag you if you'd just do it.

It is a chicken-and-egg situation. Not surprisingly, I tend to empathize with the Female Role, knowing that having to be the reminder adds to one's cognitive-labor load. The preference is to get that task done, and cross it off the list. But perhaps the Male Role feels that they want their partner's trust and the space to do it in their own time. And I understand that, too.

I think this boils down to *urgency*. The cognitive laborer has so much on their mind, they are desperate to check anything and everything off their list. When one is driven by urgency, remarks can be interpreted as "shrill" or "bossy" or "nagging." This miscommunication can cause both people in a relationship to feel unheard and misunderstood.

REFRAMING TACTIC #5: SUPERVISOR/ EMPLOYEE RELATIONSHIP

A male colleague recently said to me, when we were chatting before the start of a meeting, "My wife is like the household manager. I'll happily do anything to help, but she is the one who kind of runs things."

Combining personality and skill, this reframing tactic places a couple in a workplace metaphor. Conceptually, this tactic embraces comparative advantage. In a household with two working adults and not a lot of time, it is natural to want to avoid overlaps. So, some couples divide the household duties along management lines—one person assumes a supervisor role, and one person assumes an employee role. Both people have a job to do, and mirroring a workplace structure allows clear responsibility and accountability from both. The "manager" focuses on the cognitive labor, and the "employee" completes tasks as told. Personally, I find this reframing tactic unfair to both.

UNFAIR TO HOUSE MANAGER: Managing a perfect employee can be

a wonderful experience. But when the *House Employee* is not serious about their job, forgets half their tasks, and messes up the other half, it creates more work for the *House Manager*. And there is no recourse. Is your House Employee always late to work? You can't give a bad performance appraisal, demote your partner, or dock their pay. Is your House Employee excelling at work? You can't give a raise, a bonus, or a promotion. (If your mind is drifting toward physical rewards, let me gently remind you that would classify as transactional sex.)

This puts the House Manager in an impossible position; they can assign tasks to their partner, but there is no accountability. They just have to put up with whatever they get. In the end, they give up and take on more work—just to get things done. Everyone knows that it is more trouble to manage a delinquent employee than to do the job yourself.

While writing this book, I went to a friend's house for dinner. During dessert, I was updating the group on my research and what I had written that week. When I started talking about this reframing tactic, one man in particular took interest. When I finished, he interjected, "I get that! That's me! There's a woman that works in my office—and she is underperforming in every way. She misses deadlines, she gives false information in emails to clients—she drives me crazy. It takes so much work to constantly monitor her and make sure she isn't messing up. It adds so much more to my daily list. I often think work would be so much easier without her at all." Then he paused and turned to his wife. "My God, is that the way you see me at home?"

UNFAIR TO HOUSE EMPLOYEE: Organizational structure tends to assume that the supervisor has more expertise than the employee, and employees are expected to listen and follow instructions. We stomach these positions in our work environment because we have no choice; we all need to work to earn money. Navigating work relationships is just part of modern survival. But who wants to live in a world where your partner is thought to know more about—well, everything—than you do? How is that at all romantic? Frankly, I think competency is sexy.

Miriam and Frida have also fallen into this pattern, if only accidentally. Frida has taken on the House Manager role. She tracks what needs cleaning, assumes responsibility for all meals, guests, and laundry. Miriam isn't lazy or useless. She gets up and offers to help when Frida starts in on weekend chores. But Miriam is firmly in the House Employee role, seeing her role as supplemental and not a necessity.

REFRAMING TACTIC #6: BENEVOLENT SEXISM AND HIMPATHY

These two tactics rely on reinforcement. Bolstered by misogyny, these are common ways that our culture ensures that the Female Role is held to a higher household standard, and the Male Role is excused for a lower household standard.

The term *benevolent sexism* was first used by psychologists Peter Glick and Susan Fiske in 1996. Benevolent sexism is best defined by its opposite—*hostile sexism*. Hostile sexism is blatant disrespect to women, which is generally thought to be unacceptable behavior in modern North American culture. Benevolent sexism is not obvious or direct, but it is just as harmful. Because it is disguised as a compliment, it is harder to identify. Benevolent sexism is perpetuated in several ways, but the most important for our discussion is referred to as *complementary gender differentiation*, which is the belief that women have household talents and capacities that men do not.[6]

Everyone likes to believe they're succeeding. Who doesn't like to hear a bit of praise for working hard and doing a good job? But, although appreciation is encouraged, overemphasizing praise for a Female Role doing household work only reaffirms their assignment in the house.

- *This dinner is amazing. I never could have done anything like this.*
- *You do such a wonderful job with the dogs. What would they do without you?*
- *You make the house feel so perfect. I'd live in a dump without you.*

Saccharine praise might initially feel good; it is certainly better than being dismissed or unappreciated. But notice how the above words force the Female Role into a box, trapping them there, compelling them to maintain these high standards, and excusing the Male Role from stepping up. But because these comments are phrased in a complimentary way, the Female Role doesn't often notice that, in reality, they're being relegated to household work.

Miriam uses benevolent sexism when she praises Frida for the projects she does during school breaks. Again, I don't want to confuse this with appreciation. I fully admit, these fall on a fine line that can be hard to decipher. But, by asking yourself a few questions, you can usually determine if this is genuine praise for a job well-done, or something more harmful: *Is the person lavishing praise also the one who does far less in the home? Does the lavisher or praiser ever intend to do more, or is this language used to try and maintain the status quo?*

Kate Manne coined the term *himpathy* in her 2019 book, *Down*

Girl, to describe the disproportionate sympathy that men enjoy over women in situations of sexual abuse and intimate-partner violence. Since then, this term has been used more broadly to describe the many ways men benefit from being held to a lower standard than women. Manne herself uses the term to describe men's entitlement to domestic labor in her 2020 book, *Entitled: How Male Privilege Hurts Women.*

Himpathy can be hard to describe to those who have never felt it. When I try to characterize the himpathy I have felt in my own life, I use words such as *gnawing, uneasy,* and *uncomfortable.* It is a feeling that I am doing something wrong, though for the life of me I can't quite put my finger on what. It is the feeling I get when I think I am being too selfish, asking for too much, or asserting myself too much.

Himpathy is the reason the Female Role feels guilty when they ask their partner to do their fair share in the home; why the Female Role laughs off poor attempts at household work, or protects the Male Role's leisure time by doing more than their fair share. Himpathy, paired with the belief that "this is as good as it gets," is the reason why the House Manager forgives the House Employee's poor performance, laughing off their inadequate subpar contributions and picking up the slack.

Frida, though she is married to a woman, expresses himpathy when her mother-in-law criticizes Miriam's role in the home. Frida might not know why—perhaps it is linked to Miriam's salary or the Male Role Miriam has assumed in the home—but Frida makes excuses for her wife, insisting that she doesn't mind doing the work, and explaining that Miriam is so tired at the end of a hard week, she shouldn't be expected to cook and clean. Never mind that Frida also works a full week, and anyone who has taught school knows that being in front of a classroom for five days straight is no less taxing than an office job. Quite the opposite, Frida is probably more deserving of some downtime at the end of the week. But she still steps up to defend Miriam's comfort at the direct expense of her own.

WHERE DO WE GO FROM HERE? NEW RELATIONSHIPS

When people are dating and considering a long-term commitment, it is common for family and friends to encourage the new couple to talk about big issues. *Do you want kids? Do you expect to follow a certain faith? What are your financial goals? What are your professional goals?* But those conversations rarely go into the nitty-gritty of daily life, and it is precisely the banality of everyday life can make or break a relationship.

Establishing patterns of equality from the beginning of a relationship is always best. Take advantage of other changes happening during this time and establish a fresh routine for both of you. This is far easier than changing routines at a future date. For relationship veterans, these topics might be on your mind—as are past experiences—as you enter a new commitment. For a rookie, the idea of household balance might have never entered your mind (even more reason to initiate a conversation at the beginning of your relationship).

I wish I had some magic advice that would make this process quick, fun, easy, and painless. But honestly, discussing gender norms can be uncomfortable, and there is no shortcut to having genuine, open dialogues with your partner. Note the plural use of the word *dialogues*. Combatting gender norms, establishing new patterns, recognizing reframing tactics, and overcoming them requires far more than one conversation. Confronting a lifetime's worth of learned gender norms is not a quick process.

It is always good to start with a simple conversation. I'll give you some example questions in the box below. You might not know how to answer all these questions, and you might not like what your partner has to say. But talking through these issues helps you both move from gender-default mode into gender-aware mode, which will prepare you both for finding greater parity in your relationship.

As you think through and/or discuss these questions, remember that problems are hard to see when they are not your own. Our own lived experiences lead us to see our own truth, and can prevent us from seeing the experiences of others. I encourage all readers to be brave enough to ask questions you think you know the answer to, or questions you believe have an obvious answer. You might be surprised.

QUESTIONS TO DISCUSS BEFORE MAKING A COMMITMENT

1. Do you think the person who works fewer hours should do more housework? Why?

2. Do you think the person who makes less money should do more housework? Why?

3. Is one of you is ultimately responsible for the home, or do you see the home as a shared responsibility? Why do you feel this way? What implications does this have in terms of time?

4. What do you each value about the home? What is most important? Least? If you have differing opinions, do you think this could be due to learned gender behavior? How do you plan to address this?

5. Are both of you good at noticing? Is one of you better than the other? What implications does that have for your relationship?

6. Which one of you tends to fall into the cognitive laborer role? What can be done to recalibrate this imbalance? (The more specific your answer, the more likely for follow-through.)

7. Does one of you have a higher threshold for a mess? How are you going to address this so you are both comfortable in your home, and you share the housework equally?

8. Do you ever accidentally use any of the reframing tactics to potentially cover up gender default? If so, what can you do to rectify that?

9. Are you comfortable telling each other that you've done an invisible task? For example, do you both agree to say things like, *Hey, just so you know, I stayed up past midnight last night researching transportation options to Grandpa's house.* Why or why not?

10. How important do you think saying *thank you* is, in regard to household work? Do you like to hear it? Do you like to say it?

Finding the right place to talk is important. I discovered (probably years later than I should have) that Evan does not like having personal conversations in public. I disagree. I am fine arguing in a park or busy restaurant; it is unlikely anyone is listening to us. And even if they are, who cares? But I found, when he's uncomfortable, the conversation tends to go poorly. So now we try our best to tackle big conversations in a private, indoor space. Other people might prefer to be outside, walking or driving. It is worth the time to find a place where you both feel most comfortable.

Finding the right time to talk is also important. Some couples I interviewed for this book rely on weekly or monthly appointments for big conversations. Some couples might find a routine dinner appointment to be helpful; others prefer spontaneity. It might take some trial and error to establish what works for you.

After these initial conversations, as you share a home together, disagreements are bound to come up. That is the nature of relationships; it is inevitable that you will have different opinions about how to spend time and energy. And of course, not every argument is going to be about gender—far from it. But it is worth pausing during disagreements (or after, when you've cooled down) to consider whether a gender norm is lurking beneath your argument. If you suspect a gender issue is at the heart of your disagreement, try to blame the norm and not the individual in front of you.

Remember that gender norms frame our past, but they do not have to dictate our future. Perhaps the best thing you can do from the start is be open and honest as you discover what roles you are each performing because you feel like you have to, based on social pressure, and then work together to lighten each other's burden. If the Male Role feels pressure to make a certain salary, talk through that, and work together to jointly earn a reasonable and realistic income. If the Female Role feels pressure to maintain family relationships, discuss that, and work together to jointly maintain the social calendar.

Returning to our composite couple, I would urge Frida and Miriam to talk about the fact that they have different comfort levels with clutter, and try to come to a compromise over time. Maybe Frida finds some ways to relax her standards, and Miriam steps up to complete chores—not to her own standards, but to her wife's standards. I would want them to identify each other's triggers, and then try to diffuse tension before it arises. If dishes in the sink send Frida's blood pressure into orbit, perhaps Miriam can start her day by cleaning up the kitchen as a way to show her love.

Next, I would encourage Frida to explain to Miriam the overwhelming responsibility she feels to prepare for guests—and the judgement she would internalize if she were to fail. I would suggest Frida find the words to explain why these weekends are so important for family bonding, and why she feels such pressure to get everything just perfect. I hope that Miriam would hear those words and say, *We are a team. What is important to you is important to me. Even if I don't really understand why this matters so much, it is enough to me that it matters to you.*

At this point of mutual understanding, they can work together to prepare for Miriam's parents in a way that makes them both comfortable. Maybe Miriam will remind Frida that she does not need to be perfect, and that a bowl of ice cream is just as delicious as tiramisu. Compromise is important, and Frida can also learn to alter her expectations; once she receives praise for "less than perfect" work, perhaps she'll feel more comfortable relaxing her standards in the future. Then, when their guests give a compliment, Frida and Miriam can share in the credit. And if a future visit falls flat, they can both take responsibility for dropping the ball.

I understand this may seem like an unrealistic fairy-tale ending. I admit, life doesn't always go this smoothly. Like everything else, communication and compromise take practice. But over time, when couples see how their behavior is shaped by gender norms, they can begin to make changes. Some people are naturally comfortable with confronting the status quo and will have an easier time rejecting a mother-in-law's expectations. For others, this will be a monumental struggle. Each couple can decide how far to push back, but all possible end points begin with some honest self-reflection.

WHERE DO WE GO FROM HERE?
EXISTING RELATIONSHIPS

When you have been together for some time, you most likely have patterns of behavior that are well established, and those patterns may be rooted in gender norms. Changing established patterns is hard, but not impossible.

Typically, the Male Role is less likely to initiate change. Why would the person doing less voluntarily step up and volunteer to do more? Most likely the Female Role would have to start this conversation. In these circumstances, I suggest you avoid framing the conversation as "this is why my role in our relationship is unfair." Try to talk about how both of you are likely doing things for the relationship that you don't want to do. Remember, gender norms are restrictive to all people. Talk about how you feel restricted—and ask how your partner may feel restricted.

Sometimes it can be hard to even articulate exactly what the problem is; it is hard for the cognitive laborer to explain their role at all. Over the years I have used an activity in workshops that I have found helpful, which I will share here. This activity does not necessarily solve anything, but it can bring inequities to light.

WHAT I DID YESTERDAY

INSTRUCTIONS: Each person needs a pen and a blank piece of paper. Take twenty to thirty minutes to sit quietly while each of you writes down everything you did *yesterday*, from the time you woke up, to the time you went to sleep. The more detail, the better. Did you listen to the news while getting ready for work, or did you sneak around in a dark bedroom so as not to wake your partner? Details are important.

Try to note what you thought about during quiet times. Often our minds wander when we're showering, commuting to work, working (depending on our job), exercising, etc. What did you think about in those moments of quiet?

Honesty is essential. If you accidentally spent twenty minutes playing a game on your phone, be honest about that. If the phone call with your sister lasted an hour instead of ten minutes, note that, too.

When you're both done, place your papers side by side so you can easily see each other's work.

1. Put a star next to all the household *tasks that you did not mind doing,* for example, "ran to grocery store" or "took dog for walk." (You might have a difference of opinion on which things were done for the household. For example, one could argue "buy gift for nephew" can be categorized as duty or enjoyment. But those conversations are also important because it will help you investigate some of your core values.)

2. Put an *X* next to all the tasks that were done for your mutual benefit *that you did mind,* that felt like chores or sacrifices, for example, "cleaned drain in bathtub" or "did laundry." (This is important because you could be making sacrifices your partner doesn't need/

appreciate. This could lead to good conversations about whether or not this is necessary at all.)

3. Circle all the things that were neither work related nor family related. In other words, circle all the things that were just for you, for example, "going to the gym," "watching TV," "going to dinner with friends," etc.

4. You don't have to worry about specificity down to the minute, but generally decide how much time you each spent working, how much time you each spent doing something for the household, and how much time you each spent doing something for yourself. How do these numbers compare? Are you happy with your own number? With your partner's number? Is this reflective of a larger pattern? Is this a pattern you want to change?

*If you have more time, do this for two days. In this case, make sure you each detail one working day and one day off, so you can better capture what is done during leisure time.

If that activity feels forced, you can simply ask yourselves the questions targeted for new couples. It might be enlightening to see how much you agree or disagree on some fundamental concepts. Professional help is always a great option. While researching this book, I have spoken to both clients and counselors, and I have heard that therapy can be life changing for some. If you feel as if you and your partner need help with communication and/or compromise, professional counseling may be helpful.

If you are reading this and feel as though you are the one who is overburdened, and your partner is unwilling or uninterested in even talking about gender norms, then you have fewer options. But this doesn't mean you have no options. Start with the additional resources section at the end of the book, and then think about what you do have the power to change.

You might consider reframing a few gender roles for yourself in order to alleviate some of your burden. This does not require your partner's cooperation; it is something you can do on your own. Look for gendered behavior you can cut out of your week. No one will perish if gardens get weedy, clothes do not get ironed, holiday cards are skipped, or "DIY dinner" is enacted every other night.

Whatever you choose, if you decide to reject a gender norm in order to lighten your load, be prepared for pushback. You might receive negative feedback outwardly or in a passive-aggressive way. Talking this over with a friend or family member might be helpful: someone to support you, to be an ally, and to hear you vent when you need to. Remember—you can only feel shame if you accept it. Rejecting shame is hard, but it is possible.

On the other hand, you might even find that no one else cares either—that you were carrying around this responsibility for years, with no one to hold you responsible but yourself. Like norm perception theory from chapter 2, you might find that everyone else is also performing gender norms—and you are not the only one who needs a break.

SUPPORTING CHARACTERS

It is unrealistic to expect any couple to take on gender norms alone. Couples do not exist in bubbles, so we should not expect them to make changes in bubbles. We, as a culture, perpetuate gender norms, so we, as a culture, need to work together to bring about change.

A few years ago, Evan and I were faced with a hard professional decision. For most of our relationship, we have been able to compromise, or be creative, and figure out win-win solutions that satisfy us both. But in this one circumstance, the decision was zero-sum; we could not both get our way. We were both offered professional opportunities at the same time, and geographically we could not do both. For the first time, we had to make a very tough decision.

For Evan, the choice was easy. My opportunity (which was related to writing this book) was something I had long worked for, and he didn't have to think about it twice. He insisted that, this time, we choose my opportunity. He was satisfied turning his offer down.

I agreed, but—surprisingly—I agreed reluctantly. I fully admit that I was falling into patterns of himpathy, and even though I recognized the reframing tactic for what it was, I couldn't change the way I felt. I worried about being the reason Evan had to give up a career opportunity. Yes, I knew intellectually that I had supported many of his career opportunities in the past. But the decision was still very hard for me. I was far more comfortable in the "giving" role than the "taking" role. The whole situation left me feeling guilty and conflicted.

So, I did what I do whenever I have tough decision to make; I called my mom. And then I called my closest friends. And then I ran it by a colleague. I even ran it by one of Evan's colleagues. Every single conversation ended with someone validating our decision. I heard, "Kate, you have supported Evan's career for years and worked around his job. This is your turn. Do not give this up." I heard, "I can understand why this makes you feel uncomfortable, but you are doing the right thing." I heard, "He loves you and supports you, too. You have to do this. He won't resent you—if anything, he might resent you if you don't take this opportunity!" Over the course of about a week, I heard many voices validate my feelings, endorse my decision, and encourage me onward. I almost wept with gratitude; it was exactly what I needed.

But it got me thinking. What would have happened if the calls had gone differently? What if I had heard from my friends and family, *He does make more money than you, maybe you should reconsider.* Or, *I don't know, Kate. This book idea is a stretch. What if it doesn't work out? Maybe you should go with Evan's offer.* Or worse, *Men end up resenting women who hold them back. Are you sure you want this hanging over your relationship? Maybe you should find a way to make it work.*

I don't know if that would have changed my mind or not, but it certainly would have made my situation much, much harder. I needed that encouragement, and I needed that validation—not just once, but from many people in my life. It took six phone calls over the course of a week before I felt I was making the right decision.

Working through gender norms is not easy. Agreeing with a theory in the abstract is simple enough, but applying change to your own life and going against what is culturally acceptable can be messy and confusing. We need support and encouragement from our broader network to make this happen. It is hard enough to stand up to gender norms as a group—it is almost impossible to do it alone.

Community matters. If you have gotten to the end of this chapter but do not see this information as relevant to your own relationship, then I encourage you to broaden your scope. Think about other couples in your life who might be working through these issues: kids, grandkids, nieces, nephews, neighbors, friends, colleagues. You might be the one who can recognize reframing tactics in others, see when couples are struggling with a gender norm, and be the encouraging voice they need to hear in order to help them through life's tough decisions.

4
INEQUALITY WITH KIDS

Tina from Indiana told me how she "accidentally" fell into a neo-traditional marriage. Like many other mothers, Tina knows that she is doing far more in her home than her husband. And she resents it. She also resents the fact that she never agreed to this situation; she finds herself trapped in a life that she never wanted. She never intended to be a stay-at-home mother; she always intended to have an equal partner. And she thought she had one. Until she had a baby.

Tina identifies as white and was born and raised in the Midwest. Her childhood home included a mother and father who role modeled an equal partnership long before the concept was trendy. Her mother tended to do chores in the home, but her father was the cognitive laborer; he tracked the family calendar, managed all the kid-related appointments for Tina and her brother, planned birthday parties, and made grocery lists. Tina didn't give much thought to her upbringing, although she was vaguely aware that her household was different than other kids'. Her father did have health issues that prevented him from doing some physical tasks, so Tina assumed her parent's division of labor had more to do with her father's health and less to do with gender. "I grew up with this great role model. I just assumed this would be my life later on."

Tina met Eric when she was in her late twenties. He was every bit the modern man; he described himself as a feminist and said all the right things about women's rights and systemic injustice. Tina always made it clear that her career was very important to her, and Eric eagerly agreed. "I remember him saying once that he would be happy to be a stay-at-home dad." Tina thought she had found a guy just like her father.

Eric was living with his parents at the time; he was an academic and had just moved back to his hometown. Because of this, the couple usually hung out at Tina's while dating. "I didn't really see his living space at his parents' house. I guess I didn't think about it." Tina was shocked when they moved in together. "I realized he had different standards [than me]. He lacked pride of his space. Like, how often he cleaned the bathroom, or changed the sheets, or he would leave a bag of groceries in the middle of the floor for days. His standards are just so low. I just started doing everything."

Occasionally, Eric would acknowledge that he wasn't doing enough in the home. In these moments, Tina felt hopeful. "I would try to make lists to help him. But it was just never sustainable. It would work for one or two weeks, and then it would go back to normal."

Charlotte came along a few years later. When the baby first came home, Tina described her husband as a *hands-on dad* and used that term as a compliment. Eric didn't shy away from changing diapers or rocking Charlotte to sleep. But Tina was the cognitive laborer. She handled all planning, all shopping, and all correspondence with the day care. She has maintained that level of work ever since. At the time of this conversation, Charlotte was two and a half years old, and Tina was near breaking point.

"Now I just do everything," she told me. Eric's lack of household participation is causing Tina psychological harm, and their marriage is suffering. Tina admitted she wasn't happy, and she told me that she and Eric argue a lot. I could hear the resignation and fatigue in her voice. "I tried going to a therapist, and that was a good vent. Sometimes Eric came and that felt productive at the time, and I was able to tell him how I felt. But nothing works. I feel pretty hopeless now. I guess I have three choices. I can hire help, which I don't know if we can afford. I can do it all myself. Or I can leave him. I think a lot about leaving him. And he begs me not to. But those are my options."

Valuing gender equality does not automatically transfer into actions, and what people talk about when dating doesn't always manifest into behaviors when they share a home. Many cognitive laborers who feel trapped in an unbalanced relationship aren't quite sure when everything went wrong; it is more of a slow downward spiral, until one person is left feeling exhausted, unappreciated, burned-out, and bitter.

I understand that defeat. And I am not naive. I know many relationships will never change, and many in the Female Role have to face hard choices alone. But as a community, we need to think outside this box and give ourselves more options than what Tina sees in front of her. We need to stop asking, *How do I live with this?* or *Can we solve this problem?* We need to phrase the question in the affirmative and ask, *How do we solve this problem? If not for ourselves, then for our children?*

CHILDREN. CHANGE. EVERYTHING.

Maybe some couples who practice household parity naturally maintain that balance after a baby enters the home. But equity is not the norm for most couples, and the caregiving workload tends to fall on the Female Role.

Data on the household transition after the arrival of the first baby surprised even me. *The Washington Post* reported, in a study of two hundred different-sex couples, many of whom openly aimed for equity in their marriage, that household parity was mostly achieved before the first baby came; both partners worked an average of forty hours a week, and both did an average of fifteen hours of housework a week. After the first baby, however, there was a dramatic shift. Women's housework stayed at about fifteen hours per week, and women added an average of twenty-two hours of childcare per week. Fathers, however, only averaged fourteen childcare hours per week, and their share of housework actually *declined* to an average of ten hours per week.[1]

So, after the first baby, even couples who had previously achieved parity fell into traditional gender norms. After the baby came, the women were doing thirty-seven hours of work in the home, and the men were only doing twenty-four hours. (I don't know about you, but I can think of a lot of things I could do with thirteen extra hours a week.)

I was eager to talk to Brigid Schulte about this topic. She authored that *Washington Post* article, as well as the book *Overwhelmed: Work, Love, and Play When No One Has the Time.* She is also the director of the Better Life Lab at New America. Schulte agrees that gender norms underpin this household labor gap. She told me, "The feminist movement has focused on advancing equity in the public sphere. And while that's critically important, we're never going to see true change until we have gender equity in the care sphere at home as well. We need to collectively come to see that all people are responsible for care, are expected to do care, are equipped to give care, and benefit from giving and getting care."

When we use the words *mother* and *father* in English, we might

110

assume these are equivalent terms. The only difference is that one describes a female parent and one describes a male parent, or at least, this was my naive assumption when I had my first child. I quickly learned, as many others do, that the social expectations we have of a mother are far greater than the social expectations we have of a father.

The expectation of "motherhood" requires more time, more emotional bandwidth, more planning, more love, more sacrifices, more patience, more judgement, more strength, more attention, and much, much more caregiving, whereas the expectation of "fatherhood" remains focused on financial provisions. Each set of expectations has its own challenges, but I find that, generally, it is harder and more time-consuming to be a good mother than to be a good father, and it is easier for a woman to fail at motherhood than for a man to fail at fatherhood. We have set the caregiving bar too high for mothers and too low for fathers. And it is time to recalibrate.

As we move forward, I want to presume a shared understanding that all humans have the potential to be exceptional parents. I will use the terms *parents* and *parenthood* as much as possible in the hope of de-gendering social assumptions. I will only use the terms *mother* or *father* if I am describing the socialized expectation we associate with each role.

Like Tina, many people assume, because the conversation occurred once, or because you had near-equity before kids, that that balance will naturally continue. But this is rarely true. Couples who want to find parity after kids need to have regular and specific conversations that go beyond deciding who is going to do what. Couples aiming for equity in parenthood need to talk about values, intentions, and expectations.

The following questions are a starting point for those conversations. If possible, I recommend preliminary conversations long before the baby/child joins the family. Of course, there is no expectation that you discuss all the questions in one sitting. Answer the questions that apply to you today and save the others for later. There is no rush. These should not feel like homework.

QUESTIONS TO DISCUSS BEFORE THE FIRST BABY/CHILD

1. Do you think that one of you is more naturally suited to being a parent? What leads you to that decision? Do you think there is a gender norm or assumption that lies at the root of your opinion?

2. Do either of you need additional parenting skills and/or knowledge before the baby comes? How can you address this need? (Consider books, therapy, talking to others, research, etc.)

3. Do you anticipate one of you will be the "alpha" parent? Or do you want to try to be fifty-fifty co-parents to the extent possible?

4. Your lives will change after the baby comes. What changes are you looking forward to?

5. What change(s) makes you nervous or anxious? Why? Is there anything your partner can do to help mitigate this stress or anxiety?

6. List three things you're willing to give up/cut back on/sacrifice to make more time for childcare and housework. (Things to consider: working fewer hours, hobbies, exercise, friends, sleep, TV, video games, etc.)

7. List one thing you are not willing to give up: something that you really want to maintain if at all possible, perhaps to maintain emotional health and wellness. (This should be other than work;

the assumption is that both of you will continue to work after all potential leave is used up.)

8. Name one baby-related chore you do not want your partner to do; something that (for whatever reason) you want to keep control of.

9. Exhaustion is a common feeling for new parents. What self-care can each of you practice when the baby comes to make sure you're taking care of yourself—and taking care of each other—mitigating that exhaustion?

10. Are you planning for one of you to breastfeed? If so, what is the non-breastfeeding parent going to do during breastfeeding hours? What can the non-breastfeeding parent take on to balance out the caretaking load?

11. Name one thing you would love to take off your baby to-do list, but feel like you would be judged if you did so. Discuss this with your partner. Is there a way for your partner to help you with this item, or can you tackle the judgement together so this list item can be eliminated?

12. Are you comfortable asking your partner for help? Why or why not?

13. If you ever feel like you are doing too much, how can you signal this feeling to your partner without putting them on the defensive?

14. What are some hobbies you would love to eventually share with your child? What are some ways to integrate those things that bring you joy with parenting—so you can do both at once: enjoy a hobby *and* spend time with your baby?

MARTIN'S BABY SHOWER

Much of our gendered behavior about what the Female Role will take on, and what the Male Role will take on, starts long before the baby is born. This is why, before we get into household roles, I want to pause and consider the tradition of a baby shower.

I have thought a lot about baby showers since I first spoke to Martin. He identifies as Latino, lives in South Texas, and works in public transportation. When he and his partner were expecting their first child, his work colleagues threw a baby shower in his honor, which was a total surprise. The event meant the world to Martin. "I hadn't even been there that long, but they threw the nicest shower for me. I walked into the break room, and boom! And at first, I thought, *For me? For a dad?* But I was so excited, I took pictures. I couldn't wait to tell my wife. It was so awesome. And they went all out; they had the tables covered, and they decorated the walls. It was the greatest thing. I really enjoyed celebrating the moment with them."

Martin's story got me thinking about the tradition of baby showers, including my own. My Ohio baby shower is one of my very happiest memories. I didn't want a mixed-sex shower; I looked forward to celebrating the occasion with a specific group of women. It was a perfect afternoon, and I loved every minute of it. But in hindsight, I cringe that, during the shower, my dad and my uncles took my husband out for beers. I spent hours opening gifts of bottles, toys, clothing, and books—everything I could ever need to be a new mom. And Evan ate BBQ.

What message did this send? This situation makes it pretty clear whom society expects to care for the baby, and who gets a pass. No wonder the Female Role feels the weight of the household on their shoulders; that work starts before the baby is even born. And the Male Role is—well, excluded.

Martin's experience was very different. The fact that his colleagues threw him a shower was a way to say, *Hey, you're going to be a dad. We're really excited for you, and we want to support you and help you enter fatherhood. So, here are some things you might need to be the best dad you can be.* After that event, Martin felt proud, he felt prepared, and he felt that this group of people had faith in him—which in turn, gave him confidence in himself. I also like that Martin's partner was not included. When a pregnant person is present, we tend to (rightly) make them the center of attention. I like the fact that "fatherhood" was enough of a reason for Martin's co-workers to celebrate.

I am not against women-only showers. As I said, I loved my own. But I do think we need to be aware of the implicit messages we are sending when we throw showers, and consider how we can alter that message. Sometimes, modern baby showers include both parents-to-be, and sometimes they are all-female. But in different-sex couples, rarely are showers for dads only. Since that conversation with Martin, I am officially a big fan of dad showers. I am not talking about a hypermasculine version of a shower with a NASCAR or fishing theme. I think we need to normalize simple showers that give dads-to-be the love, support, and tools they need to be great fathers. We need to send all parents-to-be the same messages we have sent to mothers for years: *We know you can do this. We're here for you. Here's some of what we've learned. Don't hesitate to ask if you have any questions.*

For any kind of shower, my No. 1 plea is to please skip the gender reveal. I know this was popular for a time, and I still see accessories in party stores to support gender-reveal activities and cakes. But remember, you are not revealing the baby's gender—gender is linked to identity. You are only revealing whether or not your fetus appears to have male sex organs or female sex organs. The buildup around "is it a blue cake or a pink cake?" only magnifies heteronormative assumptions: that all people identify with the sex or gender assigned to them at birth; that all people are either female or male; and that male = blue and female = pink. If a couple wants to know the sex of the baby before birth, fine. But we don't need to make the child's assumed gender identity the focal point of the shower.

My friend Melissa, whom we met at the beginning of chapter 1, asked me to include this additional note: stop asking the parents-to-be what sex of baby they would prefer. What people are actually asking is what *gender* is preferred. I agree with Melissa; this is dangerous. Aside from setting ourselves up for potential disappointment, asking a parent's gender preference only reaffirms assumptions about what baby girls are like and what baby boys are like: She wants a girl so she can put her in dresses; he wants a boy so he can teach his son to play football. Of course, we know there are plenty of cute clothes for all babies, and a child of any gender can love (or hate) playing football.

I'm not judging any showers of the past; they were products of their time, and they were all thrown with love. My own shower was a decade ago, and my dad and uncles were showing Evan love the best way they knew how. I am just suggesting that, looking forward, perhaps we can make some small changes. There are many creative ways to construct a shower around equal partnership, while still maintaining the best of our cultural traditions.

ADDITIONAL SUGGESTIONS FOR RETHINKING BABY SHOWERS

- If you are the host of a shower, you can send a powerful message about gender just with theme and color choice. A neutral shower is always a possibility, with decorations and gifts in shades of green, yellow, gray, and white. (This is also helpful for subsequent siblings who inherit the hand-me-downs.)

- A gender-neutral toy theme can send a strong message, and make people think about what is marketed to girls and what is marketed to boys. Explicitly ask guests to come with a gift appropriate for a child under the age of two, regardless of sex or gender identity. It might be interesting to see what people bring.

- In Martin's honor, host a shower just for the father-to-be. Don't give goofy gifts like a mini–catcher's mitt or a toy truck. Give him the tools needed to care for a newborn: bottles, diapers, crib sheets, and clothes.

- All-female showers can find a way to boost the confidence of both parents-to-be. For example, the host could send a note and a gift to the new dad, making it clear that great things are expected from him, too.

- If the sex of the unborn baby has been announced, you could push back on gender norms by considering a math and science theme for a baby girl; gifts could include STEM-themed books, Tinkertoys, building blocks, and Play-Doh. Or consider a caregiving theme for a baby boy; gifts could include a play kitchen, dolls, or stuffed animals.

- Consider giving gender-themed books to the parents-to-be, to help them navigate the next few years. In addition to their own copy of

Equal Partners, I suggest *Dear Ijeawele: A Feminist Manifesto in Fifteen Suggestions*, by Chimamanda Ngozi Adichi; *How to Raise a Feminist Son: Motherhood, Masculinity, and the Making of My Family*, by Sonora Jha; and *Parenting Beyond Pink & Blue: How to Raise Your Kids Free of Gender Stereotypes*, by Christia Spears Brown.

- One of the most thoughtful baby gifts I received was a basket that held twelve individually wrapped books. On our baby's one-month birthday we unwrapped the first book. This continued every month until we unwrapped the last book on her first birthday. This is a great idea: give twelve children's books that *do not* reinforce gender norms.

EQUAL PARENTS FROM DAY ONE

Once again, it is best to form patterns from the very beginning. To avoid the Supervisor/Employee scenario described in chapter 3, many couples have reported success with the "divide and conquer" approach. Instead of one person overseeing all baby-related matters, the couple splits the responsibilities. This also helps divide the cognitive burden because with each task comes the mental work of anticipation, decision-making, planning, and evaluating. Each parent holds themselves accountable for those responsibilities, and trusts their partner to get their work done. The additional resources section of this book includes further guidance on how to go about dividing chores equitably.

For now, I would like to take some time to discuss three specific issues that often challenge the household gender balance, making it hard for couples—even those who value equity—to truly find a fifty-fifty balance: breastfeeding, parental leave, and parenting style.

1. BREASTFEEDING

Sometimes, breastfeeding is an option, and for a variety of reasons, sometimes it is not. I preface this next section by saying that I am not advocating for one choice over the other; whatever a couple decides is great. But the truth is that couples who decide to breastfeed may find their caregiving balance challenged.

Bottle-feeding a baby means that both parents can share in the feeding, during the day and at night. Lucas from Texas was fostering a one-month-old infant when we spoke, and Lucas told me how he and his husband managed to split feeding responsibilities. "We find it works best for one of us to sleep with the baby. We decided that for a couple reasons—mostly because he is feeding every three hours. So, we set up a single bed in the nursery, and every other night I sleep in the baby's room, and every other night [my husband] does. Whoever isn't sleeping with the baby does all the bottle prep. So, every other night, I take the baby. And every other night I do the bottles and then I have from 9:30 P.M. to 6:30 A.M. free. That is my time, when I can do whatever I want. Sometimes I just sleep, or I can do emails. But it is my time. I know some people might object to this, but it works for us right now."

Breastfeeding, however, means that this giant responsibility sits exclusively with only one of you, and likely dominates your schedule during the baby's first few months of life. It is not simply the hours spent feeding. Being the breastfeeding parent means that you're constantly preoccupied with knowing when the next feeding is, where you will be at that time, and if the baby is getting enough nutrition—not to mention the time it takes to sooth sore nipples, deal with blocked ducts, and clean up unanticipated letdowns. If pumping is involved, the time practically doubles. It takes a lot of time to pump, store, and track breast milk.

I have a colleague who recently shared that, while she was breast-feeding her infant (night or day), her male partner was up and about in a supportive roll. "He never slept while I fed the baby. He also got up, even in the middle of the night. He'd pick up around the house or bring me a cup of tea or a snack. Sometimes he would just rub my shoulders or sit next to me. Some of my friends laughed at me— they couldn't believe I made him do that. But I didn't *make* him do anything. We agreed on it, together. It made me feel less lonely. I felt supported. It was amazing."

In this story, it was other women who tried to make this breast-feeding mom feel guilty about her husband's role during feeding time. I didn't speak to those women, so I cannot pretend to know what motivated their comments, but it feels a lot like himpathy to me. These women were expressing sympathy for the father because he got up in the middle of the night, but not the mom, because that was her job as a woman.

Chantal in Canada explained how her husband, Aiden, was supportive during her breastfeeding months—which were not easy. Chantal was recovering from a caesarian and was ready to give up. So, Aiden took it upon himself to carry the cognitive labor because he wasn't able to physically breastfeed. "He requested information from the hospital and researched breastfeeding clinics to find the right one for us. He was so supportive and helpful; he helped me with latching, and he bought me the pump. In the middle of the night, he would get up and bring the baby to me because I was so sore. He was really involved with all of it. And then he also did more housework during those months because the baby was feeding all the time."

There are other approaches to balancing out the breastfeeding burden; these are only two. The takeaway here is, if you choose this option, both parents need to acknowledge the burden that a breastfeeding parent can feel, and find ways for the non-breastfeeding parent to be as supportive as possible.

2. PARENTAL LEAVE

There is still no national paid parental leave policy in the United States. As of the printing of this book there was growing momentum for #PaidLeaveForAll, but no bill had yet gone to the floor for a vote. Workers continue to be dependent on their employers' policies: some offer paid leave to both parents, some offer paid leave only to a mother, and some don't offer paid leave to either parent. It is an embarrassing statistic that 25 percent of American mothers are forced to return to work within two weeks of giving birth.[2] Clearly, we have structural work to do to ensure all Americans have access to parental leave. We'll talk about this more in chapter 10.

For those who have access to parental leave, either paid or unpaid, there is a startling difference in uptake when you disaggregate the data by sex. According to the Better Life Lab, women average ten weeks of leave, and men average one.[3]

When I see this statistic, however, I don't feel animosity toward fathers who are not pulling their weight. I have compassion for fathers who are prevented from being caregivers to their new baby or child. Schulte agreed, and told me about her own personal experience. "There has been all this rage lately, and I get it. But we can't be angry at an individual. There are larger forces out there—our work culture, the lack of supportive public policies—policies that police both men and women into traditional gender roles. My rage at my husband was misdirected. We shouldn't feel rage toward an individual, but at the norms and systems in which we're all trapped. I realized [in] hindsight that my husband didn't have the agency to make those choices that I wanted him to make. When we had our first baby, he took two days off, and then he went back to work. That was it. It was a joke. It was only years later that I found out he felt that he couldn't ask for time off. He was worried that he'd face retaliation at work, and that would hurt his ability to provide for his family, and he had no choice. And he really regrets missing out on that time."

Even when men have access to parental leave, there is huge pressure not to take it, which makes sense when we consider the significant pressure society puts on men to provide for their family. This exemplifies our definitions of motherhood and fatherhood: mothers are critical and necessary; fathers are additional or extra. We need to change that attitude to value all parents equally, and encourage all parents to take the leave to which they are entitled.

I also spoke to David Smith and Brad Johnson about parental leave. They are the authors of *Good Guys: How Men Can Be Better Allies for Women in the Workplace*. "The de facto expectation needs to be that everyone takes all of their paid leave," Johnson told me. "It is still common to ask, *Oh, you want to take* all *those days?* or *Don't you have a wife who can stay home?* These are still common questions asked of men. Instead, employers need to help men think through how they can best use their parental leave to support their family, and employers need to help men figure out how to reenter their job when their leave is over, now that they have a baby at home to care for."

Smith and Johnson also gave an economic argument for universal participation in parental leave. When men, or any non-birthing parents, take their full allotment of paid parental leave, they not only help their partner at home—they stand in solidarity with all birthing parents. Remember the statistic from chapter 1: for those between the ages of twenty-five and forty-five, the pay gap between men and women increases by 35 percent. We would surely be able to chip away at that inequity if every parent had to step away from work for two or three months when each child was born, and we'd achieve greater gender parity when it came to promotion and pay increases.

Along the same lines as parental leave, all workers need to have access to paid sick leave so they can take a day off work when a child is sick, or even take kids for medical appointments. Smith, Johnson, and I also discussed the stigma that still exists around men taking time off work for caregiving. Smith agrees that execution of paid time is not easy for men. "It is hard. Really hard, actually. It is awkward and uncomfortable to push back on all those years of gender assumptions and norms about what men should do or should not do. But we have to do it, and with time, like everything else, it does get easier."

Smith and Johnson coined the term *leaving loudly* in *Good Guys*. They say that, too often, when men leave work to take a child to a doctor, or to care for an ill family member, they sneak out the back door and try to keep up with email, hoping no one notices their absence. But men with the power to lead by example should consider leaving loudly—stating on their out-of-office email that they are doing family work and being proud of their role as a caregiver.

While we work to achieve broader structural change, there are some things we can do in our homes to better support equity during that tricky transition when both parents resume work. Remember

Tina, from the beginning of this chapter? She did not resent the as-sumed responsibilities for the baby and the home during the weeks she was on leave. But she did resent that, after she back to work, those responsibilities continued along with her full-time job. "I did my job and everything related to the baby. *Everything.* And the housework. I just got angrier and angrier."

In cases in which new parents have access to parental leave—wonderful. But to avoid a repeat of Tina's situation, couples need to be intentional about using leave to *support* parity, instead of using it to perpetuate inequity.

OPTION 1. ONE PERSON ON LEAVE: If just one of you has access to parental leave (most likely the Female Role), it is important that the patterns you establish during leave do not continue when both parents are back at work. Both of you need to acknowledge that this is a unique slice of time that allows one parent to do more in the home. When that parent goes back to work, the couple needs to do an overhaul of their daily schedule. This includes everything from morning routine and drop-off, to pickup, evenings, nights, and days off. A conversation about values wouldn't hurt either. Do you find that your gender socialization is pushing you to value some aspects of parenting more than others? What can you do to support each other, to ensure you both find equitable time for work, caregiving, household work, and self-care?

OPTION 2. BOTH PEOPLE ON LEAVE: If both of you have access to parental care, some people like to take time together so they can enjoy a few months as a new family. I had a male colleague tell me that, when each of his boys was born, he and his partner took two months off together, and they were some of the best weeks of his life. He loved getting to know the new baby with his wife; they would sleep when the baby slept, and be up when the baby was up.

He loved not worrying about schedules and spending long days together. During those months at home, they both took on their fair share of household work; his wife breastfed and he did all the food prep and laundry. When they returned to their paid jobs (which was a harsh reality for both of them), they worked together to ensure they were still splitting the load equally.

OPTION 3. TAKING TURNS: Asynchronous leave is another option; one parent takes time off from work, and then the other does. Greta from Ontario, who identifies as white, told me about the effect her husband's leave had on their new family. (Her leave may seem long by American standards, but Canadian policies allow for longer and more equitable parental leave.) "I stayed home for over six months, and then I went back to work. Having Tony switch off and stay home when I had to go back was amazing. I didn't have to worry about day care yet. I just had to get myself dressed and out the door every morning. Our son started solid foods during that time, and he was a picky eater, but Tony had to deal with it. He couldn't pass him off because there was no one around to help. We don't have family in town, and I can't easily take calls at work. So, he just had to figure it out."

Tony, Greta's partner, agreed. "Paternity leave was really important for me. When people talk about how tedious it is to take care of a child, I get it. It forced me to be knowledgeable and in charge of everything. And it forced her to step back and trust me. It also becomes clear how much your partner does when she is gone all day. It is impossible to take someone for granted when you realize how much they do."

Greta went on to describe how her husband's paternity leave was as important for her as it was for him. "Even though it was good to go back to work, I was also jealous of the time Tony had with the baby. But during my leave, I kind of just started assuming I was the baby expert. I think we both did. But after I went back to work, it would be Saturday, and I would have to ask Tony, 'What time does the baby nap now?' Or, 'Do you think I should feed him now or wait a little longer?' I think that was a big thing for both of us. It shifted to Tony being the baby expert. And it felt a little weird at first. But eventually, it was normal."

Greta went on to tell me that after Tony's months at home, they both went back to work, and the baby went to day care. By that point, they were both confident parenting, and that dynamic remained in their relationship—and continued when their second child was born.

3. PARENTING STYLE

Parenting style is a sneaky cause of household imbalance. This situation typically arises with older kids, or at least toddlers. But it is worth talking about early so you are prepared when it occurs.

Lisa from Philadelphia, who identifies as white, told me about a recent struggle in her household. After the birth of a new baby, her three-year-old son, Lincoln, began hitting when he felt frustration. "It is just lack of impulse control, which is compounded with the new baby. So, now we are really struggling with Lincoln's hitting and his temper tantrums. My husband tried the yelling match, but that didn't work. So, I wondered, *How are we going to approach this?*" Lisa got to work researching online, reaching out to friends, and reading a few books about discipline strategies. She finally reported her findings to her husband, and they agreed on trying a time-out approach to discipline.

"It takes a lot of time. If, for example, Lincoln hits during dinner, one of us has to get up, put him in time-out, talk to him about why it is wrong to hit, and then monitor him. Lincoln can already sense that I am the softy parent, so when my husband does time-out it is shorter and easier. When I do time-out, he knows Mom will take more time with him, so he drags it out."

The impact of discipline on the household balance was twofold. First, there were the weeks of research, reading, and deliberating that Lisa did to come to the decision to try the time-out approach. This took hours away from Lisa's day, but required no hours from her husband's day. (This story also sounded like a classic example of Allison Daminger's cognitive labor cycle. Lisa took responsibility for the anticipating and research. Then she and her husband shared the decision-making.)

In this case, they agreed on one strategy. But that was just the beginning. Now the couple had to actually follow through with their time-out plan. And in doing so, they realized that Lisa was spending more hours per week disciplining Lincoln than her husband was. And those hours were hard hours. Taking Lincoln to time-out wasn't only disruptive to her schedule; those hours were emotionally exhausting.

These "hidden" patterns of our day need to be noticed. In Lisa's case, it is important to note that she was the one who researched parenting options, and she was the one spending more hours disciplining Lincoln. It was essential for Lisa that she and her husband acknowledge this and make a plan to try to counter the extra work she was doing each week.

Making the invisible "seen" is a common tactic suggested by many experts to better appropriate household chores and cognitive responsibilities.

KIDS: WHAT TAKES THE BULK OF YOUR TIME?

1. Take a moment to make a list of all your child-related responsibilities, from bath time, to day care correspondence, to video chats
   with grandparents on the weekends. Which tasks take the most
   time? Which take the most emotional energy?
2. Ask your partner to do the same. Compare lists. Try to accept
   imbalances for what they are; do not use a reframing tactic to
   excuse gendered behavior. Can you make any changes to alleviate
   the cognitive labor?
3. Take some time to talk about values. Do you partake in different
   tasks because you value different things in the home? Can you
   come to respect each other's values, and acknowledge that gender
   norms might be playing a role in your household divide?

WOMEN PERPETUATE SEXISM, TOO

I did some deep breathing before I started writing this section because I know it is going to be unpopular with some. But if we are
going to tackle all the nooks and crannies of this issue, we have to
discuss maternal gatekeeping—even if it makes us squirm with discomfort.

Maternal gatekeeping is a "set of beliefs and behaviors that may
make it difficult for men and women to collaborate in family work."[4]
Sometimes the Female Role uses maternal gatekeeping to assert
their preferences and maintain things the way they want them to
be. This often comes in the form of criticism, with the goal of limiting the Male Role.[5]

- *Oh, that outfit doesn't match at all. The baby looks ridiculous. I'll go change her.*
- *This bottle is way too hot! Are you crazy? Uh, let me do it.*
- *We can't take the baby out in this weather! What are you thinking? Good thing I'm here, or who knows what you would do.*

One of these comments in isolation would not likely have an impact on the family. But several of these comments every day, over time, sets a household tone that the Female Role knows best, and the Male Role is an incompetent buffoon. In these instances, it is hard for me not to empathize with the Male Role. If I were criticized several times a day for trying to help, it wouldn't take me long to back away altogether.

Sometimes gatekeeping can be used like himpathy, to protect the Male Role from working too hard or doing too much. This has similar results but uses a more polite tone.

- *Oh, you were at work all day; just relax. I'll change the baby.*
- *It is easier if I put the baby down after I feed her. Just watch TV. I'll join you soon.*
- *You don't really want to go shopping for baby clothes, do you? Stay home and hang out with your dad. We'll be back soon.*

This strategy might prevent the Male Role from getting hurt feelings or direct criticism, but the results are the same. These comments establish the Female Role as the expert—the one more equipped to deal with the baby's needs.

Truly committing to an equal partnership is hard for everyone. It means one partner needs to step up and do more than they were raised to do, and it means one person needs to step back and do less than they were raised to do. In theory, this seems straightforward, but in practice it can feel awkward and uncomfortable and confusing. If we are going to make it work, we need to help each other out.

Men have been socialized to believe they don't know as much as their female partners; they might doubt their own ability to parent effectively, and believe that they are not naturally equipped to take care of a baby. Researchers have observed that new mothers can play a critical role in supporting, or undermining, a partner's attempts to be a caregiver to a new child.[6] When the Male Role shows signs of uncertainty or hesitation, the best thing the Female Role can do is say something supportive.

- *I think that way is great. I might do it differently, but that doesn't make my way better.*
- *This is my first baby, too. I don't know what I'm doing either.*
- *The baby is fine! You can totally do this.*

When a woman has been socialized to take responsibility for the home and the children, it can be painful for her to step back. Doing so may feel like an admission of inadequacy or worse, a lack of love. When the Female Role shows signs of discomfort in backing away from a baby-related task, the best thing the Male Role can do is say something supportive.

- *You do not have to do everything. I've got this. I promise.*
- *Taking a nap doesn't mean you're a bad parent. We both deserve a break sometimes.*
- *I know you feel like you need to do it all, the way your mom did. But there are lots of things you do differently than your mom. This works for us.*

Mothers are not the only people who use maternal gatekeeping. All kinds of people habitually criticize men and undermine their ability to parent a newborn: relatives, neighbors, colleagues, and friends. Oftentimes, these remarks are veiled in humor, making the clueless father the butt of a joke. But really, there isn't much that is funny about undermining a parent's ability to be a good parent.

As we discussed in chapter 2, our friends and family often reinforce what they deem to be "appropriate behavior" with words of praise, and what they deem "inappropriate behavior" with words of criticism. Greta, who we met earlier, told me about a visit from her in-laws when her baby was a month old. "My husband was showing off a little bit in front of his dad. It was cute, you know. He just wanted to show his parents what a good father he was. So, when our daughter needed a diaper change, he would jump right up. Or if the baby got fussy, he would swoop in to comfort her. And I was actually feeling really proud. But then, after a few hours, my father-in-law turned to me and said, 'So what do you do?' I was speechless—just totally stunned. And the next time the baby needed something, I made sure it was me who stepped in. To prove to my in-laws that I was also a good mum. In hindsight, I wonder, if I had been doing everything, would he have said those same words to my husband? I doubt it."

For friends and family, it requires a higher degree of awareness than perhaps we are accustomed to. If you find yourself making a gendered comment, stop yourself and ask, *Is this really helping these new parents? Is this joke that funny, or is it better to keep this one to myself?* And when you make a mistake, which you will do because we are all human and we all make mistakes, just say you're sorry. A quick apology can go a long way.

For new parents, it is likely that many in your community live in gender default and will make inappropriate comments. You will likely hear maternal gatekeeping at the playground, in the office, or in line at the grocery store. Finding parity in the home requires you to be confident in your own choices, and reject those unhelpful comments when you hear them. Depending on the situation, you may choose to confront the comment, or you may let the comment go. But try not to take comments to heart or let them affect your behavior—the way Greta let her father-in-law's comment get to her.

EQUAL MEANS EQUAL

I have a vivid memory of a pizza dinner, years ago at a hole-in-the-wall dive, where the tables were uncomfortably close together. Unfortunately, I could hear every word spoken at the table next to us. It was a six-top, consisting of what appeared to be two dads, two moms, and two kids. One of the mothers was especially loud. At one point during the meal, the loud mom let out a belly laugh and said to her female friend, "I tell him all the time. 'Your money is my money, and my money is my money.' Isn't that right, honey? Ha! And you," she said as she pointed at her son with a fork, "the sooner you realize this the easier your life will be."

I have heard this saying before. And sure, it can get a laugh. But we cannot ethically advocate for dads to step up and do more if moms claim—even in jest—that they deserve special treatment. We can't have it both ways.

The double standard doesn't end with money; it can also relate to time. My neighbor once told me how frustrated she was that her husband wanted downtime at night. She thought he needed to come home from work and dive in to help with the kids. She expected him to watch the kids while she made dinner, do the bedtime routine, and then help her with chores after the kids were asleep.

But I knew from previous conversations that she was not working at the time and had three hours to herself every morning when her kids were at preschool. So, I pushed back. "Well, don't you get time to yourself every day? You've told me how much you love your quiet mornings to do what you like. Maybe your husband just needs a little downtime, too." I could tell this annoyed her, and she immediately cut the conversation short.

I understood where she was coming from. When kids are small, the evening hours can feel the longest. Everyone is tired, and getting kids fed, bathed, and to bed feels like a nightly marathon. But I also believe that *equal* must mean *equal,* and applying a double standard to one parent or the other only cheapens the overall argument for parity. One person should not have regular, protected alone time while the other does not.

We often think about chore divisions, but you could also try to frame your conversation around time, instead of tasks. Where do you spend the most time during the week? During the month? The following categories might help you with this conversation. Decide which spaces are a priority for each of you, then help each other set boundaries so you both put in your fair share of paid work and unpaid work, and have equal downtime to rest and recharge.

TIME

Work Time—Do you both have adequate hours in the week to keep up with your work hours/duties? Commute time could be rolled into this.

Chore Time—Do you both devote about the same number of hours per week/month to taking care of household work?

Parenting Time—How many hours per week do you spend with your kid(s)? Are you a single parent during these hours, or do you parent together? Make sure you're both spending about the same number of hours with your kids, and that the time is balanced between fun times and frustrating times. One parent shouldn't get all the playful hours, while the other parent is stuck with the grouchy hours.

Alone Time/Friend Time—This could be curling up with a book, going for a long bike ride, or meeting up with friends. Whatever you choose, this time is spent away from your partner and kid(s) and must be separate from work. (Playdates do not count.) This time should *not* be used for cognitive labor.

Health Time—Many people sacrifice sleep and exercise to meet work and childcare responsibilities. (I fall into this trap all the time.) But every doctor I have ever had tells me that, in the end, this wastes time instead of saving it. Taking care of ourselves and our bodies is essential if we want to take care of others. I know this is easier said than done, since I struggle with this myself. But it is something to keep on your radar.

Time Together—This can be hard to come by for those who don't live near family; babysitters are expensive, and when kids are little, it is hard to trust a stranger with your baby. But making space to be together, without the kids, is also important for many couples.

GRANDPARENTS SAVE THE DAY

It is not uncommon for grandparents to come and stay with parents when there is a new baby in the family. (I'll use the word "grandparent" here for ease, but of course that role does not necessarily mean a biological grandparent. Other family members or friends can also offer that much-needed help to new families.) Sometimes helpers come right away, lending a hand while the birthing parent heals and recuperates. Some helpers wait a few weeks and help out when both parents return to work. Grandparents that live close by can help with all of the above, making regular visits to bring food, clean up the house, or watch the baby while new parents nap.

Grandparents are fantastic; I am not in any way making an argument against them. They can be lifesavers for many couples, especially for the second, third, or sixth baby; grandparents often watch older kids while the new parents focus on the infant. But grandparents who find themselves in a home where gender equality is a goal need to be aware of their role; their presence can support—or hinder—longer-term household equality.

Claire from Michigan, who identifies as Asian American, told me about her frustration with her mother-in-law. "I know she is trying to help, and she is trying to be nice. But [when she visits] she spoils the boys so much." I asked her for an example. "She doesn't even have them bring their plates to the sink—that kind of thing. The boys get used to just standing up from the table and running off, and she happily cleans up after them. And when she leaves, it is terrible. It takes me weeks to get the boys back to their routine."

When a grandparent "slot fills" for the Female Role, the workload might feel lighter during the stay. But it makes life all the harder when the grandparent goes home. Slot filling allows both parents to fall into unrealistic patterns; the Male Role thinks he can be a great dad without doing any more work than before becoming a parent, and the Female Role has to work double time to do the jobs to which she has grown accustomed, *plus* those jobs that the helper was doing.

Grandparents can also fall into the role of maternal gatekeeper—by protecting the Male Role from doing too much dirty work, or building the Female Role's self-confidence by making some jokes at the Male Role's expense. Subconsciously, grandparents can apply their generational gender norms to this new family with statements that start with, *Well, in my day . . .* or *When I was raising kids . . .* Like anything else, one or two comments is not going to make a major impact. But grandparents who play a key role in the new family might have more influence than they realize.

I encourage grandparents to be aware of household dynamics, and to do their best to support household parity if that is important to the new parents. What specifically can grandparents do? The following advice was collected from interviews and conversations with both new grandparents and new parents.

- "It was really important for me not to step in when I thought my son-in-law was doing something wrong. A few times I had to bite my tongue, actually. But he needed to find his own way with his new daughter." (Grandma, first grandchild)
- "The best thing we could do to help was to take the older child out of the house, and let our daughter and son-in-law spend time with the new baby." (Grandpa, second grandchild)
- "I only offered advice when I was asked. Otherwise, I just

let them figure it out themselves." (Grandma, first grand-child)

- "I remember my mom actually standing up for my husband. If the two of us had an argument about something baby related, she would take his side. That gave him tremendous confidence. It annoyed me at the time, to be honest. But in the long run, I think it was the right thing to do." (Mom, first child)

- "A lot of us grandparents can't sleep through the night either. One of the things my daughter appreciated most was that I did the nighttime bottle when I visited, and let the parents both get a good night's sleep." (Grandma, fourth grandchild)

- "My in-laws are really good about reinforcing our decisions. If I make a rule, I know they're going to follow it. That is really helpful." (Mom, second child)

- "There were a few times when the baby was crying, and I was trying to take care of laundry or something, and my mother-in-law would just make a cup of tea and ignore me. At the time, I was pissed off because I wanted her to help. But now that I think about it, that is just what life is like. The baby is always crying at inopportune times. You just have to figure it out." (Dad, second child)

- "Looking back, my mom didn't help me with anything routine when she visited. She didn't clean or do laundry. She did extra things—she made a cake once, and would buy fresh flowers. So, when she left, I missed those special touches, and I missed her. But my husband and I were already doing the everyday stuff. So, our routine didn't really change much." (Mom, first child)

- "My husband and his father used to golf almost every weekend. When our first baby was born, I know [my husband] didn't want to disappoint his dad. But my father-in-law, thank God, said to him, 'No, you have other things to take care of on the weekend. Let's skip the golf trips for a while.' I was shocked, but also grateful. So was my husband. I think emotionally, he needed that permission from his dad." (Mom, second child)

Dynamics and relationships are different in every family. I know that grandparents may or may not have power in a home with an infant. I can understand how a grandparent might read this and think, *But my daughter-in-law* wanted *me to do the laundry! Was I supposed to say no?* Of course not. Everyone knows their own kids, their own situation, and what they can and cannot suggest. I simply pass along these recommendations for you to consider, and use the ones you find appropriate.

Another wonderful gift a grandparent can give the next generation is the open acknowledgment that things are different now. Expectations of parents now are very different than the expectations our parents and grandparents faced in decades past. Today, new parents are surrounded by images of Pinterest-perfect birthday parties and Instagram-worthy Halloween costumes. There is an odd pressure to pack organic bento boxes for a kindergartener's lunch, make it through a weekend with only thirty minutes of screen time, and attend every one of your kid's soccer games. Do you know how many "special" days there are on a school calendar these days? Favorite book character day, spirit days, wacky Wednesday, funky hair day . . . the list is endless. And every single one of these special days requires a parent to dig through drawers and laundry bins for an hour the night before, pulling together something that does not make your kid cry.

Yes, the previous generations were wonderful. But perhaps we are romanticizing history just a bit. Were these mothers of the past actually able to manage everything, all the time, with a smile? And even if they were successful, that experience does not mean it was the right thing to do—and it doesn't mean future generations should be relegated to repeat history.

NEW JOBS, NEW HOMES, AND ADDITIONAL BABIES

So far, we have focused on the arrival of the first baby because this is when couples are likely to experience the strongest pull toward traditional gender norms. But new homes, new jobs, and additional babies can also cause a shift in routines and a change in patterns.

Overwhelmingly, couples I interviewed shared the necessity to pause and readjust whenever there is the smallest change in routine: a new job, the addition of a part-time job, someone going back to school or starting a new volunteer position. Several teachers told me how important it was that they sat down and had a refresh with their spouse every August before classes resumed.

It is also important to stop and discuss if the child's schedule changes: attending a new day care or preschool, starting elementary school, starting new after-school programs or weekend clubs. If health situations arise, and someone receives specialized treatment or therapy, the family probably needs to readjust. Moving cities certainly requires a discussion, but so does moving down the block. The addition of a new pet also comes with responsibilities that need to be discussed, as does a family member moving in or staying for long visit.

Whenever logistics change, responsibilities change. And the dialogue about who is doing what needs to stay current. I wish we could have one big gender chat once and be done with it. But the reality of parity is that it takes dedication and ongoing work.

The addition of another baby or child is certainly cause for an adjustment.

Balancing work and home requires even more communication, even more planning, and even more coordination after additional children join the family. Take advantage of this change to sit down and have an honest conversation about what you have done right, and what you could do better in the future. The following questions might help families expecting a new child talk through some of their household issues. As before, please discuss these at your own pace. Choose the ones that are important to answer today, and leave the others for later.

QUESTIONS TO DISCUSS BEFORE ADDING ANOTHER BABY/CHILD TO THE FAMILY

1. Do you think you have fallen back on any gender norms while caring for your first child? Anything that you would like to change or readjust now?

2. Do you think your parenting style reflects the experience you had as a child? Is this a good thing or a bad thing? Do you want to repeat your childhood with your own kids—or do you want to make some changes? Talk to your partner about this and see how they feel. What was a "perfect childhood" for one person, might not work at all for another.

3. How do you feel (honestly) about how you and your partner divide up the physical and cognitive tasks in the home? Do you feel like you do too much? Too little? Just right?

4. If you are the one doing less, how do you feel about knowing you are not doing your fair share? Do you find yourself validating your actions in any way? What can you do to take more responsibility in the house—not just for a few days, but real sustained responsibility?

5. If you are the one doing more, how do feel about knowing your partner is not doing their fair share? What would you do if you had some extra time?

6. What are the best parts of the day for you? What do you look forward to the most? (Try to preserve this for each other when the new baby/child comes.)

7. Think about how life will change when the new baby comes home. Do you plan to take turns so you each have both kids at once, giving one parent a complete break? Or do you believe in the all-hands-on-deck approach?

8. Will one of you breastfeed the new baby? How can the other parent compensate for the hours it takes to feed the baby?

9. Is either of you taking parental leave for this baby? How much, and when? Are you both taking as much time as you are able, or are you falling into gendered patterns?

10. Have you both made sacrifices at work to be more present at home? Has one of you made more sacrifices than the other? How did you come to that decision?

NOTES

Before you move on to part 2, use this space to make some personal notes from the first four chapters. Consider data points and statistics, social change theory, and ways to navigate equality at life's milestones. Choose points that mean the most to you—that make the most sense in your own life.

_____

_____

_____

_____

_____

_____

_____

_____

_____

_____

_____

_____

_____

_____

PART TWO

WHAT EQUAL PARTNERS LOOK LIKE

5
FROM KING OF THE CASTLE
TO EQUAL PARTNER

For years, I struggled to put into words the differences between someone in the average Male Role and an equal partner. I found that, when I tried to communicate these concepts to friends and colleagues, my thoughts were muddled and required lengthy explanations. Unless my audience had a high level of interest, people often got distracted, and I would give up halfway through my spiel.

This was particularly frustrating because I was not defining a new thing—this behavior already existed. But there were no commonly used words or phrases to identify or describe it. I found this lack of vocabulary limiting in both personal and professional settings. Without a way to describe what we expect, how could our partners ever be able to meet our expectations?

Our social narrative is that the Male Role can and will only do so much in the home, the Female Role is the domestic leader, and nothing is going to change that. With this perspective, things are indeed unlikely to change. However, if we collectively embrace the idea that the Male Role can do more, that fatherhood can finally be synonymous with motherhood, then we allow the space for change to occur.

Here I introduce three terms that I hope will allow us to have some honest conversations, to help us better articulate what *is* and what *could be*.

KING OF THE CASTLE

The *King of the Castle* is well represented in TV and movies: Ward Clever, Ricky Ricardo, Al Bundy, Don Draper, George Jefferson, Homer Simpson, Tony Soprano . . . These TV personalities are diverse in economic class and working hours. But what they all have in common is their role in the household. Can you recall Tony changing a diaper? Ricky cleaning a toilet? Homer folding the laundry?

Kings are just as common in real life as they are in "TV Land." Sociologists attribute this division of household duty to men's historic belief that they are entitled to female labor, and women's subsequent buy-in to this social order. Masculine-coded behaviors, like leadership, decision-making and authority, do not leave room for men to do feminine-coded behaviors, like care-giving and nurturing.

In previous generations, the King was responsible for earning the family's income. Many readers might recognize their father, uncle, or grandfather as Kings. But fewer and fewer men today will likely fit in this category as the number of dual-working families has continued to rise. Regardless, despite what he or his spouse does for work, today's King still does very little in the home. This enables him to spend his free time any way he chooses: playing golf, drinking beers with his friends, CrossFit, or just relaxing on the couch.

I want to stress that the King is not necessarily a bad guy. He might be very kind. He has just never questioned why there are men's jobs and why there are women's jobs. Because he gets the better end of the deal, he doesn't bother to raise any questions about this distribution of labor. He may even appreciate what his partner does in the home—and he may say, *Thank you,* but he rarely offers to help.

If he is a father, the King may love his children very much, and play with them after work or on days off. This voluntary playtime sometimes disguises the truth. Friends and family look at this fun dad rolling around with his kids in the leaves and think, *Now, there is a great father.*

The privilege of the King is that he gets to choose when he spends time with his kids because he is not responsible for the day-to-day. It is this concept of a *choice* that is so important in defining a King. He never cooks. He does not have to clean. He does not concern himself with shopping or childcare. After work, the King's responsibilities are complete. If he has the energy or is in the mood, then he may get involved with household activities. But he does not have to. The King can just as easily lay down on the couch and watch a basketball game.

My friend Cliff recently told me a story that perfectly illustrates how a King might act when left on his own. Cliff was sitting at an airport gate on a Friday evening, eager to board and get home to Chicago. A group of women sat across from him, and it was clear they were off for a girl's weekend in the Windy City. They were a boisterous bunch, talking about what they would do and where they would eat. Then, one woman stepped aside to take a phone call, and Cliff couldn't help but hear the conversation.

"You don't know how to make mac and cheese? OK. It's OK. I have time. First, take out a pot. . . . Right, under the microwave. . . . Good. Now, fill it half full of water. . . . Sure, tap is fine. Now, put it on the stove. You want to turn the heat on high in order to boil the water. . . . It goes faster if you put the lid on. . . ."

The King not only operates in gender default—he prefers it. And he wishes everyone else would operate in gender default, too. It just makes life easier (for him).

HANDS-ON HUSBAND

In the twenty-first century, the *Hands-On Husband* is the guy we see most often on TV, in movies, in comics, and on commercials: Dre Johnson, Phil Dunphy, Mike Heck, and Bob Parr (aka Mr. Incredible.) This Hands-On Husband is not just commonly portrayed on TV; he is often the basis of sitcom humor. These scenarios are so common we hardly notice them anymore, but the slapstick buffoonery of the lovable husband or dad is often what prompts the most canned applause. For example, the husband is trying to cook an anniversary dinner when the neighbor walks in on him. The camera cuts to the Hands-On, burnt and frazzled, trying to hide the takeaway containers in the freezer. The Hands-On Husband is the butt of the joke, and these exaggerated gender roles reinforce norms we assume to be true: in the home, men are allowed to be incompetent, whereas women are responsible for fixing everything. These gender situations may be less harmful than the toxic masculinity of Tony Soprano, but they do role model how men act and how women act, which we often carry into our real lives.

Complaining about this figure might seem counterintuitive because many of us have used the term *Hands-On* as a compliment for years. And compared to the King of the Castle, it is a positive and welcome improvement. Older generations of women love to point out how wonderful the Hands-On Husband is because they were married to Kings. They tell younger people not to complain too much because the Hands-On Husband is such a good guy.

To those people I say, *Yes, the Hands-On is doing better than those in the Male Role in previous generations. But he is still not doing enough.* The defining characteristic of the Hands-On Husband is that he *helps* with tasks. He (usually) does what he is asked to do, but these are mere steps in a larger process. The Hands-On is not responsible for the process, which means he does not partake in cognitive labor. If he stopped "helping" tomorrow, the household would proceed as usual.

A neighborhood friend, Sheila, unknowingly described this neo-traditional dynamic to me. Sheila's daughter was showing some warning signs of a developmental problem. Sheila mentioned it to her husband straight away, but he waved it off as "normal kid stuff." So, Sheila took it upon herself to do extensive internet research, identified a local doctor for assessments, filed the paperwork, called the insurance company (over and over), and made the appointment. She presented her findings to her husband, who then agreed to come to the assessment. The couple listened to the doctor's report and jointly made the decision about next steps, now that their daughter had been placed on the autism spectrum.

Months later, when I saw Sheila again, I asked how things were going. She was happy that her daughter was thriving, but admitted she was personally exhausted. She said she had to alter her work schedule to take her daughter to various appointments during the week, which meant making up hours at night. "Some nights I get to bed so late, I wonder if it is even worth sleeping."

I asked if her husband was helping, and her face brightened. "Oh absolutely!" she responded. "He's a great father. He has been so helpful in making decisions about what's best for her." Note here the classic Hands-On behavior. Sheila did all the planning and thinking. Her husband only stepped in with problem solving and decision-making.

She is the one responsible for 100 percent of the implementation, yet she genuinely praised her partner for doing less than a quarter of the work.

Like Sheila, women are often the first to applaud their partners for their contribution; this unearned praise becomes an important aspect of the Hands-On Husband. Because household work is an "extra" for them and not a requirement, the Hands-On may think he deserves, or at least comes to expect, an overabundance of appreciation for his work. North American culture only reinforces this perception. When my daughter was in day care, and I ran in to pick her up at 5:01 P.M., I was met with cold eyes. Despite my eruption of apologies, those childcare workers did not have much sympathy for me. No one needed to say out loud, *You are a bad mom because you don't love your daughter enough to be on time.* That was clearly communicated without words. However, if my husband arrived for pickup at 5:01 P.M., he was met with smiles and praise.

Yes, the Hands-On Husband might be a really great guy. But I want to make this point clear: he is still not our ideal. He is our compromise.

If the Hands-On is not responsible for the household's management or cognitive labor, who is? His spouse. This person is better off than the King's partner, for sure. They do not shoulder 100 percent of the burden—there is a degree of help. One can dole out assignments, and those assignments help tremendously. But the spouse of a Hands-On Husband continues to be the cognitive laborer of the home.

Those married to a Hands-On Husband without kids may be able to shoulder the home burden and still be able to read before bed and hang out with friends on the weekend. This makes being married to a Hands-On more tolerable. But in a home with kids, the spouse of the Hands-On Husband—like the spouse of a King—may experience the same daily exhaustion that borders on depression. Like a plate-spinning circus performer, these partners spend every waking moment constantly looping through a mental to-do list, making sure that no plates drop and shatter.

THE EQUAL PARTNER

The superficial definition of the *Equal Partner* is a person who does half of the tasks that any given home requires. And yes, this is a good start. But do not stop there—the Equal Partner needs to be much more than a chore robot. The Equal Partner must anticipate half the household needs, fully participate in managing half of the household affairs, and share in half the household's cognitive labor.

The Equal Partner does not need to be told what tasks need doing around the house. He sees a full dishwasher and empties it. He notices the carpet is looking grungy, and researches cleaning options. He sees that his closet is thin, so he sets up the ironing board in front of the TV, making sure to ask his spouse, "Do you need any ironing done, too?" He makes it a priority to be an active Noticer of things that need doing

The Equal Partner shares in the management of the household. He acknowledges that tasks are but a small indication of a larger system, and he takes responsibility for half the processes of that whole system. In homes with kids, the Equal Partner does not simply show up to his daughter's birthday party with some balloons. He helps her pick out decorations, sends the invitations from his own Evite account, orders the cake a week in advance, and ties bows on all the little goody bags.

The Equal Partner is also familiar with the processes that his spouse handles, so he does not flinch when he needs to be a single parent for a week or more. The Equal Partner knows exactly what happens on a day-to-day basis to keep the household running.

Most importantly, the Equal Partner shares in the emotional burden of the family. This is the hardest point to explain to a King or a Hands-On, since the emotional burden is not tangible. But cognitive labor is at the core of household parity.

A Hands-On Husband might regularly play the "dumb dad" card in order to get out of chores, or he may use a reframing tactic, such as saying, *She's so particular* or *I do make more money than she does*. But the Equal Partner does not resort to gendered tropes.

Being human, Equal Partners have their bad days like everyone else. Everybody is sometimes grumpy, sometimes lazy, and sometimes defensive. I'm not suggesting perfection. The difference is that the Equal Partner holds himself to a higher standard and pushes himself to be better. The Equal Partner rejects the social hall pass that permits him an easier life because he finds himself in the Male Role. He does not accept behavior society assigned to him because of his gender identity. He rolls up his sleeves and does the work that needs doing.

The spouses of Equal Partners may still climb into bed at night with a long to-do list running through their heads. But they are less likely to feel alone, isolated, and resentful because they know that whatever they are facing that week, at least they can share that responsibility with another person.

We need not sell ourselves short. The Hands-On might be our reality, but there is no reason why the Equal Partner can't be the goal.

PICTURE A CONTINUUM

Some readers might feel uncomfortable with these descriptions, thinking that labels are static: the why-does-everything-need-to-fit-into-a-box perspective. I fully appreciate this hesitation, especially when it comes to queer and same-sex couples who are constantly forced to evaluate their place in a heteronormative society.

Please consider the King, the Hands-On Husband, and the Equal Partner not as fixed roles but as a continuum of behaviors, underlying beliefs, and social expectations. There are those who do not even measure up to the King; there are those in the Male Role beyond the Equal Partner who are the household's primary caregiver, and there are a thousand points in between. Though I used the pronoun *he* for these descriptions, people of all genders can take on the roles of the King, the Hands-On, or the Equal Partner.

King of the
Castle

Hands-On
Husband

Equal
Partner

Adherence to these behaviors need not be strict. Like life, one's place on this continuum shifts and changes daily, weekly, monthly. Oftentimes, work dictates when individuals are the Equal Partner and when they slip back to being the Hands-On. The purpose of the continuum is not for anyone to feel labeled or stuck in one place—but for people to begin to see the possibility for improvement.

Thinking through daily scenarios can be helpful in understanding how these roles play out in real life. Below are some common

153

everyday activities and the way that each of these three roles would likely react. If you like, choose another daily activity common in your home and think about how these three personalities would respond. Maybe you can consider dinnertime, school interactions, Halloween costumes, or vacation planning—any routine that is common in your home.

	A DAY OFF (HOUSEHOLD WITHOUT KIDS)	BEDTIME ROUTINE (HOUSEHOLD WITH KIDS)
King of the Castle	The King is mostly concerned with his own personal enjoyment, since this is his day off from work. He may meet friends to play basketball, or he may play Xbox all afternoon. He might choose to do a household project; then again, he might not. His leisure time is his own.	The King is happy to give good night hugs, but he does not get up to help, no matter what he hears from down the hallway: tears, shouts, laughter, or the words of a stressed-out mother trying to corral everyone into bed. Nor does he appreciate the patience and energy required to complete this routine every night of the week.
Hands-On Husband	The Hands-On Husband probably prioritizes his own needs for his day off first, but when asked, he will go along with what needs doing: cleaning the garage or running errands. He might, however, consider these to be "favors" to his partner, and will expect some form of praise for his cooperation.	The Hands-On Husband does not take responsibility for bedtime, nor does he see himself as crucial to the bedtime routine. If he works late or grabs a drink on the way home, he knows his partner will take care of things. But when he is called, he is happy to help. He generally knows the bath routine, and he likes reading bedtime stories.
Equal Partner	The Equal Partner is aware of the house to-do list on his days off. He makes a mental note of what chores needs to get done, what social activities are planned, and who needs to be where and when. If he wants time for himself, he plans it in coordination with his partner.	At 8:00 P.M. the Equal Partner stops what he is doing and rounds up the kids for bedtime. He might prefer the help, but he can handle the routine if his partner is away or busy. Sure, he feels drained and exhausted when the last kid falls asleep, but who doesn't? Every night is an accomplishment.

Maybe you read the Equal Partner description and laughed, thinking, *No man does THAT.* Well, yes, some men actually do. Not as many as we would like, that's for sure. But they absolutely exist.

We all have our own comfort levels, our own expectations, and our own goals. I am not suggesting that we all need to be the Equal Partner; I am sure many readers are happy with their King or their Hands-On. Maybe you just want your partner to move a few steps down the continuum, but you do not necessarily expect parity. Whatever people choose to do or not do in their own household is fine. I am merely offering some vocabulary and definitions, and I trust that you can decide how you want to use this information.

My one request for all readers is that we collectively try to be more precise with the words that we use to describe Male Role behaviors. In order to properly communicate expectations, we need to be clear (respectful, but clear) about what behaviors constitute a King, a Hands-On, and an Equal Partner. In other words, we need to call it like it is. Treating someone like an Equal Partner when they are a Hands-On only perpetuates falsehood in perception.

I talked to Daniel Carlson, a sociologist with the University of Utah, about this. He agreed, citing recent data his team collected that demonstrates that many men have an inflated idea of their own contribution. Among those different-sex couples surveyed in this study, women reported that 29 percent of household work is either shared equally or the father takes the lead, whereas the men reported that 65 percent of household work is either shared equally or the father takes the lead. Carlson explained, "This has everything to do with perception. You can't drag someone across the finish line if they think the race is already over. We need people to understand what doing your fair share actually is."

Carlson's information suggests that there are many Hands-On

Husbands out there calling themselves Equal Partners and getting away with it because, presumably, no one in their life is holding them accountable. Think about this another way: no one would stand for a clerk walking around a law firm and claiming to be a partner—someone would correct that behavior. The same should hold true for the household. Let's not falsely elevate Male Role accomplishments. Let's be honest about what the Male Role does in the home, and be honest about how those behaviors affect his partner.

Using clear words and definitions will eventually have a positive impact on the next generation. Even if we're happy in our own partnership, do we expect our children and grandchildren to replicate our relationships? Or do we want to prepare kids for the possibility of something different? Maybe you are married to a King and don't mind it in the least—but you want to help your teenage granddaughter explore a different kind of partnership, or support your Equal Partner nephew and his new boyfriend. This is when community is essential. We can't read these descriptions and think only of our own nuclear households. We need to consider how a revised vocabulary can help us better communicate with various people in our lives.

FINDING EQUAL PARTNERS

We have become adept at calling out bad behavior and listing things that men do wrong. This, of course, is important. But I find we lack examples of positive behavior and are at a loss for words when asked to describe what men do right. For this reason, the remainder of part 2 will focus solely on the concept of an equal partner, with the specific intention of answering five questions: Where do these men come from? What is their inspiration? How do they do it? What are their partners like? And what lessons can we apply to parenting boys, in order to raise a new generation of equal partners? (As a mother of a son, I was particularly interested in this last point.)

I used my own description of an equal partner to identify volunteers to be interviewed. I did not do a random sampling that is representative of North American men, nor did I attempt to make claims and draw inferences about the average person in the Male Role. I specifically and deliberately looked for those who are already different; those who do not participate in a neo-traditional relationship. Those who are intentionally and diligently working for parity in their home.

I began with my own social and professional networks. Then, to achieve a truly diverse sample, I expanded my search to specifically include men from varied ethnic and cultural backgrounds, religions, education levels, and economic classes. I admit, it was not always easy to find these guys, and it was somewhat disheartening to learn how few men out there fit my description of an equal partner. I had many people squint at me after I gave them my pitch and sheepishly answer, "I honestly don't know one couple like that."

But some people did know an equal partner in their life. Enough people told me, "that sounds like my brother" or "there's a guy at work that might fit this description." I would reach out with an initial email and proceed with some preliminary screening.

I admit that I had to abandon several men during the process. Many men determined this wasn't an accurate description during the email screening. Many more read through my criteria and thought they met the description, but when I asked them to discuss the checklist with their partner, they came back and told me their partners had set them straight—that they did nowhere near 50 percent of the household work. There were a few men who made it past the screening and all the way to the interview, but their stories made it clear they were not truly equal partners. These men all fell out of my sample set.

Those men that met my definition were invited to do an interview. From there I relied on snowball sampling—or rather, asking each interviewee if they had someone else to recommend. Some did not—others recommended two or three guys they knew. That is how, over the course of about six months, I conducted forty interviews.

I spoke to men living across the United States, and some in Canada. About 50 percent lived in a suburb, 30 percent in an urban area, and 20 percent in a rural area. I spoke to men who identified as African, Afro-Caribbean, Appalachian, Bangladeshi American, Black, Cajun, Chicano, Filipino American, Japanese American, Latino, Native American, Polynesian American, South Asian, and white; Bahá'í, Catholic, Christian, Jewish, and nonreligious. I talked to a man who described his childhood as "the epitome of entitlement" and another who told me he grew up "almost homeless."

I spoke to men with PhDs and men with high school diplomas. I spoke to men working shifts in the fields of construction, water treatment, agriculture, and oil refinement. I spoke to men with white-collar jobs representing private, government, and nonprofit sectors. I interviewed just one man in the medical field; he is a clinical psychologist. I spoke to teachers, professors, and coaches—including one NCAA Division I basketball coach. I spoke to two stay-at-home dads.

I spoke to men who had kids, men who did not have kids, and one man who was expecting his first baby. I spoke to men in their twenties, thirties, forties, and fifties. I also interviewed men with a range of family incomes. No matter the income level, I specifically chose to interview men whose households *did not* depend on a nanny or any other full-time household help. I believe full-time help is an economic luxury unachievable for most in the middle class, and I wanted lessons learned from this book to be applicable to a wide range of families.

The men I interviewed are not perfect. I am sure every one of them would want you to know that. They are human, they make mistakes, they can be selfish and stubborn, and they have arguments with their partners—just like everyone else. I am not putting these men on a pedestal for doing their fair share. I am using the same words I would use for an equal partner of any gender; they are doing their fair share in their household, and that work is greatly appreciated.

I also spoke to several of the partners of these men. I admit, at first, my primary objective was to simply verify information. I wanted to know if these men were truly equal partners, or if they just had an inflated sense of their own household contributions. But I quickly realized these partners also had a wealth of information to offer. Their stories appear in chapter 7.

Although these stories are relevant for a much wider audience, I cannot claim that the information shared is representative of all men who would identify as an equal partner. For this reason, as I continue, I will use the abbreviation EP40 when I reference this specific group of equal partners interviewed for this book.

ORIGIN STORIES: WHERE DID THEY COME FROM?

I was only able to identify one universal truth: all of the EP40, either during childhood or adolescence, had some kind of exposure to another way of life. The importance of this commonality was simple—the EP40 grew up knowing there were other ways to do things. Not one of them grew up believing that everyone did things the same way they did things; they were each aware of different ways of living, and this opened them up to the idea of trying new things as they grew up.

For first-generation Americans, it was emigrating from their birth country to the United States. For second-generation Americans, it was listening to stories from their parents and grandparents. One man said his European mother always offered a counterpoint to experiences he had growing up in the United States. Another man learned a great deal from his mother's Panamanian boyfriend.

Aunts and uncles were role models, and travel was a powerful experience for many. Several told me about a teacher, coach, or professor who inspired them. For those living in a rural area, having friends and relatives in the city was important. For those living in the city, time spent in the country was important. This finding provides some insight that may be helpful to the greater community. Yes, the nuclear family has a huge impact on a child's upbringing. But the village can also play a significant role in a child's upbringing. Some of the EP40 were hugely impacted by people they saw only once a year.

My research also identified five other origin themes. Not one man could tick off all the boxes, but every one of the EP40 told a story that fit into at least one of the following themes, and many fit into two or three. Collectively, the EP40 made it clear that they believe these themes were integral to their eventual roles as equal partners.

THEME 1: SINGLE MOMS

About 25 percent of the EP40 were raised by single mothers, and that experience was paramount to the men they would become in the future. In all cases, the fathers were either not present or only minimally so, which left the vast majority of parenting and care to the mothers.

We met Martin in chapter 4 in the conversation about baby showers. He was the third of six children, and his abusive father left his mother when Martin was twelve. As the eldest male, friends and family told a young Martin that he was now the man of the house, and it was his responsibility to step up and take care of the family. We spent a fair amount of time processing that experience. "How messed up is that? Telling a boy that age that he is the head of the house? As if a boy that age can take care of a home." It was Martin's mother who helped him find his way. "I couldn't support them financially, obviously. But my mom taught me how to help the family in other ways. She taught me how to do dishes and how to sweep and how to hand-wash the clothes. What it took to run a home. I would also help with my younger brother and sisters when she was at work."

Martin now uses these skills and this attitude in his home with Evie. They have been married for eight years and have two daughters. "Just like when I was a kid, I see something that needs doing, and I do it. It is a way to show [Evie] that I love her."

Izaiah grew up in Barbados. Izaiah's mother didn't make much money, but she managed to provide a safe and happy home for her son and her daughter. Izaiah describes his mom as fiercely independent, and he told me she is by far his biggest role model. "I grew up watching her work very hard. She was very careful with money." Helping around the house was expected of Izaiah and his sister; everyone in the home did their fair share to keep the family going. "She taught me that if I needed my soccer uniform clean, I needed to do it. That task was part of the work that came with enjoying soccer. . . . I am so thankful for my mom; she helped me feel like I could do it on my own. She taught me that I didn't need to depend on a female to cook and clean for me; that I could do it myself."

This dynamic has carried over to Izaiah's relationship with his wife, Jalecia, whom he married shortly after our interview. He spoke about not wanting to be a burden on Jalecia, the same way he hadn't wanted to be a burden on his mother. He specifically dismissed the idea that he might be entitled to domestic labor because he is male. "Taking care of myself and my household is important. That's not a burden; that's part of living. I don't want anybody doing my laundry. Call me weird, but that is something I can do on my own. . . . What is so important that I couldn't take an hour out of my day to do some washing or prepare a meal? I think success is when we both feel like we're supporting each other."

I found these stories of the past applicable to parenting today. We need not falsely assume that for a man to be an equal partner, he must have that behavior role modeled to him as a child. Neither Martin nor Izaiah had equal partner parents, but their moms were quite capable of teaching them the respect and work ethic needed to be a full partner later in life. (These EP40 happened to come from single-mother homes, but the same lessons could be learned in any single-parent household.)

THEME 2: JUSTICE AND MORALITY

Although a few EP40 grew up in households where gender equality was a specific focus, many more spoke about justice and morality in a broader sense. This wider net, which includes civil rights and human rights, was often the gateway to understanding other forms of oppression. In some cases, faith played a role in shaping their worldview and how to treat other humans. I heard stories from men who identified as Bahá'í, Catholic, Christian, Jewish, and Muslim talk about the role religion played in their upbringing. EP40 boys who grew up in households where "justice and equality" were key values had an easier time understanding harmful gender norms when they were older.

James was one of seven boys growing up, and he identifies as African American. His childhood home consisted of a mom and a dad and six brothers. James's dad followed Black Nationalist philosophy and passed those lessons on to his sons. "Dad taught me about respect and pride and grace. About learning from those who are different than we are." That foundation gave James the vocabulary to talk about racial inequalities, and it prepared him to understand other forms of oppression later in his life.

Years later, it was James's mother who introduced him to gender inequalities. "She told me this story, from when she was a girl. My mom's high school math teacher automatically gave all the girls in the class a D; he just didn't think girls were meant to study math or science. College wasn't ever an option for her, with a D on her transcript. I asked her, 'Why didn't you fight?' And she told me there was no fight to fight. It was just the way things were." Instead, James's mother got married and poured herself into her sons. "But eventually, her husband, my dad, became part of the structure that held her back. And she resented him for it." James had compassion for his mom because he could recognize oppression. Now he intentionally and specifically tries to be an equal partner in his own marriage because he doesn't want to be part of a system that holds his wife (or any other woman) back.

Remy was aware of inequities from a young age. His nuclear family included his mom, dad, a little sister, and his grandmother.

Remy identifies as white and Cajun; he was born and raised in southern Louisiana and still lives there today. Remy's family did not have much money when he was growing up; they always rented their home, which meant moving a lot. "I decided, on my own, that the system was rigged. I watched my dad get fired and the impact that had on our family. My dad worked hard, but unlike the American dream, he wasn't rewarded. I didn't have the words for it back then, but basically, I hated racism, I hated oppression, and I hated control that led to marginalization."

When he was nine, Remy's family left the Catholic Church and joined a Black Baptist church. Through that experience, he made many new friends but lost many others. "Lots of family and friends left us at that point. But my mom didn't care. My dad wasn't around much, so my mom was the man of the house. [She taught me to] hate racism and not to care about what other people thought."

Remy's mom did not, and has never, discussed gender inequality with him. But it was easy for Remy to apply the lessons around justice, which he learned as a kid, to the concept of gender. That philosophy helps tremendously in his marriage. "Sharing household labor is just the right thing to do. Work has never been a choice for either of us; we need the money and we both need to work. But she shouldn't have to do more work at home because she is a female. We both do what needs doing because the end goal is to spend time together. I would not enjoy laying around while she is working, and vice versa."

THEME 3: EXPERIENCE IN CAREGIVING

Caregiving is coded as female work. Whereas girls may grow up babysitting and taking care of younger siblings and cousins, boys are often excluded from that opportunity. But several EP40 had the opportunity to give care at an early age, and that had a big impact on the subsequent decisions they made about partnership and family in the future. Martin, who previously shared his baby shower story, told me that there were always kids and babies in his home: first his younger siblings and then his nieces and nephews. He is glad that he had exposure to babies and kids when he was young, and he thinks that experience helped bring out his nurturing side as an adult.

Born in the mid-1960s, Logan grew up in the South and identifies as white and Bahá'í. He described his father as a workaholic, and he says he didn't know his dad well before his parents divorced. Logan's mother got remarried, and a few years later a little brother came along—Dylan. Logan was fourteen when he became a big brother, so he was perfectly capable of taking on a significant role in Dylan's life. "I built him a little seat on the back of my moped, and we drove around town together. I suppose part of it was my mother needed childcare—but she really gave me the chance to take care of him. She trusted me. It was during that time I learned that I wanted kids of my own, that I really liked being around children." I am chalking up the facts of this story to the 1970s, and doubt many people would allow a toddler on the back of a moped these days. (Logan agreed.) But the lesson around caregiving remains.

That experience was vital to Logan's marriage years later, when he and his wife were expecting their first baby. "Because of my experience with Dylan, I started out with more knowledge of babies than my wife. I knew what the temperature of the formula should feel like; I knew about changing diapers; I knew that babies cry and sometimes there's nothing you can do about that. I knew that babies take time, in a very intimate way. And I am still just so grateful for that early experience." Logan's involvement with baby Dylan gave him the confidence to be a father and an equal parent years later; in his family, there was no option of maternal gatekeeping because he was the one with the expertise. Logan ended up having five children, who are now between the ages of seventeen and thirty. Logan is also a proud grandpa to his first grandson.

Caregiving can also be life changing when men experience it as a young adult. Allen identifies as white and grew up in Nova Scotia. He was the eldest of four boys and would look after his little brothers from time to time, but it wasn't until he got a job as a summer camp counselor that he really had the opportunity to experience caregiving. "My first few years, I was eighteen or nineteen years old, and the boys in my cabin were little—like seven, eight, nine. They were little boys. I had to remind them to brush their teeth, and at night I would tell them bedtime stories. When they got homesick, they needed hugs, and sometimes they would wet the bed. I learned really fast that I could either make that kid's summer awful, or I could pretend I spilled something and clean up the sheets before anyone realized. It was an obvious choice." During our conversation, Allen realized those summers really normalized caregiving for him. "I learned that being masculine doesn't mean being unavailable."

Ash grew up in a military family and moved every few years. His father worked long hours and traveled a lot, so Ash spent most of his time with his mother and his sister. He went to college after graduating from high school, but didn't have much direction. After two years, he dropped out and found a job as a day care bus driver. "The students would arrive at day care in the morning. I was responsible for [picking them up and] dropping them at different elementary schools around the area . . . [then in the afternoon I would pick] them up and return them to the day care center." He told me that caregiving came naturally to him; it brought out a paternal instinct. "The part I enjoyed most was, at each elementary school, we would all get out of the bus and walk the kid up to the door. To say goodbye and wish them a good day." I asked if he did this as a safety precaution. "Maybe. But mostly I think it was because I was building a little community. It was just instinct. I had it then—even before I had my own kids. I knew what to do naturally, without thinking about it." Ash eventually left this job and went back to college. He later heard that the new driver dropped the kids off at the curb, and that made him feel a little sad.

Incidentally, Allen and Ash both went on to become teachers and fathers.

THEME 4: OTHERED

The term *othered* has roots in sociology. Academics use this term to describe a group of people treating a subset of the group as different, lesser, or not belonging. But now, even Merriam-Webster approves of using the word *other* as a verb.

About 75 percent of the EP40 were othered at some point in their life. This came in various forms, most commonly in issues related to race, class, ability, gender identity, and/or sexual orientation. Men described feelings that ranged from "not fitting in" to being bullied and physically assaulted. Feelings of being othered were strongest in men who did not have an affinity group in their community, for example, the only Brown kid in a very white suburb, or the only kid with a disability in his high school.

I also heard stories about being othered from mainstream masculinity. This affected boys who, in their teenage years, were small, skinny, nerdy, unathletic, and/or overly shy. All men I spoke to seemed perfectly aware of the adolescent male pecking order and how they fit into it. Some possessed a few masculine traits that enabled them to fit in, if even superficially. Remy explained, "I never really felt like I fit in. But I could get by and make friends because I was funny and good at sports. For boys, if you're athletic and you can make other kids laugh, you'll be left alone."

A few of the EP40 were not othered themselves, but learned those lessons by working closely with marginalized groups. Ethan grew up in Maine. As a white male from a middle-class family, he didn't feel othered during his childhood, but he started to understand the concept when he began working with special needs kids in college. "My work has completely shifted my worldview. My interaction with [those children and families] has shaken up all my preconceived ideas about caregiving and family and education."

These stories about othering very much fit with known research. Psychiatrists refer to this as "altruism born of suffering." The idea is that, once a person goes through a traumatic experience, they are more likely to empathize with another person who has gone through a traumatic experience.[1] This seems to explain why a person who has been othered in their life would have more compassion and understanding toward their partner. Of course, there is certainly no guarantee; but a person who has been othered may have a greater opportunity to understand another who has also felt alienated. In this case, it appears that many of the EP40 used their othering experience for good. Those feelings of inadequacy, exclusion, and injustice made them more capable to empathize with their future partners.

THEME 5: NEGATIVE ROLE MODELS

One doesn't necessarily require that correct behavior be role modeled to them; sometimes we learn by watching what *not* to do. About 50 percent of the EP40 told me stories about men in their lives who set a negative example; these descriptions varied from emotionally distant men, to absent men, to men who exhibited some form of toxic masculinity. Several EP40 also told me about their experiences with abuse, violence, alcoholism, drug addiction, and trauma. But with help, they were able to break their destructive cycles, instead of perpetuate them.

Lucas is one of those men. We first met Lucas in chapter 4, when I shared how he and his husband, Aaron, take turns feeding their foster baby every other night. Lucas is now a successful teacher, husband, community member, and foster father. But those identities did not come easily for him.

Lucas identifies as Latino and grew up in Texas. His parents divorced when he was three, and he is a survivor of childhood sexual abuse. He lived with his mother while growing up in an unsafe household with severe economic challenges. "There was a remarkable absence of positive role models growing up. My dad later died in a federal prison while facing drug charges. I was not meant to succeed."

Lucas only had negative role models at home, but that experience propelled him to look for support elsewhere. He eventually found positive role models in his teachers. "School saved me. It saved me from my home life. It was the safe space I needed as a kid. My school friends later became my chosen family, and we are still very close." Lucas grew up knowing what he didn't want to be: he didn't want to be an abuser, and he didn't want to have a substance abuse problem.

He saw what could happen to people in those circumstances, and he wanted something different for himself.

Those ideals hold true today in his marriage with Aaron, and in the work he does. Now a teacher himself, Lucas intentionally reaches out to kids who are survivors of abuse or are being systematically oppressed. He aims to create spaces built on safety and trust, so students can come to him and ask questions.

REPETITION MATTERS

Unsurprisingly, none of the men I interviewed believe that one single person or experience made them who they are. Many of the EP40 grew into who they are over time because of repeated messages around equality and healthy masculinity. This concept about phases and repetition was especially central to Charles's story.

Charles grew up in Virginia. He identifies as African American and Christian. The consistent people in his life growing up included a mother, two siblings, and a large extended family. When I asked him to tell me about his childhood, he automatically divided his first eighteen years of life into four phases. This was important because each phase exposed him to different people and taught him different lessons. According to Charles, it was the sum of all these phases, and the repetition of messages, that made him the man he is today.

- Phase I, Ages 5–11: Lived with mom, siblings, and stepfather. Stepfather did not shy away from housework and frequently cooked for all the kids.
- Phase II, Ages 11–13: Lived with mom, siblings, and mom's boyfriend. Boyfriend was in the Air Force and brought structure and discipline to the house. His respect for

Charles's mom was intentional. Academics became a focus, and Charles started to believe he had the potential to go to college.

- Phase III, Ages 13–16: No men in the home: just Charles, his siblings, and his mother. The three kids divided all housework among themselves, as his mother had to work very long hours to provide for her family. "It was a 'let's make it work' kind of time. Mom used to say, 'Someone better have one of my uniforms pressed before I come home. I don't care which one of you does it—but someone better do it.'" Learned how to divvy up chores with older sister.

- Phase IV, Ages 16–18: Older sister moved out. Charles took over care of his younger brother when his mom worked, and did all the household work. Learned how to do cognitive labor: making lists, grocery shopping, managing a budget, etc.

Charles believes it was the positive influences from each period in his life, plus the ongoing relationship with his grandmother and his church community, that taught him the value of a work ethic, independence, and compassion.

Tim identifies as Filipino American and Catholic; his parents immigrated to California, where Tim was born. Tim grew up in a home with his mother, father, grandfather, and three older brothers. Tim's mom was the parent who was career focused, and his dad was the parent who took care of the home. In this way, Tim differs from most of the other EP40, as his parents role modeled a reversal in gender norms. The behavior of Tim's mother seems to fit the description of the Hands-On Husband.

But when Tim met and married Sarah, she automatically stepped into a traditional Female Role without any conversation. "I was raised to be taken care of," he admits. "Sarah is the third of nine kids—she has been taking care of siblings her whole life. She was raised to be a mom. We just fell into these roles, despite my own childhood home."

Tim explained that he was a true believer in the concept of gender equality, but he wasn't good at living those values. He worked a lot, and Sarah was basically a single parent when their first child was born. They lived with Tim's parents, so Sarah had help. But she didn't want the help of her in-laws, she wanted a partner. Sarah eventually reached boiling point. She told Tim that she was leaving with the baby—that he was welcome to join them, but she would no longer stay in her in-laws' house. Tim and Sarah began therapy, and that was what got them through their most difficult years.

One positive experience wasn't enough for him. Tim required repetition. The combination of household role modeling, an insistent partner, therapy, supportive friends, and years of intentional work made him the equal partner that Tim is today.

MEN'S GLASS CEILING

For a while, I was frustrated by the lack of universal commonalities in these men's stories. Then I realized I was looking at this issue from the wrong perspective. It was less important to focus on where someone came from, who raised them, or where they went to school. What is more important is how someone lives their life today. Anyone, from anywhere, seems to have the potential to be an equal partner.

This is an important point because it counters many common tropes we hear about men and household work:

- *His mother always did things for him; he just never learned. It's not his fault.*
- *His father was like that, too; he just doesn't know any different.*
- *He just wasn't raised that way.*

All of these statements, which we have all heard thrown around in casual conversation, blatantly excuse gendered behavior because of an underlying assumption that we are all destined to repeat the past. Of course, the past is important. We are each the product of our lived experiences; identity and childhood dramatically impact who we are, the choices we make, and the opportunities we have—or do not have. We need to be aware that people in positions of privilege often use the myth of the "self-made man" to perpetuate cycles of inequality through their actions, behavior, speech, and control of the law. Institutional oppression is very real and has profound implications. I would never diminish anyone's life experience, or be so presumptuous as to make judgements about how a person responds to lifelong, systemic oppression.

But I think we can acknowledge our past *and* refuse to allow history to dictate our future.

Based on the EP40 interviews, life experience does not need to be determinative. Lucas came from a very challenging childhood characterized by poverty, trauma, and violence. Martin spent weeks of his childhood in a shelter with his mother and his siblings, hiding from his abusive father. Remy came from a household surrounded by men who exhibited toxic masculinity. Izaiah described the men from his childhood as tough and emotionally distant. Yet all these men are now the people they want to be, not the people society raised them to be.

Help is certainly important. Lucas and Martin give credit to programs run by nonprofit organizations. Remy and Izaiah credit their mothers for showing them how to love and be loved. All four of these men were recipients of kindness and patience and empathy during their lifetimes. We should not assume people can break cycles and become equal partners on their own. But we should also not assume people cannot be equal partners because of their background.

Knowing this, I have little patience when I hear men use the line *It just isn't the way I was raised* as an excuse for doing less in the home. I think of men like Lucas and Remy and Martin and Izaiah, and how hard they worked to be who they are today, and I realize how empty that excuse really is.

The glass ceiling is a common metaphor used to describe the unseen limits society puts on a woman's professional ambition. But we need to start using the term *glass ceiling* for men, too. This metaphor is also an excellent description of the way society protects men from household work by lowering our expectations of them, which prohibits them from doing more. I imagine Logan and Ash would be angry at the insinuation that they couldn't be a true partner in their homes. I think we need to think differently about men as partners and fathers, and stop putting limits on male capacity. Anything else is, ironically, patronizing.

6

TOWARD EQUAL PARTNERSHIP

In *The Will to Change: Men, Masculinity and Love,* bell hooks reminds us that "most men have not consciously chosen patriarchy as the ideology they want to govern their lives, their beliefs, and actions. Patriarchal culture is the system they were born within and socialized to accept." All Americans are born into our current gender culture; none of us chose it. But from here, we each have to decide where to go.

Though most men don't *choose* patriarchy, many men go with the flow—benefitting from their position within the system. Because the EP40 take on the Male Role in their relationships, it would be culturally acceptable for them to sit back and do less in the home, allowing their Female Role counterparts to do more. But these men do not. They intentionally chose another path. *Why?*

Four motivational themes emerged from my interviews: providing for their families; love and happiness; supporting their partners; and connecting with their kids. These themes are not mutually exclusive; many EP40 would probably agree that several of these themes, or even all of them, provided some sort of motivation for their actions.

Together, these motivations demonstrate that the EP40 do not see their role as an equal partner as being a sacrifice. No one gave any indication that they were forced into this lifestyle, unhappy with their choices, or bitter about the amount of work they do. This is an important point, echoed in Daniel Carlson's work at the University of Utah. He explained to me: "Asking men to forego their privilege and do more household work is really looking at this issue the wrong way. Being an equal partner is actually more rewarding—it actually improves relationship quality. These are not competing interests. There is more evidence to support the equity perspective."

MOTIVATION #1: PROVIDING FOR MY FAMILY

In chapter 2, we discussed the concept of breadwinning—how taking care of a family in an economic sense has long been coded for the Male Role. The EP40 impressed me with their interpretation of this long-standing expectation; they still believed in the concept of the Male Role providing for his family, they just broadened their definition of *providing.*

Matthew identifies as white and Catholic and grew up in what he describes as a pleasant New England suburb. His father was a groundskeeper, and his mother was a nurse who worked the night shift. Matthew has three siblings, and he spent a lot of childhood hours with his brothers and sister. Their family followed more traditional gender roles, and Matthew describes his childhood home as peaceful and happy. Although his mother was the cognitive laborer, his father always took a great interest in his kids and still does.

When Matthew and his future wife, Janie, started to talk about marriage, he knew her job would always take priority over his. As a doctor, she had greater earning capacity than he did. Janie was also ambitious and highly capable; her talent was recognized and she was frequently promoted. When I interviewed Matthew, he and Janie had two children—the youngest was just two months old. Janie was on parental leave at the time, but Mathew knew, once she went back to work, she would return to long hours and heavy responsibilities.

With Janie earning enough money for their family of four, Matthew had to ask himself, *What is my role?* "I started to think, *How am I going to provide?* so to speak. Everything has value. The skills that I have to take care of the house, that provides. And the skills I have to take care of the kids, that provides. Even if I can't be the one bringing in all the money, I can still be a partner and provide for my family."

Matthew switched jobs to ensure his work was more compatible with Janie's schedule. Knowing Janie couldn't be the parent to leave work early when the kids got sick, Matthew found a job that would give him greater flexibility. In a capitalist society that tends to value income above all other indicators, I appreciate how hard that probably was for him. But he explained, "You have to think about your self-worth versus the money that you make. It's different, really. There is value in taking care of your kids and not chasing a career. I am still providing for my family."

I tried that language out with other EP40, and it resonated time after time. Providing for one's family was a huge motivating factor for them—but *providing* was interpreted broadly. Sometimes money is not what your family needs most.

Ryder was born and raised in Michigan to a mother he affectionately described as a "hellfire." He identifies as white, and he doesn't consider himself religious. Ryder often got into trouble growing up. "Normal kid stuff," he explained. He met Bethany while he was working in Alaska. They married, started a family, and eventually moved to rural Virginia to be closer to Bethany's family. At the time of our interview, they had two children, ages four and five.

Ryder was a stay-at-home dad. When he did work, he worked in construction. But for a while now, he has been staying home to take care of the kids. He explained, in his matter-of-fact way, that Bethany simply had the capacity to earn more money than him. It just made sense for him to take on a domestic role. "Bethany is taking care of money right now. She makes enough for our family. What our family really needs me to do is the other stuff, taking care of the kids and doing the cooking and the laundry." He was honest with me about how hard that job was. "Staying home full time is more challenging than anything I had ever done before. . . . But for me, it just boils down to what matters. I don't need a big home or other people raising my kids. Time is the biggest currency, and right now, I have lots and lots of time with my kids."

I was curious how Ryder felt about not working. *Did it bother him?* I was glad for his honest answer. "Well, I don't write it on a hat or anything. I do find myself purposefully not asking what other men do, like at the playground, because I don't want to answer back. But I am not really embarrassed either. As time goes on, it gets easier." Ryder did not see himself in this role indefinitely; it was a short-term childcare solution, motivated by his desire to provide for his family.

MOTIVATION #2: LOVE AND HAPPINESS

Romantic love was very much present in many of my conversations with the EP40. I was pleasantly surprised by how many men told me long, sweet stories about how they met their partners.

We first met Martin in chapter 5. He is the man from South Texas who was told to be the "man of his house" at the age of twelve. Now Martin is married to Evie, and they have two small children. He talked for a long time about how he met Evie and about their wedding. "I am still crazy about her. She means so much to me. Being with Evie and the kids, I am living my best life. I am happier now than I have ever been before. I get so much joy from being a partner and a father." I suggested that perhaps he was painting a rosy picture for me. I am married, too, after all. I know the reality of relationships. Martin laughed a little and agreed. "Sure, not every day is a great day. But I always love her. We can always talk about stuff. And then maybe the next day is better."

Boubacar also had a love story to tell. He is a first-generation American, born and raised in Francophone West Africa—thousands of miles away from Maryland, which he now calls home. Boubacar identifies as African. He is a practicing Muslim and the father of two children, ages four and seven at the time of our interview.

Boubacar explained that his parents were not at all representative of traditional families growing up. His paternal grandfather practiced polygamy, and his grandmother was the last of four wives. His father grew up watching the rest of his family marginalize his mother as she struggled to care for her children. Boubacar's father made the decision that he didn't want to live that way, and he raised his kids to value equality between men and women. "As a child, I would do the same chores as my sisters. We would all fetch water and firewood. I remember scrubbing the pots in the yard. After cooking, the pots would be so black, and I was told to scrub them to make them shine. The women in the village would pass by and yell, 'What are you doing washing the dishes? No woman will marry you!'" Boubacar chuckled. He was raised to push back on gender

179

norms. He didn't mind those small confrontations, and still doesn't today. "I was not raised to be a typical man in my culture."

Rebecca was a US Peace Corps volunteer in Boubacar's village. They fell in love and married. Boubacar and I talked about the difference between superficial happiness (eating a delicious meal or buying a new TV) and deep happiness. Boubacar made it clear that his relationship with Rebecca brings him deep happiness and contentment. "Islam tells us that men must support women. How can you support her if you leave her all the work, and the kids, and don't do your part? Doing domestic work is my duty."

MOTIVATION #3: SUPPORTING MY PARTNER

Nathan identifies as white and Jewish. He was raised by his mother and never met his father. Nathan is now married to Madeline, and they are both academics. Together, they are raising their first child—who was just under a year old when we talked. During our interview, Nathan spent a fair amount of time discussing his wife's career.

Nathan told me that Madeline has always been the more ambitious of the two of them. From the beginning, she always had bigger, loftier professional dreams. Madeline is now very successful in her field. "When she gets accolades, it is more valuable than if I got them. It matters so much to me that she is successful. I am very proud of her. . . . And I feel validated; I feel happy and satisfied that I could help her achieve her dream. I am happy to contribute to something meaningful." Watching her succeed, he explained, actually means more to him than his own success.

Nathan frequently shows his love and support by consciously taking on part of the emotional burden of their homelife. He learned very quickly that, with a baby in the house, not running out of "stuff" is critical, so he has taken on this responsibility. We joked about the catastrophe that comes when you run out of staples like formula or diapers. Nathan consciously monitors their household inventory to determine what they have and what they need, and then he is the one who finds time to go shopping. He believes this is one way he can show his support of Madeline's career. Making sure the house is in order is Nathan's way of giving Madeline cognitive freedom, allowing her to either work or rest when she is at home.

Henry lives in Washington, DC, with his male partner, Reza. Henry identifies as white, and Reza is Iranian American. They do not have children. When they first moved in together, Henry believed their partnership resembled true parity. Then, Reza decided to go to medical school; at that time Henry decided he was going to take on the bulk of the household work. Henry told me about the long and grueling hours that Reza worked. Henry knew Reza would clean their house on his off hours if need be, but Henry decided he would rather do more housework so the two could spend quality time together when they had a day off together. I asked Henry if he ever felt at all bitter. "Not at all. I am happy that I am in a place in my life, and my career, when I can do this. I work from home, and this is how I can support him."

Henry expressed pride in Reza, but he took that a little bit further than anyone else I interviewed. "I feel proud of him, certainly. But I also feel proud of myself for the act of supporting Reza in medical school. He is doing something really wonderful, and this is my contribution to his career. And that is really important to me."

Other EP40 talked about supporting their partners—not in terms of career or profession, but in terms of emotional health. Logan, whom we met in chapter 5, was the guy who drove his little brother around town on his moped. Years later, he and his wife have five children and live in Hawaii. Logan was certainly motivated by his love for kids, but also by his commitment to his marriage and his concern for the emotional health of his partner. "The plan is—I mean if all goes well—you're going to have lots of years together after your kids are out of the house. And I didn't want [Noriko] to be resentful or bitter toward me. . . . Being an equal partner means investing in her, as much as my kids. . . . You need to think about the long game, and really invest in [your partner]. Show them that they matter."

Jack is the guy who described his childhood as "the epitome of entitlement." Jack identifies as a white urbanite who was born and raised in Seattle. He traveled around Asia during his twenties, and then he took a job with a nonprofit in the United States that facilitated study-abroad programs. "When I was traveling in Japan and Southeast Asia, I started to really understand my privilege. I also started to understand that Americans tend to associate themselves with work and money, but the rest of the world doesn't really do that. What I did [for work] became less important [to me]."

Jack met Brenda, they married, moved to Vermont, and started a family. At the time of our interview, their kids were three years and four months old. Brenda has the more strenuous job; Jack has the more flexible one. He believes that his time in Asia helped him be more comfortable with his own professional goals—or lack thereof. "I am really comfortable with my own focus on family. I see it as a point of pride that I am more attuned to my kids than to my work." He says that he and Brenda are good about averaging a fifty-fifty balance, but he makes a special effort to step it up at home when her work gets busy. I asked him if his motivation was pride in her professional accomplishments. "Not so much her professional achievements, no. I am more concerned with her emotional and mental health."

When Jack knows Brenda is coming home late from a long, hard day, he will not only put the kids to bed, but also pick up the toys, do the dishes, and vacuum if there is time. He wants her to have a clean and orderly house to come home to. "I need to do this so she has a sanctuary to come home to. So she can collapse and refuel." Jack saw the direct link between the state of the house when Brenda got home and what kind of mood that would put her in. He fully admits he isn't always perfect, and we all know there are those nights when the kids do everything in their power to derail your plans. But Jack's goal has always been to make as nice a space as possible for his partner when she comes home from a long day at work.

Jack does not see his actions as a sacrifice. "If anything, my actions are selfish because I am not giving up anything. I am gaining a great marriage and a great relationship with my kids. I guess I can't do what I want, when I want. But that just comes with parenthood."

MOTIVATION #4: CONNECTION WITH MY KIDS

Three-quarters of the EP40 were fathers, with children ranging in age from a few weeks to thirty years old. Every one of those men expressed that their kids were a huge motivation behind their household behavior. They all valued their deep relationships with their children, and they believed that building a deeper relationship came from spending a great deal of time together. With time, of course, comes care. There was taking care of the children directly, such as feeding, bathing, dressing, and helping with homework and activities. And there was the care that took place in the house around the kids, to facilitate the family as a whole: shopping, cleaning, planning, cooking. The EP40 fathers value both, which makes them very intentional parents.

Ash's children were in college at the time of our interview, which I appreciated. Most of the fathers I interviewed had little kids, and they spoke of relationships they hoped to have in the future. Ash, however, had the luxury of looking back and telling me about the kind of relationship he has now. We met Ash in chapter 5; he was the preschool bus driver who eventually became a sixth-grade teacher.

"[Growing up] I was always hiding things from my parents because I was scared about getting in trouble. So, I kept things from them. Lucia and I always wanted our girls to talk to us. When mistakes are made, we may be stern, but we always want to be talking. . . . I really credit Lucia for that, she is a great communicator. When we met, I was more like my father and I held things in. She taught me how to communicate with her and with our girls."

Ash and I talked about how exhausting it can be to parent little kids, and he described how his work schedule enabled him to do so much of the everyday care when his kids were young. He and Lucia tried to split the work down the middle. But being a very present father was important to him, and aside from the usual ups and downs, he has loved being a parent. "I admit I now miss doing the physical tasks, like doing their laundry and singing them to sleep." For Ash, all those little-kid tasks transitioned into a solid relationship with his girls when they were teenagers. He felt that, because he was such a strong presence in their life as little kids, it was only natural to maintain a friendship as his girls grew up. "You're just there in different ways [when they're older]. Maintaining presence and being there in good times and bad times—just listening. Active listening."

Jacques lives in southern Louisiana and identifies as Native

American. He grew up with two older half-siblings, a mother, and a father. His dad spent most months of the year away from home working on rig boats, leaving Jacques's mother to take care of the kids and the home. "My siblings are much older than me, so I sort of grew up alone. They both struggle with drug addiction, then and now, so mom was always having to deal with that. It was a rough life. I knew she loved us, but she's a tough woman."

Jacques became an uncle when he was ten, and he loved being around his niece and nephew as a teenager. "I always loved kids, and I knew I wanted to be a dad." He also knew he did not want to work on rig boats his whole life, nor did he want to inherit the drug problem his siblings struggled with.

Jacques met Morgan in high school. After graduation, she continued her education to become a clinical psychologist. Jacques found work in the oil industry, but unlike his dad, he took a job at the oil fields so he could come home every night and spend time with his kids. He and Morgan started a family when they were in their early twenties. When I interviewed Jacques, his kids ranged in age from ten to twenty-two. "My parents are of the old style. But I didn't need a woman to serve me. And I don't expect someone else to raise my kids. I can do for myself."

Jacques told me he loved being a dad: he loved caring for his kids when they were small, and he loved being a part of their lives now that they were older. Even though his oldest daughter has moved to California, Jacques described their relationship as close. They text and talk daily, and they visit whenever possible.

I asked him how it felt, looking back, to be the kind of parent that he was. "Well, it feels good. It's my greatest accomplishment, to know that you were part of that. And not just as a part-time dad who came around once in a while. . . . Morgan and I always tried to raise the kids to be caring people. Honest people who help those that can't help themselves. I am so proud of all of my kids."

HOW DO THEY MAKE IT WORK?

The next step was to investigate how the EP40 made the day-to-day reality work. We already discussed how gender norms and cultural assumptions impact the lives of the Female Role and the Male Role. What did these men and these families do to counter cultural pressure? In my conversations and interviews, I specifically tried to get to the root of shared emotional labor. As Tim expertly summed up in our interview, "Sure, congratulations, you found each other. But now you have to find a way to stay together." I identified seven common strategies that helped the EP40 maintain household parity.

STRATEGY 1: QUALITY COMMUNICATION

Communication was a core theme in nearly all of my interviews, which is why I chose to list it at the top of my strategies list. Of course, *communication* is such a catchall word; it can mean everything and nothing at the same time. Thankfully, the EP40 were very specific about which kinds of communication were helpful and which kinds were unhelpful.

First, there is logistics communication. This is the everyday stuff, the "who is going to do what" communication. This can be monotonous and repetitive, but it is absolutely critical to EP40 households. *Are you picking up the kids or me? Do you have time to stop off at the hardware store or should I? Do you have to work late tonight? OK, I'll do bath time. Can you take over for fifteen minutes? I really need a break.*

Whereas a lone CEO can keep plans in their head and carry out actions without discussion, co-managers need to constantly keep in touch to make sure they're both on the same page in order to successfully mitigate gaps and overlaps. The EP40 communicate with their partners throughout the day, every day, through a variety of methods: in-person conversations, text, emails, voice mail, family calendars, shared notes on phones, and actual, old-fashioned lists taped to refrigerator doors and kitchen cabinets. In my conversation with Jacques, we both agreed that deciding what to eat is often more time-consuming than the actual cooking. He explained his family's strategy. "We text back and forth during the day to come up with dinner; then I pick up anything we need on my way home from work. That way the decision doesn't fall on either of our shoulders."

Constant communication can also help divide the emotional burden. Saying the "anticipating" tasks out loud helps both people realize what needs doing in any given day or week, and then the pair can distribute work more evenly.

But the deeper, emotional communication is what the men I interviewed talked about in more detail. They talked about the critical skill of being able to read your partner and pick up on their unspoken signals. And they expressed the need to truly know each other as people.

Boubacar talked extensively about what healthy communication meant to him and his relationship with Rebecca. "Yes, communication is important. But it goes beyond verbal and nonverbal. Saying, *I told you to do this* is not communication. It goes deeper." Boubacar believes that the foundation of day-to-day living is agreeing on shared values, and understanding the other person's past and present. "It is not just telling her what I need, but understanding what she needs. *Is she tired? Is she struggling? Does she need my help?*" Boubacar went on to explain that, when he notices Rebecca is worn down, he tries to step in before she has to ask. Because he understands her values, he knows what he can do that she will appreciate. Because he understands her triggers, he knows what not to do—or what he can take care of to mitigate her frustrations. And when he isn't sure about her feelings? When he is confused by her signals or not sure of her intentions? He makes time to ask her, and listen.

Robbie identifies as Black and Christian. He grew up in Ohio with a single mother and two sisters. His childhood was a tough one, and he had two unsuccessful marriages following his high school graduation. Robbie described his move to Texas at the age of twenty-eight as a rebirth—a way to leave his past behind and start fresh. "I had to hustle up down here. I didn't have any blood family to rely on and needed to provide for myself. I had to learn how to do that—how to take care of myself. But I learned. I didn't know what a good marriage looked like back then, but at least I learned how to be responsible for myself." Three years later he met Lydia at a friend's birthday party. He was attracted to her confidence and her independence. The two dated and married. At the time of our interview, they had two kids, ages five and seven. Robbie also has one twenty-year-old child from his first marriage.

With the added experience of two unsuccessful partnerships, Robbie was in the position to articulate what it was that made his relationship with Lydia so successful. "Communication is 90 percent of the whole doggone marriage," he told me with a laugh. "And not just what you say, but really understanding where your spouse comes from, and respect their position and opinion." Robbie echoed Boubacar's message, explaining that knowing your partner deeply helps to frame your communication for the life of the relationship. "Lydia was raised in a middle-income house, went to college, had family vacations. I mean, she went to Hawaii with her family. And I was a welfare kid who went to SeaWorld once." Robbie said that, even after years of marriage, they still see the world from very different perspectives. When he and Lydia have a disagreement, it often boils down to perspective and lived experiences. Remembering and respecting each other's past, Robbie stressed, is essential to connecting on a deeper, emotional level.

Hector identifies as Chicano and also lives in Texas. In the first minutes of our conversation, he told me that he grew up in a violent and abusive home. But his life story is far more about breaking cycles, and less about living them. Like Lucas, Hector credits a high school program for helping him become his true self. "They helped me formulate ideas around healthy relationships and healthy masculinity. They prepared me for my life with Marisol." Hector completed high school and college, and he found a job at a nonprofit organization as a child advocate working on behalf of child assault survivors. Marisol was a volunteer at that organization. They married and now have one child, who was eleven years old at the time of our interview.

Hector talked a lot about how he and Marisol don't only have the task of processing their own internal balance, but also have the task of processing the daily microaggressions they face in everyday life. They have to be each other's rock, which isn't always easy. "The reality is that communication is even more important in families of color. On top of processing chores and logistics, we have to process the oppression and abuse and prejudice that we experience outside the home. Because that is just our reality. We work really hard at forming a partnership of protection for our family and our community."

STRATEGY 2: LOTS AND LOTS OF TIME

The EP40, especially the fathers, stressed how important time was for them. Lamenting modern family schedules was a popular topic of conversation. I know this from personal experience, too. Mornings are scheduled to the minute to make sure everyone is up, dressed, and fed, and lunches and bags are packed for school and work. There's the drop-off routine and then a reprieve of several hours while everyone is at work, school, or day care. At the end of the day, there is the race to pick everyone up on time, and some families chauffeur kids around to sports, tutoring, music lessons, or after-school jobs. Then comes an intense urgency to get home before the hangry sets in. There's dinner and homework; for the little ones, add in books and bath. Once the kids get in bed, you might have time enough for one deep breath before diving into the dishes, cleaning, work emails, laundry, or whatever tasks needs doing that night. Some parents muster the strength to start their job on a night shift. Others fall into bed for a few hours—only to get up and do it all over the next day.

The men I interviewed believed that real relationships emerge from these monotonous weeks, as each family proceeds through the daily routine together. Spending time together helps with communication—the more you are with your partner in the kitchen or in the car, the more chances you have to process the emotional tasks required by the family. Time together also builds relationships with your kids; every parent knows that the sweetest, most memorable moments are rarely when everyone is in matching outfits, posed for a photo in front of the fireplace. The best moments come during random car rides, bath time, or morning chatter over bowls of cereal.

Logan, the father of five, and I talked a lot about time. He believes that there is a strong correlation between time together and taking on an emotional burden. When you spend a ton of time with your toddler, you notice she tends to get hungry at the same time every day. So, you know to bring along extra snacks if you go out for errands during that time. When you spend a lot of time with your third grader, you notice that his pants are getting too short, and you realize he need some new socks, too. When you spend a lot of time cooking and cleaning up, you notice what your teenager eats and does not eat, which influences your meal planning and shopping list. So much of what we know about our kids is through observation; if you aren't taking the time to observe, how do you know what they need?

Aiden would agree. Aiden is a father of three children; the oldest was six at the time of our interview. Aiden was born and raised in British Colombia, but he now lives in Ontario with his wife, Chantal. Aiden's father passed away when he was very young, and his mother raised him and his brothers alone. Aiden attended an all-boys school and didn't have many female friends growing up. He told me he was a bit shy and uncertain of himself when he started dating.

He met Chantal when they were both living on the West Coast, but she soon got a job promotion that took her across the country. Aiden moved with her, and they married. He was happy when they got pregnant with their first baby. "I think the instinct, if I understand correctly, is that most males put in more time [at work] when they have kids. But I'm sort of the opposite. I want to work as little as I need to. Sure, it's hard sometimes. Your brain fries and it can be so boring." Aiden firmly believes that his time is much better spent with his kids than at work. He works for the airline industry, which allows him flexibility. He took advantage of Canada's care and nurturing leave policy to take time off and care for each of his kids after they were born. Aiden feels that, like Logan, the quantity of the time he spends with his children is essential to being the parent he wants to be.

STRATEGY 3: ASSIGN DOMAINS AND FOLLOW THROUGH

Think back to chapter 3 and the reframing tactic of Supervisor/Employee. If we reject the idea that one person should be the overall House Manager and one person should be the overall House Employee, then we need a strategy to facilitate co-managers. The strategy that appears to work best with these men is the "divide and conquer" approach. Most EP40 couples split up the categories of work that are required to make their household function (food, laundry, day care, dog, etc.) and assign domains to each person.

As a reminder from chapter 3, when you split this list, try not to rely on personality or skill set. Remember, many skills we take into adulthood we gain through a gendered upbringing. Try to assign domains based on comfort level and preference.

Each person is then responsible for completing their domains, day in, day out. This means the totality of the domain—the anticipation of needs, the planning, and the actual physical tasks. Each person also needs to step back from their partner's domains and refrain from micromanaging. Yes, this can be hard; I know from personal experience. But the beauty in this arrangement is, whatever domains your partner has, you do not need to think about. You can cross it off your to-do list; it is not your responsibility.

Zack identifies as white and grew up on the East Coast. His parents made a good income, and Zack and his twin brother had a privileged childhood, complete with vacations, stability, love, and a good school.

When Zack was little, he began exhibiting characteristics that were considered feminine, which were frowned upon. He remembers overhearing his father remark that he "talked like a girl" and Zack knew, somehow, this was disappointing his dad. So, he began making a conscious effort to be more masculine and more athletic in order to please his parents. By the age of ten, Zack had managed his mannerisms so his behavior better aligned with the expectations his community had for a boy.

The twins were blue-eyed blonds. "There was this constant narrative that followed us—people were always saying, 'I bet the girls love you two!' We heard that over and over. And even though I was behaving correctly, under the surface I felt a lot of stress. . . . Gay was not a positive image [at that time and in my suburban community]. . . . I just didn't want to disappoint my parents." As he grew older, Zack only got better at performing traditional masculinity. He was athletic in high school, had lots of friends, and met his parent's expectations by "drowning in activity."

Zack came out when he was in college. He told his brother first and then his parents. His mom cried. But his parents told him that they still loved him, and still supported him. Zack met Greg after college; they moved in together and married. They hope to be parents one day, but as yet, they do not have kids.

When the two first moved in together, Zack admits he brought some of those more masculine-coded traits that he taught himself over the years into his home with Greg. In other words, he fell into the Male Role (and allowed Greg to fall into the Female Role) without thinking too much about it. Over time, Greg helped him to see what was happening; they talked about it and worked on it. Now both men feel like they have found a balance much closer to parity. "Even though now I probably still do more of the masculine-coded tasks, there is nothing that I would not do. . . . Neither of us play the martyr. I think that is important because we both tell each other what we have done for the other and hold each other accountable."

For part of our interview, both Zack and Greg were on the call together. They explained how Zack does all the food shopping and cooking, and Greg does all the dishes and laundry. They have each committed to taking care of different domains, and they trust each other to fulfill their commitments.

STRATEGY 4: CREATE ROUTINES

Some EP40 and their partners had jobs and work routines that required a more equitable balance. Ethan, whom we met in chapter 5, talked a lot about this topic during our interview. As a reminder, he is a special-education high school teacher. He did not feel othered growing up, but he came to appreciate the impact of marginalization through his work with kids with special needs and their parents.

Ethan's partner, Alexis, is a nurse. They have two children, who were, at the time of our interview, one and two years old. Ethan's work schedule follows the academic calendar, and he works Monday through Friday, whereas Alexis works three twelve-hour shifts at the hospital each week—two weekdays and every Sunday. When she is on duty, calls and texts are nearly impossible. "Our routine is specific. When she is at work, I am pretty much a single dad. I do everything that day; get them up and dressed, pack lunches, drop-off, go to work, pick up, come home, get everyone fed and in bed. If they have a cold, I handle it. On Sundays I have the kids all day."

This unyielding regimen has helped Ethan and Alexis maintain parity. They do not have extended family in town. The days she works, Ethan knows he is the only adult in the room; there is no one else to pick up any slack.

This routine of Ethan taking the kids for three days a week, every week, has also helped him take on half of the family's emotional burden. "I think ahead because I've come to realize the negative impact of not planning. For example, not having food in the house for Sunday would be a huge pain. I'd have to pack both kids up and take them to Costco or something." I thought about having to do a Costco trip with two kids under three, and shuddered. "So, I always make sure I shop beforehand. This forced disruption has been really good for us." Ethan says constant communication is important, and he told me he appreciates that he and Alexis don't keep a tally on who does what for any given day. They don't have a big chart or follow each other around with a checklist. They both notice what needs doing and do it. Over the past few years, they have come to trust each other; no one needs to manage the other.

Allen's routine is to cover his household graveyard shift. We met Allen, the camp counselor, in chapter 5. Now he is married, and he and his wife have three kids. At the time of our interview, they were eighteen months, three, and four. Allen's wife was able to access parental leave after each birth, and she pieced together many months at home with the kids. But Allen's job did not allow him to take extensive time off. He became aware that his wife was bonding with the kids during daytime hours, and he was missing out.

To counter the gendered effects of the schedule, he took on the nighttime routine. Since their first child was born until today, Allen has assumed all responsibilities that occur between 11:00 P.M. and 7:00 A.M. "If the little one needs a bottle, or if one of the older ones has a nightmare, needs a cup of water, or wets the bed, that is all me. Then I get up for the day about six and get everyone dressed and fed." During these eight hours, Allen's partner has time to sleep and refuel, and Allen gets to have intimate time with his kids. "Now we both have a strong emotional connection to them. If they're hurt or crying, they're just as likely to come to me as they are to go to her. And I am really proud of that."

I asked Allen how he managed to make it through work after a hard night with the kids. He laughed and admitted that there were many days he was terribly sleep deprived and moved like a zombie at work. But he believed that caring for children all day was more emotionally taxing than his paid job. He firmly believed that his wife needed off hours at night in order to effectively parent during the day.

Lucas also talked to me about his family routine. We have met Lucas before. He and his husband, Aaron, are currently caring for a one-month-old foster child. Lucas is a full-time teacher and is also working on his master's degree, so if anyone knows the value of time—this is the guy. He and Aaron also rely on routines, with specific times that each of them is responsible for the baby, specific times when they are not responsible for the baby, and specific times when they can be together as a family. He talked quickly and with an urgency I could appreciate. "We rarely sit still," he told me.

Lucas added some additional thoughts about how to make routines work that I found insightful. "[When you build your routine], you need to set correct and honest expectations about what you can each do. Assumptions set us up for failure. [Aaron and I] are careful to link expectations with reality and actual behaviors." Maintaining reasonable expectations is key to preventing disappointment in their home. Neither man volunteers to do something they know they can't handle, nor do they ask the other to do something that is unrealistic.

STRATEGY 5: FIND SUPPORT OUTSIDE YOUR HOME

Mothers have long formed groups and networks for support. These are often built into our social order, which makes it even easier for women to sign up and join. Community listservs abound with new-mom groups, and some hospitals and birthing centers bring groups of women together who are all in the same trimester of pregnancy. As soon as kids go to day care and school, there is always one outgoing person in the Female Role who collects everyone's information and starts a group chat.

These groups—formal or informal—serve two general purposes: they offer resource support by connecting everyone to needed information, and they offer emotional support from women going through a similar life stage. I rely heavily on my networks for resource support, and to cover a range of needs, I rely on multiple groups. I have one group chat for the moms associated with my son's class, one group for the moms associated with my daughter's class, and two groups of moms in my community—one for the city and one for my small neighborhood. I lean on these networks all the time: *Where can you buy X? Do the kids have early release on Friday, or did I dream that? Where are the best sledding hills for little kids?* Within minutes, my networks come through for me.

The emotional support is also an important element of networks. Is it 7:00 P.M. and you haven't thought about dinner? Send a quick vent text, and within minutes, your mom friends will forgive you, empathize with your busy schedule, and assure you that PB&Js make for an excellent meal. Women's networks, the good kind anyway, are always there to validate your feelings and reassure you that—despite your many mistakes—you are a very good mom.

Men do not traditionally belong to parenting affinity groups. There are no men in my children's school lists, and the few on the community listservs are not particularly active. This leaves men with fewer options. When men have a question about parenting, they have two choices: ask their partner or turn to Google. When men need to vent or need someone to tell them they're a good dad, again, they have two choices: turn to their partner or suck it up.

This gendered system of ours is harmful for both. For the Female Role, it puts more cognitive labor on their plates. For the Male Role, it makes it even harder to network and connect when they want/need to. And the overall system simply reinforces a gender binary. This is, unfortunately, our social norm, but it may be changing. The EP40 have started to realize that having a supportive network can be exceptionally helpful, and they're taking steps to join and create networks in their neighborhoods.

We met Chase all the way back in chapter 1. He was the man who felt pushed out of his daughter's life and wasn't able to be the dad he wanted to be. I am happy to report that Chase's life is much better now. He did experience some exceptionally painful years during his divorce and custody battle. But now he is remarried and has a third child—a daughter who was two years old at the time of our interview. Although he struggles to rectify strained relationships with his older children, he can be the dad he has always wanted to be with this third child. "I do all the things with her I didn't get to do with the older two."

Chase has found comradery with a group of men in his community, a group of other dads who care. They get together with their kids for weekend playdates, exchange emails, and during the pandemic, they kept in touch via text. Chase always thought his own apprehensions and uncertainties about being a dad were unique to him, and he has taken great comfort in learning that other men are going through the same things. "I don't feel alone anymore. This group has been so healing for me. We all share our struggles and we ask each other questions. This group of dads has given me so much confidence. I always wondered, *Do I have what it takes?* I never had help or people I could go to and ask questions. But now I do."

STRATEGY 6: PUSH BACK WHEN YOU EXPERIENCE GENDER NORMS

The men I spoke to continually talked about how they have to push back against harmful gender norms in order to reaffirm their own family values. This can happen with family, community, and friends.

Hector talked about how he and Marisol have to push back with family members who abide by much more traditional gender roles. This was a bigger issue in the early days of their relationship, but it still continues today. "When we first married, we actually moved to be closer to Marisol's family. And her family conforms to traditional norms about men and women. After a while, we started falling into those patterns, which in the end was one reason why we moved away again. But we still visit often."

Hector and Marisol love their extended family, so they work to find that delicate balance of living their own gender values while remaining respectful and kind. Their way is not to start a big argument or cause an intentional disruption. Rather, Hector and Marisol quietly and deliberately try to continue the household relationships they have in their home even when they are visiting family.

Marisol told me that a common point of contention is food preparation and serving. In her family, men expect to be served by women—and women assume their job is to serve men. Marisol and Hector don't agree with this, so when they visit family, she does not serve men, and Hector does not sit around with the other males and wait for his food to come. They are well aware that their break from family patterns and norms can be awkward for everyone. I asked them if their behavior led to uncomfortable moments. Hector immediately agreed. "Of course! The older generations—even our generation—you can tell they just don't really understand us. It can be very uncomfortable sometimes. They rarely say anything direct, but they give each other looks. . . . But in the end, we need to be true to ourselves—and we don't have shame about that. So, we just can't allow people to shame us for how we behave."

Boubacar talked about how he had to push back on community when he was first married. At the time, he and Rebecca were living in West Africa, but not the country of his birth. The compound where they lived was small, and everyone knew everyone else. Rebecca worked many more hours than he did, so Boubacar took care of their home. "I did the washing in the open and hung it up to dry. Even the underwear. A typical man in my culture would never do this, but I was proud to work against the stereotype." Boubacar made me laugh during our conversation. He fully admitted that sure, he could have hung their "smalls" inside to dry. He knew he didn't have to hang their underwear out in the yard for everyone to see. But he wanted to make a statement about who he was; he was perfectly content and confident in washing his wife's underwear. He knew no one would ever say anything; they would just talk behind his back. This was his way of putting the issue out there in the open—literally on display for everyone to see.

Sometimes, pushing back means knowing when to walk away completely. Remy from Louisiana told me how he finally had to distance himself from some high school friends. After years of trying to ignore their behavior, he finally decided enough was enough.

Remy used to hang out with his old buddies on Thursday nights. He admitted he always felt a little different, but he had known them for so long, he just fell into a social routine. Remy explained that many men in his community, both friends and family, appear to bond by cracking jokes about their wives. The old "take my wife . . . please" kind of comedy. Growing up in this environment, he had become numb to it. "I had just known these guys for so long. They would bash on their wives and stuff when we were out, which I don't do. I would just keep quiet and drink my beer."

About a year before we spoke, Remy was out with the guys as usual, when his friends began making inappropriate and crude jokes to their female server. Remy was mortified. When the server left the table, he told the guys that what they said wasn't cool, and he asked them to consider how their "jokes" might have made the server feel. "But it didn't work at all. It just got so much worse. They actually called her back to our table, if you can believe it, and they said, 'This guy here says we're bullying you. Did we offend you? We didn't offend you, did we?'"

Remy took a long pause. I asked him how the server responded. "What was that woman supposed to say? Of course, she said, 'Oh no. It's all just fun.' And she laughed it off. But that was it for me." Remy and I talked about how differently that would have gone down had he just one other ally at that table. But he knew he was in the vast minority, with no one to back him up, and he just didn't want to be part of that group anymore. All his years of pushing back had not worked. The only thing left to do was to leave.

(Remy hasn't been back for Thursday night beers since. But following strategy 5, he found a new group of men with whom to socialize—men who don't need to use misogyny as a bonding mechanism. Remy is much happier with his new group of friends.)

The EP40 all have to set values for themselves, and that means reinforcing those values when they are challenged. Some have an easier time than others; I interviewed some men that admitted they lived in a progressive bubble where they rarely had to push back. But other men found that affirming values was just part of their everyday routine.

STRATEGY 7: RECOGNIZE UNEARNED PRAISE, THEN REJECT IT

Because men have historically done so little in the home, the men who do step up to take on more domestic responsibility are often the recipients of a great deal of admiration. The EP40, not surprisingly, are very often the recipients of unearned praise.

Ethan told a story that made me laugh out loud. When Alexis went back to work after their first baby was born, Ethan had long Sundays to fill. There happens to be a microbrewery within walking distance of his house, so when the weather was nice, he would take the baby for a walk and drink some beer. Sometimes he would meet friends, and sometimes he would sit alone.

"This place is in a little shopping plaza with a grocery store, so there's a lot of traffic. And we would get a lot of attention, mostly from older women. They'd all pull over and want to talk to me. And basically, they treated me like a hero for taking my baby to a bar. It became a running joke with my wife—we wondered how long it would take those people to call child services if a mom was at a bar with a baby. And sure, it was a joke, but there was an element of truth there. I know if it was Alexis and not me, she would have gotten a very different reaction."

We know that unearned praise can be detrimental. When society applauds men for doing simple domestic or family-related tasks, we disproportionately inflate the worth of those contributions. And sometimes we inflate egos, too. This is why the EP40 are so careful to notice unearned praise. Whatever they do or say in the moment will differ depending on the situation. But in their heads, the EP40 think to themselves, *I am only receiving accolades because of our broken gender norms. I am not doing anything exceptional. I am just doing my job as a partner/father.*

For the rest of us out there who might be that grocery shopper who sees Ethan out with his cute baby, I wondered what the appropriate response would be. How do the EP40 wish people would act when they are out with their kids? Ethan wished he was just ignored because he felt so bad for being praised for just doing his job as a dad. Other men admitted that perhaps a little encouragement was good; after all, parenting is hard work and we all need a bit of a boost now and again. The best answer we could collectively agree on was to treat all people the same. If you are the type that likes to give parents a little encouragement—go for it. But be conscious to give out praise evenly to all parents. If you would never consider approaching a random woman to tell her that she is doing a great job with her kids, then maybe you should not say anything to a dad in the same position.

STRATEGY 8: DON'T BE AFRAID TO BE EMOTIONAL

The word *vulnerable* came up over and over during interviews. The EP40 explained that it is important for them to be comfortable exhibiting vulnerability in front of others, and for them to create the emotional space for others to be vulnerable with them. These two concepts are cyclical; when others demonstrate vulnerability to you, you are then better equipped to demonstrate vulnerability to others and thereby create space for others to be vulnerable. The EP40 also talked about the harm that was done in their lives when role models were unable to demonstrate vulnerability and failed to allow them to be vulnerable themselves.

As a sidenote, I understand some people may have a negative reaction to the word *vulnerable*. For many men, vulnerability is synonymous with crying or perceived weakness. John Badalament, author of *The Modern Dad's Dilemma: How to Stay Connected with Your Kids in a Rapidly Changing World,* suggests using the term *emotionally courageous* instead. Feel free to use whichever you prefer. I believe it is more important to embrace the concept than the language attached to it.

The most common negative stories about vulnerability revolved around the fathers of the EP40. Many shared memories about an emotionally distant father—a man who might have been physically present but with whom they lacked a deeper connection. Lack of vulnerability affected the relationship many of the EP40 had with their fathers, and this became an obstacle to their own development as partners and as fathers.

- "I still do not really know my father. He doesn't express himself. He keeps everything on the inside. He puts up this wall between him and my mother, and between him and me."—Anik, New York (Bangladeshi American)
- "I had an emotionally disconnected dad who worked a lot. My mom did everything at home, which included carrying out my dad's orders. I struggled with anxiety in school, but my dad made it clear that was not OK. I felt a lot of shame.

I didn't understand how to 'man up' and do what others did."—Alex, Vermont (white)

- "I never knew my dad as a person. I had no sense of him as a person. I think it stems from his immigrant experience. He had no family or friends and felt very isolated."—Tim, California (Filipino American)
- "I never doubted that my dad loved me. But he was incapable of showing affection or emotion. Still is. So, it becomes really hard to do it yourself. His limitations became my limitations. It takes work to overcome that. And it has been a long process of growth."—Tony, Ontario (white)

The men who reported these stories were eventually able to be emotionally close to a partner, to share their feelings, and to listen to others. But developing those skills took time and practice; many of them are still working at it. Some of the EP40 managed to build a stronger relationship with their fathers as adults; some still struggle to connect with their dads, while simultaneously trying to foster positive bonds with their own children.

But most EP40 conversations about learning how to express their emotions were positive. For example, many men told me how important it is that they can be their own true selves with their partner. They appreciated the opportunity to show emotions that men are typically discouraged from sharing: fear, sadness, inadequacy, uncertainty, frustration, embarrassment. Some men mentioned that they were natural criers, and told of the relief they felt after suppressing that urge for years and then finally finding someone who didn't mind them letting their emotions out.

Martin talked a lot about his "soft side," which wasn't often valued while he was growing up. But his partner loves that part of him, and even encourages it. Martin told me a story about how he had to travel for work on his birthday one year, and he arrived home very late, after his wife was asleep. But on his pillow, she had left him a card and a teddy bear as a gift. It was the first time Martin could remember receiving a stuffed animal as a gift, and it touched him. He still loves that little bear, and even more, he loves that his wife gave it to him.

Ash talked about his appreciation for his wife, who accepted him for who he was and the job that he wanted to do. "You get different reactions being a male teacher. Some women aren't exactly ecstatic about that idea. [When I met my wife], she knew I wasn't going to make a ton of money, but she has always made me feel great about my career. She's proud of me." Ash imagines many men have to posture for their families; to bring home more money and provide more things. He was grateful that his wife accepted him for who he was and helped him do the job that he loved.

The EP40 also talked about learning to show their emotional side with other men, and specifically with other dads. Keegan Albaugh is founder and president of Dad Guild in Burlington, Vermont. Worried about national statistics that linked heart disease and depression to men's lack of an emotional connection, and aware of his own desire to connect with other dads raising young kids, he started the organization with just a handful of members. Within a few years, his membership list has grown to over four hundred.

Dad Guild offers a variety of ways for dads to connect. They run playgroups on the weekends for dads and their kids, and they host Dads Night Out once a month for adults only. Keegan told me that he specifically and intentionally tries to create a space for dads to be vulnerable with each other, not in a formal group way, but little by little—role modeling different ways for men to talk to each other and connect. "We make it an intention to talk about how we are feeling. By putting it out there in front of a bunch of dudes, it normalizes talking about this kind of thing . . . [when there is an event, I'll walk around] saying stuff like, *Hey, it's been a really hard week for me—how about you?* Just to normalize that kind of dialogue."

Dad Guild is a perfect example of how social change can happen. Keegan explained that, even though their group is just for the greater-Burlington area, there is a ripple effect when their members use their Dad Guild skills in other friendships. "A couple of guys have told me that they are reconnecting with old friends, guys from back home, outside the state. They are trying to talk about the kind of stuff in those relationships that we talk about in Dad Guild. When I hear those stories, I think, *Oh, this is really cool.*"

THE INTERSECTION OF GENDER AND RACE

It is human nature to categorize things. For this reason, I understand why there can be a desire to compartmentalize gender and race as two separate social constructs. But some issues are layered and complex, and they do not fit neatly into one box or another. In these cases, I think it is best to dig into the nuance, and talk about how issues around gender are compounded for people of color.

Nearly half of the EP40 identified as men of color, and many of those eighteen men told me explicitly that it was not possible to compartmentalize their identities. I do not think it would be possible to end the conversation of "how they do it" without specific mention of "how they do it while balancing issues around race and racism."

We met Izaiah in chapter 5; he was born in Barbados and credits his single mom for teaching him how to care for himself. Izaiah does not have children of his own yet, but working in higher education means he is always surrounded by young adults. He knows he is a role model to many, and he takes that seriously. Izaiah intentionally reaches out to those on campus who might need some extra help: students of color and first-generation Americans. This story is an account of one of those occasions.

"I was having a conversation with my students. And we were talking about hair, which is a common subject in the Black community, and I shared my opinion about natural hair. And I made a comment that if I had a daughter one day, I would not allow her to straighten her hair before she was eighteen, and then after that, she could make her own decisions."

Of course, Izaiah's objection to straightened hair wasn't about control over a daughter; it was about pride in Black women's bodies, and the philosophy that Black people need not follow white standards. "How we are to act is modeled on the white man. That's the norm. Whether we want to admit it or not, that is the norm. That is the blueprint for all of us. What the white man does, over time, that becomes normal for the rest of us. Following that blueprint, in my opinion, has not served us well in any point in history."

But a student in his presence disagreed and called him out. "One student, a young Black woman—let's just say she wasn't happy about that. She told me, and these were her words, that I did not have the right to police my daughter's body." So, here was a collision of values. This story helps illustrate an unavoidable issue that combines race and gender.

I found Izaiah to be a thoughtful, soft-spoken person. I asked him how the conversation with this student turned out, and he explained in his calm voice. "Well, I thought about it, and she was absolutely right. If that is something my daughter wants to do, I'll need to be OK with it. . . . I think we need to be open and honest about our challenges for ourselves, in our own spaces . . . [because] this is important to me."

I heard over and over that many of the EP40's experiences as partners and fathers had as much to do with race as they did with gender. And the consensus was that the intersection was felt most acutely when it came to parenting. If white fathers feel judged when they are out with their kids, men of color have even more intensified experiences. (I think back to Ethan's story about taking his baby to a bar, and I wonder how a Black man would have been treated in that same situation. I believe we all know it wouldn't have played out the same way.) Although the following stories are specifically about parenthood, I think they can apply to any caregiver or guardian in a child's life: family, friend, neighbor, teacher, or coach.

Hal grew up as one of the few minorities in a predominantly white community in Montana. Hal identifies as Japanese American; he has a Japanese American father and a white mother. He told me that his father was the stoic *model minority*, a term often used in reference to the Asian American community. Hal's father did not allow his emotions to run too high or too low.

When I asked about this topic, Hal told me directly, "Racism plays a huge role in parenting. The way women feel unfairly judged and held to a higher standard—which is true, they are—but men of color can experience that as well. You don't want to be the Brown guy with the kid who is dirty or unkempt. We dress our kids over-the-top when we go out, to counter those stereotypes. There is a continued social pressure and community pressure to continue to be the perfect minority. Make no mistakes."

Hal told me a story that illustrates how quickly a normal situation can turn to fear for men of color. "One night, it was after dark, and I am trying to get my toddler in her car seat. And I was really struggling to get the baby in that car seat—ugh—remember how hard that can be? I mean, she was kicking and screaming, and honestly, I was feeling pretty good-natured about it. And then I saw a neighbor's porch light go on, and then I immediately felt shamed and judged, like I was doing it wrong." I asked Hal if he had those feelings because he was a man or because he was Brown. And he immediately responded, "Both." He couldn't separate the two. When he saw that light go on, he reverted back to those childhood feelings of being watched and judged. He was doing the best he could to parent his toddler, but he was afraid his best wasn't good enough.

Thankfully, this particular story has a happy outcome. Hal kept struggling with his daughter because he didn't have a choice; she had to get home and to bed. "And after a couple minutes, my [white] neighbor came out and didn't say a thing, but he started helping. And in the end, it took two grown men to get that toddler in the car seat. And no words were spoken. But at the end, he gave me a hug. And that was his recognition of my insecurities, and how I [still] have a fear of being judged."

We met James in chapter 5; he was the man whose father taught him the principals of Black Nationalist philosophy. When I broached the intersection of gender and race, James brought up the myth of the absent Black father, and how that has affected him as a parent. "I don't want to play into the stereotype of the deadbeat dad, which is the narrative in Black communities as well as the nation. I find myself overcompensating to not be that guy, or at least to not be perceived as that guy."

James does not buy into that myth himself, which is good because that is exactly what it is—a myth. The Centers for Disease Control published a report back in 2010 demonstrating that of all American fathers, Black fathers are the most present in their children's lives, whether they live with that child or not.[1] But that doesn't matter; the mere presence of that narrative in American culture is enough to force James to rethink who he is as a father.

Will identifies as Polynesian American and was born and raised on the West Coast. He grew up in a predominantly white community and, like Hal, felt pressure to be a model minority. As one of only two non-white kids in his high school, Will was careful to behave as was expected in order to be accepted in white circles. It did not surprise me when Will said he did a lot of performing growing up.

Like others, Will spoke about how his experiences as a child have manifested in his adult behavior. "I was well aware that I was one of two Brown kids in a white society. I knew that no matter how good or smart I was, people would still assume I was stealing or up to no good. So, I always had to be on the defensive. To this day, I do an Ironman scan when I am out in public with my kids, making sure I know where the exits are, making sure I could protect them if I needed to."

Will also spoke of being concerned about how he is perceived in public. He told me that his skin is dark, but his son is fair and presents white. And his son is a person with autism and prone to public outbursts. "It happens a lot that I am out with my son, and he gets angry, and I have to physically restrain him and carry him out—to remove him from that particular situation. And every time I think, *It is just a matter of time before someone calls the police, and then police are going to get involved.* On top of this already very difficult situation. It goes back to when I was a kid—no matter how good of a dad I am being, people assume the worst in me."

Each reader will likely have a different reaction to this section. Perhaps you feel a sense of solidarity with others who share experiences similar to your own. Or maybe it made you think more deeply about your own unseen privilege. (When I first heard these stories, my reaction was the latter.) But whatever our past experiences, we need to remind ourselves that race, like gender, is also a social construct, be open about the fact that social norms put far greater pressure on dads of color, and be as enthusiastic to rewrite norms about race as we are to rewrite norms about gender.

7

EMBRACING EQUAL PARTNERSHIP

It is important to see both sides of an equal partnership, so, while talking to the EP40, I became increasingly curious about their partners. I wanted to know what these people were like and how they felt about the domestic divide in their home. I was curious what could be learned from investigating the other half of these partnerships.

In chapter 5, I introduced three personas/terms: the *King of the Castle,* the *Hands-On Husband,* and the *Equal Partner.* I did so in order to establish a shared vocabulary so we could effectively talk about the person performing the Male Role. I also feel that it is helpful to articulate the behaviors of the person performing the Female Role in these relationships.

COUNTERPARTS IN NEO-TRADITIONAL HOMES

Like the personas in chapter 5, the following are descriptions of behaviors, not people. One person could easily experience all three of these feelings in one month or even one week. These descriptions are not static, but are a way to help us better understand the reality for the Female Role when operating in a neo-traditional home.

As with the personas in chapter 5, I never presume that any one individual is "stuck" in these situations. For the examples below, I matched people and personas relative to the stories they shared with me during their interviews; in that one moment of time. There are multiple external factors that dictate how a person feels on any given day: work responsibilities ebb and flow; sometimes our network is supportive, and sometimes it seems to disappear; some months kids are very needy, and other months more independent; sick parents or family members can dominate our schedules for pockets of time; potty training a new puppy has left many of my friends at the end of their rope. The Female Role in neo-traditional relationships likely drift in and out of the types below based on their given situation on any given day.

EMBRACING THE FEMALE ROLE

Embracers are the people in the Female Role who genuinely like being in the Female Role. Embracers do not necessarily believe in a universal sexual division of labor; they might be feminists who support gender equality broadly. But personally, Embracers are happy with their own personal situation. They often feel pride and satisfaction in keeping a nice home for their family, and often show their love by *doing*: cooking, cleaning, baking, preparing. One could even go so far as to say an Embracer's identity is partially linked to her domestic role, and she draws a sense of confidence and empowerment from her ability to take care of her family.

A colleague, Wendy, is a great example of an Embracer. Wendy identifies as Black, and at the time of this conversation she was in her early sixties. She and Moses have been married for nearly four decades. Wendy is a mother, foster mother, and grandmother—

and, might I add, one of the most genuine and selfless people I know.

"My kids do things differently in their home, I understand that and I am grateful for it. My sons-in-law enable my daughters to have the careers that they have. And I hope my son will do the same if he ever chooses to marry. But Moses and I, we are OK with our routine. I take care of him. Oh, I know he is a little lazy, but I get to keep the house as I want. I don't have to make any compromises. And I can afford to hire help now, with cleaning and such, which makes my load easier. I have no resentment toward Moses. He has been a good husband. I love him as I loved him the day we married."

Wendy and Moses were both working full time, but they no longer had children in the house, and their own parents were deceased. Like many others in her situation, Wendy could perform the Female Role with some ease. With no caregiving responsibilities and a lifetime of confidence, she was able to take care of Moses and have plenty of time for herself. I do not know how she felt twenty or thirty years ago, nor how she might feel next year. But when we spoke, at that moment, I would say Wendy was a great example of an Embracer. She is in a neo-traditional relationship, and she is genuinely happy. She is a natural caregiver through and through, and doing for others (including her husband) brings her joy. She does not at all believe that every woman should be an Embracer—not at all. But she herself is perfectly content with her life.

ACCEPTING THE FEMALE ROLE

This category describes those in the Female Role who accept their role in the home, but would not go so far as to say they are happy with it. If they were able to snap their fingers and have their partner do more, they would. But they have also found a way to get through each week without too much discomfort. To do this, *Acceptors* are likely to have part-time or flexible work schedules and/or strong support networks, for example, grandparents in town who can babysit at a moment's notice. It might be easier to be an Acceptor if there is some disposable family income to pay for camps, a cleaning service, or meal-kit delivery. The Acceptor is probably good at prioritizing, and has come to understand which tasks are required and which tasks are optional. When one is strategic about which balls to drop, one can sometimes get by without too many people noticing what hits the floor.

We've met a few Acceptors in this book. I would say that Frida, our composite Female Role from chapter 3, would identify as an Acceptor. She would like Miriam to do more, but mostly seems at peace with her role as the cognitive laborer in the home. Lisa, who we met in chapter 4 (her son was the child in the hitting stage) would likely fall into the Acceptor role. Lisa wasn't angry or exasperated in her interview; she knows her husband doesn't do as much as he could, but she has family nearby and a solid network of friends to help.

I'd like to tell you Edward's story at this time, to illustrate how men can absolutely find themselves in the Female Role. Although not as common, many men (no matter the gender identity of their partner) perform the Female Role in the home.

Edward identifies as Black and Christian, and he lives on the East Coast. He and his husband have been in a relationship for over a decade, and they have been married for just about five years. But Edward's story begins years before he met his current partner. Edward became a single father at the age of fifteen, when he and his high school girlfriend accidentally became pregnant. She was not ready to be a mother, and left the three-month-old baby girl with Edward.

I asked him, "Did it ever occur to you that you also weren't ready to be a parent?" He did not hesitate. "No, not for a second, to be honest. I knew that little girl needed me. My father was not in my life; I did not know him at all. So, I much preferred being in a difficult situation and giving her the environment that she needed. I wanted her to feel wanted. . . . It wasn't about gender; it was about being a parent." Edward and his daughter lived in his grandmother's house for about five years, which allowed him to graduate from high school, work for a few years, and save up some money. When Edward turned twenty, he and his daughter were able to move out and start a life of their own. He was grateful that he could finally parent the way that he wanted to, without comment or criticism. "My mother and grandmother were unattached. They provided stuff, like making sure I was fed and had clothing. But there was no emotional support. And that is what I want to give my daughter. I just wanted my own space to live my life with my daughter in the way I wanted."

Edward told me that he thrived once he had his own house. He worked, provided for his daughter, managed to go back to school himself, and put her through college. His daughter is now grown and has two kids of her own. Edward remains very close to her, and he loves being a grandfather.

Edward explained that, after years of doing all the domestic tasks, female-coded work was second nature. He is comfortable making lists, managing the calendar, and keeping the house tidy. These are actions ingrained in his character after being the only adult in the home for so long. And generally, he doesn't mind so much. When he got married, he slipped into the Female Role, and his husband slipped into the Male Role, though they never had a pointed discussion. Once in a while, Edward gets frustrated and wishes his husband would do more. But most days he is accepting of this routine.

COPING WITH THE FEMALE ROLE

This persona is similar to the Acceptor, but I believe the key difference is best measured by the amount of "frazzle" they feel. People who are *Coping* are frazzled; of course, they wish their partner did more—they are barely at peace with their situation. A person who is Coping feels the full weight of being the cognitive laborer, and they are drained as a result. Those Coping might not have the support network that the Acceptor has. I think we all saw quite a few women move from being an Acceptor to barely Coping during the coronavirus pandemic, when support systems and self-care options literally disappeared overnight. Without reliable help and periodic moments of relief, many in the Female Role watched both their professional lives and emotional health deteriorate.

People who are Coping also rely on prioritization, and they might drop more balls than their Acceptor friends. They also might get less sleep, sacrifice the majority of their free time, and/or cut big corners at work.

I believe Melissa fits into this category. We met Melissa at the beginning of chapter 1 of this book; her's was the first story. She has two kids and was struggling to manage virtual learning and work during the first COVID-19 lockdown. At that moment, she was frazzled, frustrated, emotionally drained, and very tired. She knew she was the cognitive laborer in her home, and she didn't like carrying the responsibility on her own. She loved her partner and appreciated what he did—but she deeply wished he did more. She was barely keeping up with her family and with work, and she wondered how much longer she could sustain the intensity of her schedule.

RESENTFUL OF THE FEMALE ROLE

For this person, feelings toward one's partner have started to turn. This person feels resentment and even animosity toward their partner. Someone who is *Resentful* feels unheard and ignored; they may or may not have reached out for help, but either way, they probably feel alone and trapped. Their schedules and responsibilities feel like a physical weight on their body, dragging them deeper and further out of control. I hope those who are Resentful have a way to vent; it might even help to have friends who are also Resentful so they can validate each other's feelings.

Tina, whom we met in chapter 4 as the example of "accidental inequality," would likely be in this category. Tina thought she was marrying a feminist man, like her dad, but over time she kept doing more and he kept doing less. When I spoke to her, she was suffocating from a combination of her work and household duties; she had little time for fun or self-care, and she knows that she is unlikely to sustain this for the duration of her relationship. She is starting to believe that she would be better off as a single parent.

LEANING DOWN

There is one additional behavior that needs mentioning and could be combined with any of the above personas. *Leaning down,* a term coined by philosopher and author Kate Manne, is a takeoff on the title of Sheryl Sandberg's book *Lean In*. Manne uses this term to describe a coping strategy that women sometimes use to lighten their own household load. Instead of reappropriating work to a partner, many women assign work to other women: cleaners, nannies, babysitters, or even female family members.

I am not suggesting that we should ban cleaning services and babysitters; those economic transactions can be beneficial to all participating parties. But there is potential for harm if the Female Role uses her "economic power" to hire domestic workers (disproportionately women of color) to do physically exhausting work for a low wage and no benefits. Anyone outsourcing domestic work should be mindful of an employee's work-life balance; salary, benefits, and work schedules should be fair and respectful. (We discuss job quality in greater detail in Chapter 10.) After all, that nanny or that house cleaner is also probably trying to balance her job, household, and caregiving responsibilities. And she may or may not have the ability to outsource her to-do list.

I always appreciate when people are open and honest about their paid and unpaid help. When we try to mask the fact that some of us have cleaning services, nannies, eldercare support, dog walkers, helpful grandparents, or a laundry service, it is easier to keep up the appearance that women are magically doing it all. By being open and fully acknowledging those that make our lives easier, we send a signal to younger generations: *Don't buy into that "having it all" stuff. There's always a trade-off, and no one is perfect.*

EQUAL PARTNERS OF EQUAL PARTNERS

I want to return to talking about parity and how to get there. This section could be the same as the one in chapter 5 because the counterpart of an equal partner—is simply another equal partner. This relationship is characterized by a conscious divide of the physical and cognitive tasks of the home, so over the course of the relationship, both people enjoy the same (or similar) amounts of paid work, unpaid work, caregiving, and free time. In chapters 5 and 6, I talked a lot about how men manage to fill this role, knowing that the Equal Partner is quite different than the Male Role that society prepared him to fill.

But trading in the Female Role to be the Equal Partner is also tough. Stepping back can be as hard as stepping up, especially when one has been raised to link the worth of a woman to the domestic space. This may force female Equal Partners to change the way they think and to challenge their own values. They may be forced to reject criticism from others and find confidence in their own actions.

This was the primary focus in my interviews with the partners of the EP40, who I am going to refer to as the EP+. This group includes fourteen partners of the EP40, plus two additional women who are each in a relationship with a woman. Though smaller in number, the diversity of this group is similar to that of their male counterparts. I spoke to women living in California, District of Columbia, Idaho, Illinois, Massachusetts, Ohio, Ontario, Oregon, Texas, Virginia, and Washington. These women were in their twenties, thirties, forties, and fifties. Four did not have children, and twelve were mothers. They were all employed and came from a variety of professional backgrounds, including academia, law enforcement, education, accounting, social work, therapy, and nonprofit work. These women identify as Afro-Caribbean, African American/Black, Latina, South Asian, and white; Catholic, Christian, Hindu, Muslim, and nonreligious.

My conversations with the EP+ naturally fell into three broad categories, which I will use to describe the wealth of information this small group had to offer: getting together, being together, and being together as a family.

GETTING TOGETHER

Role modeling equality is fantastic—but we also need to talk to young people directly and tell them that equality is not the norm: it takes hard work, and it should never be assumed to be the default behavior. For that reason, I found the stories in this section helpful for those already partnered, but perhaps they are even more important for younger people to hear. This is the one chapter of this book that I will ask my kids to read when they are teenagers, hoping that this combined advice might plant a seed or two for when/if either of them starts to think about sharing their life with another.

KNOW YOUR WORTH

I started off most conversations with the EP+ with the question: Did you intentionally look for an equal partner, or is this relationship a happy accident? One admitted it was purely a happy accident, and a few said their situation was a bit of a hybrid. But the majority of the EP+ said that gender equality was a key value of theirs, and they specifically looked for someone else who shared that view. However— before we even get to the moments when these women met their future partners—a few of them reminded me that a relationship starts long before two people meet.

Lydia is married to Robbie, whom we first met in chapter 6. Lydia was born and raised in Texas, and lives there now. She went to college at Howard University in Washington, DC, and interned in New York City; both experiences gave her a perspective very different from growing up in her hometown. Lydia identifies as Black and

Christian, and she says it is a combination of her upbringing and her faith that made her the person she is today.

"My older brother was really instrumental in helping build my self-worth, not only as a woman, but as a Black woman. He taught me not to settle. . . . I saw my time in DC and New York as an exploration, not only of new places but of myself. I constantly thought, *What kind of person am I now? And what kind of person do I want to be?* I did not like New York; it was just not my kind of place, but I used that time to grow. I read a lot. And my faith guided me through much of that time." When Lydia came back to Texas, she bought a small house with her savings and invested her time and energy on being independent.

Lydia got married later than many of her friends, and she got a lot of grief from girlfriends who thought she was being too picky. But Lydia rejected that idea—she said she would have preferred to stay single than to be in a bad relationship. She knew her own value, and she was looking for someone of equal value—not value in terms of money, but value in terms of integrity. "You have to be comfortable with yourself first. [By then] I knew my own value, and I didn't waste time with men who I didn't think were worth it." If you remember, Robbie told me in his interview that it was precisely Lydia's independence and confidence that was attractive to him when they first met.

As an interesting sidenote, when Lydia started dating Robbie, many of her friends did not approve. "Some of my friends were skeptical of the twice-divorced guy with a transit job. But I have always believed that it isn't about where you have been, but where you are going. . . . It isn't about money or status or who your employer is. It is about loving God, respecting me, and respecting yourself. And

Robbie was all of that." I asked Lydia what those friends think now. "Oh, they have eaten their words. They get it now!"

INITIAL ATTRACTION

Ellen Lamont at Appalachian State University researches modern dating patterns. She has found that, although many women claim to want equal partnerships, they tend to follow strictly gendered dating patterns, for example, expecting their date to plan and pay for dates, or expecting their dates to initiate sex. Women in Lamont's study stressed the importance of men feeling like they are in control during dating. But then, no surprise, these same couples have a difficult time shifting to a more equal balance once they marry.[1]

I heard a different story from the women I interviewed. At the time of our interview, Lauren and her husband, Adam, had been married for just over a year. Lauren identifies as white, and Adam identifies as Chinese American. They met while they were both studying on the East Coast. "I was attracted to Adam because he strikes the right balance between kind but not condescending. He made me feel attractive, without ever being demeaning." I asked if Adam was in control of their dating life, and she rejected this idea right away. She said they split the cost of dates and started on equal territory from the beginning. "Adam is also better with emotions than I am. He is better at talking about feelings. I like that about him, and appreciate what he has taught me." Lauren fully realizes that Adam's tendency to initiate dialogue about emotions is often interpreted as female-coded behavior, but that doesn't bother her at all. In fact, that was what attracted her to him in the first place.

Chantal had a similar story. We met her husband, Aiden, in chapter 4. Chantal is from Quebec, and Aiden is from British Colombia.

"I dated some terrible guys. They were focused on looks and superficial things. Aiden was different from the beginning. He had a gentle voice. He cared about me and often put my feelings first. He cares about people in general, actually. That is one of the things I love about him most. I remember one of our first dates; we were driving into the mountains to go snowshoeing. And I kept thinking that I could just picture us doing this with a few kids in the back seat." It was precisely Aiden's quiet nature, his willingness to listen to Chantal, and his respect for her opinions that made her realize this was the person she wanted to marry.

VALUES CHECK

It is common advice that new couples talk through life's big issues before making a commitment: *Where do you want to live? Do you want kids? What religion to do you want to follow?* But the EP+ thought it was also important to make sure their potential partner shared in their value of gender equality—not just passively, in a "check the box" sort of way, but in a way that indicated they deeply understood misogyny and patriarchy and believed that gender equality was something worth working toward.

Jalecia is now married to Izaiah, whom we met in chapter 5. (They were cohabitating when I first met them, and married a few weeks after we completed our interviews.) They do not have kids, but are open to the idea in the near future. Like Izaiah, Jalecia was born in Barbados and identifies as Afro-Caribbean. She was also raised in a single-parent home surrounded by strict gender norms. She came to the United States for college and then stayed for her master's degree and PhD. She is now completing her postdoctoral work. I asked her if it was hard to balance the cultural norms she learned in Barbados with her own values around gender equality. She laughed. "Oh no. I know I am 'that person.' I butt heads with a lot of people; I always have, and I am OK with that. But my close friends, those people in my little bubble, it is important that they have the same gender values as me. Or, OK, maybe they're not 100 percent with me, but they're as close as it's going to get."

Jalecia had the same expectations for a partner as she did for her friends. As she dated, she was always clear about her own professional goals. But knowing that few men would push back on a working woman these days, Jalecia would test the values of her dates by bringing up more sensitive topics. She would bring up her support of transgender people and talk about how she does not ascribe to the gender binary. "I made it clear to any guy I was dating that whatever the gender identity of a child, that is OK by me." In the context of other positive behaviors Izaiah demonstrated, his agreement with that statement was an indication to Jalecia that his values very much mirrored her own.

Ashley is married to Will, whom we met in chapter 6. Ashley identifies as white, and she met Will when she was in college. Ironically, they started dating while taking the same gender roles class in their senior year. (Will admitted that he only signed up for the class because he needed a ride to campus. Ashley had a car, and offered to give him a lift.) Their relationship started with car pool small talk, and they are now married with three kids.

Gender was not a topic that Ashley was particularly interested in, and she admitted she took the class for some easy credits. But it ended up being helpful for her and Will as they got to know each other. "Taking a gender roles class was a total accident, but it ended up being super helpful. It forced us to have a lot of really specific conversations and self-reflect about things that I ordinarily would not consider." Ashley told me that having deeper conversations about gender inequality, experienced sexism, and healthy masculinity set a good foundation for their partnership.

TURNING VALUES INTO ACTIONS

As we have discussed many times before, valuing gender equality is a great start. But plenty of people who value equality do not take the steps to operationalize it into their daily lives. This is something that many of the EP+ looked at closely: *Are these potential partners really capable of living their values? Or are they just saying the right words to placate?*

Jalecia was convinced that Izaiah was true to his words by the way he took care of himself. They dated for many years, and then they lived together before getting married. During that time, Jalecia was able to witness him being independent: taking care of his own space, keeping his apartment clean, doing his own laundry, and ironing his clothes without making an issue of it. If you remember, Izaiah was the man whose mother taught him how to be independent from a woman, and that precise skill was one of the reasons Jalecia decided to continue with their relationship.

We met Marisol and Hector in chapter 6; they live in Texas with one son. Marisol was convinced that Hector would be a good partner because of his job. The fact that Hector was devoting his career to the safety of children showed Marisol that he was truly committed to the values he believed in. "The first time I ever saw him, I was a volunteer at this family center, and he was working there full time. He was in front of a group of kids, and I saw them interacting, and he was incredible." This wasn't a position that paid a lot, nor did it offer Hector prestige or power. Mirasol knew that he was doing this job because he loved it and because he cared about kids; that was proof enough for her.

We have not yet met Ted and Leigh. They both identify as white and Christian. Ted grew up in Indiana, and Leigh in central Illinois. They met after college through a work project and started a long-distance relationship. Eventually, they married and moved to the same city; at the time of our interviews their kids were ten and thirteen.

Leigh and Ted did not live together before they married. So, I asked Leigh, how did she know? How did she know Ted wasn't all talk—that he was capable of actually living his values? "Early conversations were really important. First of all, Ted was authentic. He wasn't trying to be anyone he wasn't; he was honest about his strengths and his weaknesses. But there were a few actual things that gave me the hint. One was that he made time for my work, listened to me talk about my work, and was genuinely excited for me. . . . I'll never forget this one email—we didn't live in the same city at first and so did a lot of emailing back and forth—and he wrote, 'Your dreams are becoming as important as my own.' That was an amazing thing for him to say. And I believed him."

GETTING TO KNOW EACH OTHER

Communication *before* commitment came up in nearly every interview—not just the usual chitchat, but raw, honest, dialogue about the impact that gender inequality and misogyny have on women's lives. Of course, this doesn't occur every day, but it was a regular and important part of these couples getting to know each other.

I asked Leigh if she remembered having specific conversations about gender when they were dating. She said that her definition of equality has changed since they married nearly twenty years ago, but yes, they did talk about it. "I noticed that I wasn't the one to always bring things up, and I really liked that. He would initiate those conversations, too. That was an indication that it wasn't just me making this an issue—this was something that was also important to him."

Lauren also had a lot to say on this subject. She and Adam also had a long-distance relationship. Soon after they met, Adam left to study overseas for a year. So, their courtship was mostly over Skype and email. I asked her if it was hard to get to know someone when they lived on the other side of the world. "Actually, not at all. I thought it was great. We got to know each other really well, and I felt safe saying anything to him because there was no risk. He wasn't part of my everyday routine. I had nothing to lose." Lauren found that distance forced them to communicate on a level that they wouldn't have likely found had they lived in the same city. "There were also no distractions—no friends, or bars, or movies. We just talked—a lot. And that is still the basis to our relationship. Take the pandemic lockdowns, for instance. Adam and I spent months in the same tiny apartment together. And it still wasn't enough. When we all went back to work and a normal routine, we actually missed each other."

While dating Izaiah, Jalecia found that they weren't communicating well, and her issue wasn't just with him—it was with her friends and her family members, too. "I had gone through some tough years, and I didn't know how to deal with what was going on. I didn't have the words to explain how I felt." She and Izaiah took a break, and Jalecia started seeing a therapist. That experience was life changing; it gave her the tools and confidence to go back to Izaiah and make their relationship work. "I resisted it for so long because I didn't know what I was missing. But that has hugely impacted my relationship—for the better. Since then, communication has been a big part of our partnership. On most days, we talk for at least thirty minutes without any TV or phones or computers. We think of this as our quality time, undistracted, to check in with each other." These daily conversations aren't always deep. Sometimes they just tell each other stories from work, or they talk about family or current events. But that undistracted time to just talk and connect is foundational for their partnership.

I asked the EP+, "If you could give a young woman advice about relationships and finding the right match—what would you say?" The following list is a compilation of what I was told, and I believe that this is a great tool for people of all genders. Feel free to make a copy or take a picture of this box and send it around to the young people in your life. This list isn't a magic recipe for success, but reviewing these suggestions can't hurt.

EP+ ADVICE ON CHOOSING AN EQUAL PARTNER

- Know yourself first. Set boundaries and determine your deal breakers when you are single. Then hold yourself to those boundaries when you start dating.
- Don't just have the "gender talk" once. It should be an ongoing dialogue.
- It is common for the Female Role to ask, *Would you support my career?* And when the answer is yes, it is accepted and the conversation stops. But no one should be satisfied with that simple answer. It doesn't give enough information. Ask more questions: *Would you move if I had a great job offer? Are you open to taking family leave if we have a baby? Would it bother you if I made more*

money than you or had a more prestigious title? Would you be willing to turn down a promotion if we needed your time more than your money? Are you willing to sacrifice for me in the same way that I am willing to sacrifice for you? These are the questions people of all genders need to ask potential partners.

- Make sure you can tell your partner anything. Anything! There should be no topic you can't raise and discuss. And make sure you are truly being heard.

- Remember the coronavirus lockdowns. Ask yourself, *Would I be willing to be locked in an apartment with this person for a year?*

- Have your partner reflect on their own upbringing and talk about whether or not that is what they expect in the future.

- Initiate conversations about equality and systems of oppression. Does this person truly understand how women, especially women of color, are forced to live differently than men?

- You should both be making an equal effort when dating. Is this person making as much of an effort to see you, get to know you, and support you, as you are with them?

- If dating a man, find out if they had female friends growing up. This can be a good indication of his respect for women, and if he is aware of a female perspective and female experiences.

- Don't lose yourself in a new relationship. Maintain your relationships with friends, colleagues, and family.

- Jealousy and possessiveness may seem cute at first and can be misinterpreted as an indication of love. But it gets old, fast. Too many people realize this too late.

- Ideally, you are two complete people who complement each other. No one should "save" anyone else.

- Don't role model Female Role norms from the beginning; do not even pretend. If you want to cook a nice meal, great. But the next time, let them cook for you. You want to show the real you, not an idealized unsustainable version of you.

- Make sure you can survive on your own—financially and emotionally. You never want to be trapped by a relationship.

- Choose someone who makes you feel safe. Watch how they handle anger and extreme frustration. Then ask yourself, *Do I still feel safe in these circumstances? Is any of that anger ever directed at me?*

- Don't shy away from talking about hard topics. Anything that matters to you, should matter to your partner.

- Challenge your own gender norms all the time. It should never be assumed that women are more enlightened simply because they are female. Plenty of women are misogynists, and plenty of women buy into misogynist behavior.

- Practice self-care. Encourage your partner to do the same. The better you can both take care of yourselves, the better you can both take care of others.

- Find allies in your partner's family. Look for people whom you can talk to, who will listen to you, and who will believe you.

I would also add that teaching young people the terms *King of the Castle, Hands-On Husband,* and *Equal Partner* could be helpful. Discuss how these behaviors are different from each other, and how they counter common perceptions about household balance. Be honest about what effects each of those behaviors have on a household.

BEING TOGETHER

In chapter 6, I talked about the seven most common strategies that the EP40 use to make their relationships work. I was curious what people coded for the Female Role would have to say about the same topic. When it came to the core relationships between two people—without any children in the home—there were three clear themes.

1. YOU ARE NOT LOSING YOUR VALUE

Because men traditionally hold power in the public and professional spaces, women have long held power in the domestic space. This has been the only realm in which many women have been able to exercise their expertise, capacity, and authority. So naturally, if we want to alter gender norms and allow men more responsibility in the home, many women will see this as a lose-lose proposition. They still don't have power in the public space, and now they are losing power in the private space.

One can deeply internalize being raised with the explicit expectation of becoming the domestic manager, and some women of the EP+ still felt responsible for the state of their domestic spaces. I asked the EP+ directly, "Do you think your value has at all diminished because you now share this role with your partner?" Lauren rejected this idea outright. "No, not at all. Adam's involvement actually makes me feel great. I do not feel diminished in the least." (Lauren was also the higher-income earner in her household, which may or may not affect her opinion.)

Jalecia admitted that she has felt that tug and has to fight against it. She had her own Thanksgiving story to share to illustrate her point. "I slept in that day. When I got up, I found that Izaiah had walked the dog, cleaned the house, and had dinner in the oven. All the food prep was done—there was literally nothing for me to do." I asked her how that made her feel. "Well, I admit, at first I thought I had done something wrong. But then I caught that innate thought in my head; I caught myself following a gender norm that I intellectually do not believe in." This internal conversation led her to talk about it with Izaiah. *Why did he do everything without her? Was he upset? Was he trying to prove a point?* "Ends up, Izaiah wanted to be lazy the rest of the weekend and watch football. He wanted to get all his work done now so he could lay on the couch for three days and not feel guilty. And I realized, *Oh, that makes sense.* And then it clicked that this was my relaxing day, and I'd do work later that weekend. And then it didn't bother me at all—and I felt much better about it."

I liked what Jalecia said about challenging that innate thought in her head. Self-regulation is one of the five components of emotional intelligence. It is the ability to keep our raw emotions inside and project a more measured and appropriate reaction. This is precisely what Jalecia did. She had an immediate reaction to Izaiah's work in the home based on her own gendered upbringing. But then she snapped herself out of gender default, realized what was happening, and changed her own mind. Instead of allowing guilt to overtake her, she talked about her feelings with her partner, realized his perspective, and decided to enjoy her day off and a holiday dinner with friends.

2. DIFFERENT DOES NOT MEAN BETTER

My colleague Wendy isn't the only one that likes things just so. Many people are particular about household things: the way dishes are washed, or how cabinets are organized. One rare benefit to being the household manager and cognitive laborer is that one can do things precisely the way one wants to. So presumably, the trade-off in an equal partnership might be that now we have to compromise on how things are done in the home—accept our partners' ways as different but not worse. Knowing this was the case in my own home, I asked the EP+ about it directly.

Marisol laughed a little bit at this question. "Oh sure, he folds clothes differently than I do, for one. And sometimes when he goes grocery shopping, he comes back with an odd ingredient that confuses me. But in these times, I think—*Well, I didn't have to do laundry or go to the grocery store.* And I'd rather have that time than to be 'right.' . . . I think this is hardest at the beginning of a relationship, when you're trying to blend two ways of doing something into one. But with time, it gets easier. You get used to each other and you learn how the other person works."

Speaking of new relationships, Dylan had lots to say about this topic, and it was timely as she had just moved in with her fiancé about six months before our interview. Dylan grew up in Florida and identifies as Black. She finished college in Florida, and then moved to California to begin medical school. She met Sasha during her residency.

Sasha identifies as Latina and white and is also studying to be a doctor, but she is a few years behind Dylan. At the time of our interview, Sasha was doing her internship year; although Dylan had occasional on-call hours, the bulk of her work was conducting research from home. This arrangement greatly limited Sasha's hours to devote to the home—and gave Dylan ample opportunity to do housework and shopping during breaks.

Dylan described herself as an "aggressive list maker" and organizer. She also admits she likes things just so. I asked her, "Do you ever redo chores that Sasha did because you think she did a subpar job?"

This interview was done on a video call. When I asked that question, both women gave each other a sideways glance before laughing. Clearly this was a subject they had discussed before. "I try not to do that because it just sends the wrong message. It tells her, *I don't appreciate what you did.* And that's not it at all. Let's just say I am getting better at knowing which things are really important to me—and which things don't matter as much. The really important things, I just do before she has the chance. Then it is done my way, and we avoid that argument. And the other stuff, I just appreciate her time and let it go." But the look on her face while she said that suggested "letting it go" wasn't always easy.

Dylan and Sasha had one idea that I had not heard during interviews, which might be helpful to other couples. Dylan explained that for the next few months, Sasha had greater work commitments than she did, and she would be working the night shift. This wasn't necessarily going to go on for years—just a finite period of time. But for that finite period of time, Dylan was willing to do more than 50 percent of the work.

Instead of thinking about the number of hours, Dylan thought more in terms of percentage of time. "She is home so little, and she has to sleep, too. So, she might only have two free hours in her day before she heads into work; I don't expect her to use all of those two hours to clean. But if she spends thirty minutes, or a quarter of her time, that is enough. That tells me that she is still making a conscious effort to do things for us, and that is a nice way for her to show me that she loves me."

I thought this was a great way to manage equity for those periods of time when one person is balancing something big that detracts from the average balance of the home, for example, a new job, an ill parent, or a volunteer project. I am not sure how long this could go on without some resentment building up, but for a set period of time, this makes sense. We all know that household parity doesn't mean splitting the load fifty-fifty every day; that is simply unachievable. Our lives shift and change, as do responsibilities throughout the weeks, months, and years. Finding ways to maintain an equitable balance through extraordinary times is a necessary strategy for the long term.

Perhaps it was Lydia who had the most to say on this topic. She had two points to make, each of equal importance. First, she told me that, of course, marriage is about compromise, and that includes compromising about how the other person does things. She also seemed to employ a similar tactic as Dylan. "Of course, there are things he does that slightly annoy me; that is normal. For example, I am very particular about how things are hung in the closet. I can't help it—that's my thing. I just want it done a particular way. So, I tend to just do it before he can, and then it isn't an issue. Occasionally, when he does the hanging before me, however, I just let it go. Doing it again just creates more work for me." Lydia also thought that redoing a chore would be an unnecessarily spiteful and disempowering move, and one that would do more harm than good.

I asked, "What if a chore was done so poorly, that it created a problem? For example, half the clothes get shrunk in the wash?" I admit, in my own home, Evan gets on my case about how I wash the pots and pans. And I hate it. But I also have to admit, when I do a poor job, it affects his cooking the next time they're used: greasy spots smoke, or taint the taste of a future meal. So, even though I don't enjoy his mini-lectures about how to clean a pan properly, I have to admit he has a point.

Lydia agreed—that is different and that would call for a conversation. You'd have to talk it through, and talk about the consequences of doing a subpar job. But that was not an issue in Lydia's home; the differences between her and Robbie truly came down to different—not better/worse.

Then Lydia made her second point, which was reminiscent of maternal gatekeeping. "There are women out there, and I know some of them, who don't want to lose the power in their house, and they maintain that power by tearing their husband down. But that is only working against us. I believe in affirmation and not tearing down. Robbie helps in the house because I don't tear him down every time he does." Lydia's perspective was that when people got too much negative feedback, they simply stop trying. So, she used affirmation with her entire family, and she appreciated it when Robbie and the kids treated her the same. "I openly relinquish power and control in my home."

3. HOLD EACH OTHER ACCOUNTABLE

Did the EP+ have to hold their partners accountable? Yes! Some thought their partners would still do close to half the work without their encouragement, and others were certain their partner would slip back into a neo-traditional role if they didn't keep them on task. But nearly all of them agreed that some level of monitoring and accountability was helpful—in both directions.

We met Hal in chapter 6. Hal is the guy who told the story about struggling to get his toddler in a car seat. During her interview, Hal's partner, Michelle, talked a lot about accountability and how to do it in an open and respectful manner. "For physical tasks, Hal jumps right in. But the emotional load is harder. Because those management tasks are invisible, they're hard to notice. This is where we have to focus our work and just keep communicating and keep talking, or else I will feel resentment . . ." Michelle finds that, when holding Hal accountable, she tries to frame it in terms of structural misogyny and not of them as a couple. "He understands structural racism because he has experienced it. So, he better understands structural sexism. We actually talk about the intersection of skin color and oppression a lot. I am glad for that . . . [framing it that way helps him] listen to me without getting defensive."

I appreciated that Michelle was so open about how hard being in a relationship was. Maintaining an equal partnership does not mean flipping a switch; it is a lifelong commitment that requires hard work. And of course, we are all human. We make mistakes, say petty things, and act like jerks. She fully admitted that she and Hal had their fair share of immature moments. She knows she doesn't always handle it well when Hal struggles to keep up his end of the bargain. "I know I can be passive-aggressive sometimes, it just happens, even though I tell myself not to. And [when I do] it never ends well. It is usually always better if I just bring it up, and we can talk through it."

When I asked Ashley if she ever had to readjust and remind Will to do more, she answered without hesitation. "Of course. Constantly. Over and over. Those conversations aren't futile—they move us along, but they still have to happen. Especially after we had our first baby." She sighed—a big, long sigh—then added, "All the touchy issues come with kids."

Now Ashley and Will have a set time to talk each week about domestic jobs and family logistics—typically on Sunday evening as they are looking at the week ahead. That time allows both of them the space to bring up hard topics; it isn't just tolerated, it is expected. She explained that, in the past, before they had this set routine, she might fester about an issue for days before bringing it up. In her mind, it had been brewing for a long time. But from Will's perspective, it came out of the blue. That moment might be the time *she* wanted to have that heavy conversation, but it wasn't right for Will. He would resent it, she would dig in deeper, and it nearly always led to an argument. Dedicating time to communicate about bigger issues has been an important way for them to avoid those spontaneous disagreements.

Having a designated time also solves the "bossy" or "nagging" problem we discussed back in chapter 3. If you schedule regular check-in times (either every night, like Jalecia and Izaiah, or weekly, like Ashley and Will), you create a time when you both expect each other to sit down, remind each other what is going on and what needs doing, and hold each other accountable for that responsibility. The EP+ find that follow-up questions can be helpful: *When do you expect you'll have time to do this? Do you need any help in creating enough time for you to get this done? If this task is too hard for whatever reason, do you want to trade something with me—something you think you can do more easily?* Shared calendars and lists on smartphones can also serve as reminders, relieving the Female Role from constantly having to follow up, follow up, follow up.

BEING TOGETHER AS A FAMILY

As we have discussed previously, a household workload changes exponentially when children join the family: infants, school-age kids, teenagers—they all require a ton of work. And it is precisely during these years when equal partnerships may be the most critical.

REJECT PERFECTION

One word that many mothers often use to both describe the expectations others have for them, and the expectations they have for themselves, is *perfection*. But it is virtually impossible to be the consummate professional at work, be a supportive and loving partner, maintain an exercise routine, volunteer in your community, keep your house clean and tidy, and be an intensive parent. Yet for some reason, people in the Female Role collectively try over and over to achieve this mythical perfection.

The women I spoke to had in common a dislike of the idea of perfection, and an intentional rejection of this expectation. Like the EP40 trying to disregard unearned praise, the EP+ try to disregard perfection.

Lydia brought up this topic before I could ask her about it. "I think a lot of women think their worth is wrapped up in perfection. But being perfect is both unattainable and subjective. My definition of perfect is probably different than yours. So, it really is a losing battle." I asked her how she rejected perfection in her own life. "As a mom, I have let the little things go. I think of the kids first—I have learned to give of myself what I am willing to give, and not expect the same back." Lydia agreed that she and Robbie have both let standards slip since having children, for example, allowing the carpet to go without vacuuming a few extra days, ignoring the Lego mess until the weekend, or ignoring the weeds in the front yard.

Ashley shared a story about her attempt to reject perfection while simultaneously taking steps to protect her own reputation and not feel resentful of Will. The year their daughter started kindergarten, Ashley got a new teaching job that required her to be at school very early. Will had more flexibility in the morning, so they decided he would be the parent to get the kids up, ready, and dropped off at school. Ashley was fine with this arrangement—but she did worry about what her daughter would look like at school. She feared that she would show up in mismatched clothes and crazy hair. Ashley knew that it was her, not Will, who might potentially be judged for that situation.

To diffuse possible issues in the future, she called the kindergarten teacher before school began. "I basically told her what our family situation was, and warned her that my daughter would probably be a hot mess when she got to school every day." I asked how the teacher reacted. "Oh, she was fine with it. She even offered to help with my daughter's hair!"

One could look at this situation and criticize Ashley and the teacher for colluding to let Will off the hook, and/or criticize Will for not learning how to braid hair. But I think this is a great compromise—or at least a great transition step. Changing gender norms isn't going to happen overnight. In the meantime, many people around us will continue to judge us by the old standards. So, while we work toward equality, I believe that it is perfectly fine to make a few allowances along the way. It was smart of Ashley to give the teacher a quick call; it set her mind at ease, unburdened her from unnecessary criticism, and allowed Will to proceed with the morning routine in his own way.

Sarah is married to Tim, whom we met in chapter 5. I used Tim's story to illustrate the importance of repetition in establishing new gender norms. Sarah identifies as white and Catholic. She grew up in Iowa with six younger siblings. Between her parents' belief in traditional gender norms and the hours she spent as a caregiver for her younger siblings, Sarah grew up very comfortable in the Female Role. It wasn't until she and Tim had kids, and she had to balance work and motherhood, that she struggled. If you recall, Tim and Sarah were close to divorce when their first child was a baby. They both credit the success of their marriage to a combination of therapy and their mutual commitment to following their therapist's recommendations.

Sarah and I spoke about the "extras" that seem to come with extreme modern expectations of perfect parenthood: the long lineup of extracurricular activities, elaborate birthday parties, and organic lunches. We happened to do our interview in December, and Sarah lamented about the "You've Been Claused" package that had recently arrived on her doorstep. I knew exactly what she was talking about because we had the same thing go around our neighborhood in October. In the fall it was "You've Been Boo-ed," but it is the same idea. You hear a knock and run to the door, only to find a "surprise" bag from a mystery neighbor. Inside is a cornucopia of kid treasures and a note instructing you to pass the fun along to another neighbor. I commiserated with Sarah; we both felt frustrated that these activities tend to add to a mother's to-do list. I laughed out loud when Sarah described her reaction to the cheery "You've Been Claused" bag on her front porch. "NOW, on top of everything else going on, I had to run out and find the perfect gift for my kid to drop off at another poor, unsuspecting mother's door. Moms—we just fuck ourselves over all the time."

Keeping up with perfect parenting seems to require a few more hours of work each year. Think back to the statistic in chapter 1 that stay-at-home moms in the 1970s did fewer hours of childcare than working moms in 2020. Although this revised philosophy of parenthood was initially linked to upper middle-class families, new research shows that parents across the United States, from a variety of socioeconomic levels, believe this is the best way to parent.[2] However, it is becoming clearer that these heavy demands on the modern parent might actually be unattainable. Sarah and other EP+ seem acutely aware of these social parenting pressures, and they are willing to edit their schedules to bring stress levels down. For example, they could limit each child to one or two extracurricular activities at a time, agree to attend just a few games each season, or agree to host birthday parties every other year.

WORK THROUGH THE GUILT

Guilt was a key theme that came up with just about every one of the EP+. This is also something I struggle with, so these conversations resonated with me. People in the Female Role may push back on society's unrealistic expectations of motherhood, but they might feel really, really guilty in the meantime.

Chantal feels guilt frequently, but she talks about it and then pushes through. She does not let guilt impact her decisions or her actions. "I feel guilt when I have to work late and can't pick up the kids from day care, or when I have to work on the weekend and can't go with the family to the park. In those moments, I think I am not doing enough." I asked her, "Do you ever leave work earlier because of that guilt?" She considered the question for a moment. "No. I always try to come home as soon as I can. So, if I am working late, it is for a reason; there is something important I have to do before I go home."

Chantal said that, although it doesn't make her change her schedule, it does bother her sometimes. "One time, I said to Aiden, 'I think the kids hate me.' It was one of those days that they wanted Daddy for everything. And he was so sweet. He said, 'No, that's not what I see. They adore you.'" Chantel found it helpful to talk about her guilt and insecurities with her partner. Sometimes, just talking it through made her feel better. I think this is a good message for everyone with a friend or family member who might be facing mother-hood guilt. If someone comes to you with feelings of inadequacy, validate her feelings, contextualize the conversation in cultural gen-der norms, and assure her that she is indeed a fantastic parent.

I was especially curious to ask Sarah about guilt because she comes from such a traditional background. How did pushing back on gender norms make her feel? Sarah openly admitted that she feels plenty of guilt. Watching Tim step up has meant that she has had to step back, and that means she has had to let things go. "It is hard to realize that I don't have to be the one to do everything for every-one. I've had to work through the guilt and the expectations, and give up being the gatekeeper to my kids and their feelings. In the process, my husband and my kids have become so close, they are real buddies now. Sometimes my son goes to his dad when he needs comforting, and even though it makes me a little sad, it's also really wonderful. I really think women are doing their partners and their kids a favor when we step back and allow them to form their own re-lationships independent of us."

"I KNOW I HAVE IT GOOD"

At the end of the day, the EP+ know they have solid relationships. Marisol used the word *gratitude* a lot when speaking about Hector. "I work in a school with primarily female teachers, and they talk a lot about their husbands and boyfriends. They talk about how frus-trated they are about how little men do in their home. And I just feel grateful that I have a very different life. It makes for some awkward moments at work, but mostly, I am just grateful."

I asked Chantal if she ever wonders what life would be like with a different kind of man. She laughed and said, "I think I would yell a lot more." But humor aside, this is spot-on with research that says couples who have equal marriages tend to argue less, have lower divorce rates, and even better sex lives.[3]

None of these women felt that their relationships were undeserved; they all felt perfectly deserving of the love and respect their partners offered them. And they wished they were living the norm and not the exception. They wished their friends, sisters, cousins, and neighbors had situations as good as theirs.

Sarah fully realizes that she has a relationship different than most women. "Sometimes I worry I am setting our daughter up for disappointment because I worry that she won't ever find anyone like her dad." I assured her that we all just have to work together to raise our sons to measure up to the standards that we have for our daughters—to prepare kids of all genders to be capable of equal partnership.

8
THE NEXT GENERATION
OF EQUAL PARTNERS

My daughter, like many other girls her age, owns the *Bedtime Stories for Rebel Girls* series. These books are full of beautiful illustrations and inspiring stories about great women who did great things. We reflect on those stories and talk about how she, too, can be anything she sets her mind to. My husband and I tell our daughter daily, directly and indirectly, that she does not need to conform to outdated gender norms. She can follow her natural instincts, even if they happen to be male-coded characteristics. And we try to role model that behavior in our home, so she doesn't perceive our words as empty.

But how are little boys being raised? Are they also reading *Bedtime Stories for Rebel Girls*? Are they also taught about strong women and female leaders? Are they given permission to exhibit female-coded traits? We have excelled at empowering our girls to break free of harmful gender norms, but, except for a few pioneers leading the way in alternative masculinities, I am not convinced we are doing enough to encourage our boys to break free of harmful gender norms.

Perhaps the most exciting aspect of the research behind this book was looking for lessons about the future. We know that gender is still a powerful motivator when it comes to setting household routines, and we know that progressive attitudes about gender norms do not always translate into actions. What I needed to learn—as the mother of two children, one who identifies as a boy and one who identifies as a girl—is what can we do to help the next generation of people be better than ourselves? What can we do to break this cycle and raise our kids to embody a full set of desirable attributes, regardless of sex or gender identity?

After talking to the EP40 and the EP+, I identified the following five approaches to raising boys. Any reader with children in their life—from kids they see on a daily basis to kids they only see a few times a year—can start doing these things today. Although these ideas are specifically targeted for boys, and meant to counter traditionally masculine gender norms, they are certainly applicable for raising children of all genders.

To ground these recommended approaches in research, I interviewed three experts (who are also all parents) for their reactions, and to see if they had additional advice to share. Gary Barker is the founder of Promundo and MenCare. He has advised the United Nations, the World Bank, numerous national governments, and key international foundations and corporations on strategies to engage men and boys in promoting gender equality. Ted Bunch is an author, educator, activist, and lecturer working to end all forms of violence and discrimination against women and girls. He is chief development officer of the anti-violence organization A Call to Men and the co-author of *The Book of Dares: 100 Ways for Boys to be Kind, Bold, and Brave*. Sarah Schoppe-Sullivan is a developmental psychologist, professor of psychology, and director of the Children and Parents Lab at The Ohio State University. She is widely published in the areas of fatherhood, maternal gatekeeping, and household change after the first baby.

APPROACH #1. PRACTICE AUTHENTICITY

Will talked a lot about authenticity. If you recall, Will is Polynesian American and grew up on the West Coast. His dad role modeled a classic form of masculinity: tough, athletic, in charge. "Dad was always polite and kind to women. But he was also a well-respected athlete and coach in our community. He always told me growing up, 'I want you to be better than me.' And I took that to mean athletically. He wanted me to be better." Will himself was athletic, and he was successful with high school sports. But he wondered, *How could he be better than someone so amazing?*

Will was also one of two non-white kids in a very white town. Between his community's expectations and his father's expectations, Will didn't have much of a chance to be authentic.

Things began to change when he was in college, beginning with the gender roles class he took with his future wife, Ashley. "I admit, at first I only took this class to get a ride to campus. But this class ended up being really good. I opened up to looking at and rethinking social norms. I thought about masculinity, and what it means, and what it means to me."

Ashley and Will were both college athletes. After graduation, Ashley became a teacher/coach, and Will got a full-time coaching position in college athletics. They now have three kids, who at the time of our interview were eight, eleven, and thirteen.

Will talked a lot about the importance of authenticity. After "performing" for so many years, Will is grateful that he is finally at a place in his life when he can be his own true self. He remembers the way men performed masculinity to him when he was young, and in contrast, he is trying to role model something very different to his kids and his team today. "I don't keep my thoughts inside anymore; I say them out loud. I tell myself—*Just say something.* When I don't know something, I make sure to say it. When I disagree or am uncertain or scared or confused, I admit it. I don't have to be perfect. I am one of those rare coaches who doesn't believe winning is everything." Certainly, coaches want their team to win games. But Will says he spends just as much time on the development of the whole person as he does on game strategy. "And I recruit young men specifically into my program, and I am up-front about what I do. So, they know exactly what they're in for."

Years later, Will found a way to reconcile the goals his father set for him. He finally decided that he was never going to exceed his father's athletic achievements, but he could be a better partner than his father was, and he could be a better father than his father was. "This is how I am better. I am a better dad, and I am a better husband. And I am really proud of that."

Robbie had a lot to say about authenticity, too. Remember that Lydia is his third wife, but Robbie explained that Lydia is the first woman who loved him for who he was, not for someone he was trying to be. "The first time I got married, we were so young. She wanted to be married to a tough gangster, and that is what I pretended to be. My second wife was a white woman, and I was always conscious of how I was behaving and whether or not it was appropriate for her and appropriate for a biracial couple." Having those relationships as comparisons, Robbie is relieved that he can finally be his true self around Lydia. Ideally, home should be a safe place; it is exhausting to keep up a charade around those closest to you. Robbie appreciates that now he can now be in a relationship without pretenses. He doesn't have to be brave or tough or in control; he can just be himself.

We have not met Violet yet. Violet identifies as white and grew up with a mom, a dad, and a sister in a small southeastern college town. For the first four decades of her life, Violet was perceived as male, a condition known as *gender dysphoria*.

Before she transitioned, I interviewed Violet as one of the EP40. In that interview she told me about her upbringing and her family; they were loving but gender traditional. Violet, always interested in gender, sought out books on the topic and was inspired by feminist friends. It was the mutual rejection of traditional gender norms that initially attracted Violet to Georgia; they met, married, and, at the time of our interview, they had two children under ten.

Violet understands the importance of authenticity. "When I was perceived as a man, I was very unhappy. I could not function very well with all the gendered stereotypes that were projected onto me. It wasn't simply that I was a different kind of man; it's that, on a psychological level, I am a woman. [This made it] incredibly difficult to function, because I was alienated from myself. Before transition, I went through multiple, long, debilitating depressions. One of the deepest of these occurred when my children were still quite young. During the worst months of this depression, I was unable to function beyond the most basic activities of daily living. Actually, my motivation and decision to transition was due, largely, to my realization that I could not continue to live my life in a way that was impacting my children and wife so negatively."

Being truly authentic to herself, and living as a woman, has been a turning point in Violet's life. "[It] has made me a better parent. It has improved my life in every dimension. Since transitioning gender both socially and physically, my emotional well-being and ability to care for and be a role model for my children has increased in remarkable ways. For me, authentic self-expression means that we love ourselves enough to challenge what we have been taught about how to be in the world."

This first approach may seem counterintuitive for this section because it is more about our own adult behavior, and less about the behavior of our children. But role modeling authenticity will allow the next generation to be authentic themselves, instead of growing up behaving in a way they think they are supposed to. We don't want boys to have to repeat the experience of Will, Robbie, or Violet. We don't want boys to be forced into inauthentic behavior like Zack, who in chapter 6 told us that, at a young age, he felt the need to manage his effeminate mannerisms to please his parents. Our goal is for the next generation to grow up true to themselves, which ultimately starts with our own behavior.

Sarah agrees that fathers should feel free to do things differently than their dads, to reinvent masculinity, and to break new ground in what it means to be a dad. "There is evidence that dads are already doing this, demonstrating more nurturing behavior than previous generations, and we need to continue to give each other permission to do things differently. It is OK to reshape who we are, and possible to simultaneously appreciate the past while reinventing your future."

Ted confirmed why this is so important for young boys; they won't know how to be their own genuine selves unless they see that role modeled by others. "Boys need to be able to show a full range of emotions in order to be their full authentic selves. That is what brings out the authenticity—to be able to react with a variety of feelings, in a variety of environments. Not all boys and men like sports. They might like dancing or the arts. And that is good! We need to reimagine—not redefine—but reimagine boyness." It isn't about comparing a man to a man, or a boy to a boy, but accepting each person for his own unique self.

APPROACH #2. TEACH BOYS TO ARTICULATE THEIR FEELINGS

Empathy came up over and over in my conversations with the men I interviewed, but perhaps Mike helped me find the best words to describe why this is so important for young boys.

Mike is from California and identifies as white and Bahá'í. Growing up, his mother set a good example for him, as she challenged gender norms in her life and her work. "She wouldn't allow statements like 'boys will be boys' used around her. And I know she worked toward equality with my dad. Dad didn't always do great, but Mom led and he generally went along with it. He was at least open to it."

Now Mike is married to Rosamund, and they have two children who at the time of our interview were six and just under two. Mike has a degree in clinical psychology and runs his own family practice. He specializes in men's issues and parenting teens. I asked him what work concepts he applied to his own relationship. Without a thought, he mentioned empathy and compassion. "Compassion is my number one priority. I try to ask myself, *Why is this hard for her? How can I better support her?* I know I can't fix her problems. But I can be there for her." Mike believes that, hands down, one cannot be an equal partner if one doesn't have the capacity to empathize with another person and to show them compassion.

So, how does this relate to the next generation? In order for men to have the ability to empathize, they first need to learn how to articulate their feelings. Mike intentionally works to build these skills in his kids. "Boys are generally taught to understand two emotions—joy and anger. But there are dozens of other emotions that we need to be able to feel so we can empathize with our friends, partners, kids, etc. You can't have compassion for others if you, yourself, don't understand shame, embarrassment, humiliation, fear, and sadness."

Mike knows that little kids don't often have the vocabulary to articulate feelings, so he works hard to help his son find the right words to match his emotions. "I rarely accept anger from him. I know that most times, when he is expressing anger, there's another emotion underneath that. I have to figure out what is behind that anger." Mike believes, both professionally and personally, that helping his son learn how to feel and articulate a range of emotions will help him be a better adult.

Mike stressed the importance of allowing kids to feel disappointment and sadness. Those are valid feelings, he told me. Modern parents often swoop in and try to fix kids' problems, which Mike believes is a great disservice to them. He believes it is better to allow children to sit and feel those feelings. This will better enable them to be empathetic toward others in the future.

Sarah confirmed that all humans are capable of empathy; it is a learned behavior. We just need to take the time teach it to each other, and to our kids. She also added that we can't stop at tapping into emotions; we also have to learn how to control them. "This is an important piece for men to role model to boys—how to regulate emotions and how to control their anger, so they do not harm themselves or others."

Gary linked this approach to mental health. "This is also at the root of many men's undiagnosed depression. If the only emotion you can express is anger, and the only manifestation of that anger is the use of aggression toward others—whether it is verbal or physical—if we only give you this one thing to express your multitude of feelings, that could be causing you sadness or sorrow or humiliation; that just isn't healthy."

Ted elaborated on the fact that we teach boys to *solve* problems, but not how to *process* problems. When a boy tells his friend that his parents are getting divorced, the friend doesn't ask, *How does this make you feel?* We need to teach boys how to process their own emotions, and how to process feelings with one another. This reminded me of the hundreds of conversations I have had with women who say, "I don't want him to fix anything. I just want to talk about my feelings, and for him to listen to me and discuss things with me." Ted agrees. He added, "This is one of the most uncomfortable things for a man to do. It is like a foreign language—and many men even experience anxiety when a partner asks us to process feelings because we don't know how to talk about emotions. You have a flat tire? Fine, I'll go fix it. But I don't know how to talk to you about how the tire got flat, or how you felt when it happened. When men are asked to process emotions with a partner or a friend, they freeze. And the reason for this is because we're not teaching boys how to articulate their feelings."

APPROACH #3. CALL OUT BAD BEHAVIOR

Adults regularly correct children's behavior on a slew of issues. This is just part of being a parent, stepparent, guardian, coach, or teacher. Issues around gender are no different. It might be a bit more awkward to correct a gendered mistake than, say, biking on the wrong side of the road or leaving a wet cup on a wood surface. But kids don't know they've made a mistake unless we (gently, kindly) point it out to them.

This begins when children are small, when gentle reminders or explanations help them to form opinions about the world and how it works. Zack and his husband, Greg, spend a week every summer with their niece and nephew. Last year, when the kids were only three and six, they were pulling out some toys to play with in the afternoon. The girl chose a doll and handed it to her uncle. This prompted a snide comment from her older brother; essentially explaining that Uncle Zack doesn't want to play with dolls because he is a boy. "We corrected him and said, 'Oh no—Uncle Zack loves to play with dolls; dolls are for everyone.' And then I made sure to play dolls every day during that week." Zack was glad he was the one who was there when his nephew made that comment, but it made him wonder what other comments his nephew said throughout the year. "He has such strong ideas about gender, and he's so young. I keep thinking, *Does anyone else take the time to correct him?*"

Kids start to perceive gender roles from a very young age, and the gender messages they receive outside the home might be more traditional than inside the home. Zack's nephew could have picked up his ideas about girls and dolls from a friend, classmate, cartoon, or neighbor. This means we need to be vigilant about correcting mistakes in these early years.

This gets tougher as kids get older. Ethan, who is the special-education high school teacher, talked a lot about how he deals with aggressive behavior, both physical and verbal. "We need to hold boys accountable for aggressive behavior. [When they act out] we have to explain why oppression is bad and give them some alternative behaviors. *Don't do this—but you can do this.* [We can't just tell them no; we have to also] give them the skills to succeed." Ethan believes this also links with teaching empathy; we have to help boys understand how their actions affect others, and help them feel compassion.

We first met James in chapter 5. As a college coach, he finds himself in the awkward position of correcting the behavior of young men—not boys. By college, his athletes have achieved a great deal of independence, which can make them harder to reach. James realizes that, as their coach, he has a unique influence with this group of young men; he knows his players listen to what he has to say. He does not take that lightly.

Like his father did for him, James tries to help the young men on his team work through issues around justice and oppression, and help them to recognize mistakes they make that might cause others hurt or harm—even if accidentally. He addresses sexual violence and gender issues head on, even if he happens to overhear an off-hand comment on the bus or in the locker room. James also had some great ideas on how to use social media to his benefit. "I make it a point to follow [all my players] on social media, and I have a word with them when they like or repost something oppressive. I am just honest with them, and I ask things like, *Do you agree with this? What do you think about it? Is this something you want to put your name behind?* It is a good way to initiate some of those hard conversations that don't come up during a usual practice."

I will also note that James is a big fan of empowerment. "I treat my players like men. I give them the tools they need to do things themselves, and then I sit back and trust them to make good decisions. This way, they can look back and feel pride in their accomplishments."

Gary agreed about calling out bad behavior, but warned about snapping back with a quick "don't do that" response. We should not police every mistake a boy or young man makes. That could drive their private lives underground, where we can no longer be an influence at all. Instead, respond by asking questions and open up a dialogue. "The key is staying in relationship with the boy. So often our discipline or punishment sends boys away, rather than requiring them to stay in dialogue. We need to help them make sense of the harm they may have caused."

Ted added that beyond discipline, we need to get at the root of the problem, and involve a larger community in that conversation. "If a group of boys does something wrong, then it would probably be a good idea to involve the whole class [or the whole team] in a conversation about why that was wrong and how it impacted others. I would even consider bringing their fathers [or father figures] in, too, and including them in a broader conversation."

APPROACH #4. FORGIVE MISTAKES AND MOVE ON

As important as it is to correct bad behavior, it is equally important to allow boys to make mistakes.

We have met Hal and Michelle in previous chapters. I mentioned that Hal is Japanese American and that he grew up in a white suburb in Montana. Hal's dad was the high school football coach, and Hal also played football. "Growing up I thought my father did more than he actually did. It wasn't until I grew up that I realized how little he did around the house. And really, he was even a little sexist."

Hal tried his best to follow his father's lead, and it wasn't until college that he started to see the world differently than before. In class he watched a documentary titled *Tough Guise,* which introduced him to the field of masculinities. "Before, I would have called myself a jock, but I had a real awakening after watching that film. They do a good job of showing how images in pop culture make men bigger and more powerful, and how images of women started to shrink." Hal had always understood racial inequity, and in college he was able to understand the intersection of race and gender. Hal became interested in anti-violence work, and after graduation he took a job at a nonprofit organization that works in combatting domestic violence. He met and married Michelle, and they had two children. At the time of the interview, the kids were six and ten years old.

When we spoke about mistakes and how to correct them, Hal explained that we can't shame boys to the extent that they will no longer listen. Kids are kids; they make mistakes—it is how they learn. If we berate kids, or hold mistakes over their heads, the learning ends, and they become resentful. Yes, we need to correct mistakes. Then we need to forgive and move on.

Hal was also very clear that we need to be aware of how children of color are held to a different standard. "We're scared to let our Brown and Black kids make mistakes because, of course, there is fear they will be disproportionately penalized. So, we hold them to a higher standard—which goes back to the concept of a model minority. We have to break out of this social pattern. We have to let all kids make mistakes; we have to let ourselves make mistakes. And when mistakes happen, we just call it out and we move on. We can't allow ourselves to be shamed because we achieve something less than perfection."

Henry would agree. He was the man supporting his partner, Reza, during medical school. Henry spoke about allowing mistakes as well, but in the context of LGBTQ+ children. "For too long we have sanitized our community, which also happens in other marginalized groups. Gay couples and queer kids feel like they have to be squeaky clean to participate in the mainstream. We need to collectively allow everyone mistakes, and allow everyone growth."

Both Hal and Henry talked about how privilege allows children to make mistakes. It is a luxury to make a mistake and not have that mistake tied to your identity. Often, when a white boy makes a mistake, it is seen as just a mistake; something to be forgiven. But if a Black boy makes a mistake, all Black boys are seen as guilty. When a boy who identifies as queer makes a mistake, the behavior is linked to his sexual orientation. Hal and Henry wish all teachers, parents, coaches, and community members could allow kids to just make mistakes, simply because they are kids.

Sarah agreed that this is in line with what academics know about discipline. We need to correct the mistake/action/behavior—not the person. "Perhaps the child said something wrong, but *he* is not wrong. He might have said something sexist, but he is not necessarily sexist." It is also good to acknowledge whether mistakes are made due to a lack of information or a lack of experience. "Explaining and discussing the situation may be the only thing needed to prevent a repeat in the future."

Gary added that accountability has to be relational. We can't just give out a heavy penalty and hope the problem goes away. That is the easy way out, and that is not how learning happens. "We need to call out problems, but then send the message, *I'm not going to walk away. I am going to stick it out with you. And we're going to get through this together.*"

APPROACH #5. ENCOURAGE FEMALE FRIENDS

Many of the men I interviewed talked about how important it was to have female friends throughout their childhood and adolescence. Not romantic relationships, but platonic friends. Some gravitated toward female friends when they were othered from the guys; others had female friends in addition to their male buddies. These female friends helped many EP40 refine their worldview—when you have friends who are women, and you hear their struggles being a woman, it is easier to "see" sexism as a man.

John talked a lot about his female friends during our conversation. John was born in Mumbai, India, to an upper middle-class family. His father took a job overseas when he was seven, which provided the family with more money but left his mother to raise John and his younger brother alone. The extra money meant John was able to attend a private high school. He did well academically, was active in sports, participated in many after-school programs, and had lots of friends. He didn't feel othered; he felt accepted. John had the luxury of spending his free time studying or doing activities because his mother and grandmother saw to his every need. "I would come home with a filthy soccer uniform, and by the next morning it was magically clean." He admitted that most of the families he grew up with role modeled a stereotypical household divide. "As a male, I was actually discouraged from going into the kitchen."

But John started to see another side of life when he befriended several young women in high school. I asked him why he sought out female friends—was it that he was rejected from the boys? "No, not at all. I was captain of the soccer team. I had many good guy friends, and we're actually still close. I just found girls to be considerably more mature at that age; we were all sixteen, seventeen. And that appealed to me." Many of his female friends felt trapped; they were smart, they got great grades, and yet they were being forced into marriage as soon as they graduated. "They told me lots of stories about the social pressure they faced. Many of them faced early marriages. . . . I learned how to listen, and I internalized those stories. These were important things that were impacting their lives. I've always valued independence, individuality, the ability to have aspirations and goals. And these girls were being limited." It is no wonder that when he later met his wife, it was precisely her independence and her individuality that sealed his attraction.

This is something we can all encourage with the boys in our lives. Sisters and female cousins are fantastic, when available. For all-boy families, parents may have to be even more intentional. When kids are little, adults can arrange playdates and activities with kids of all genders to normalize mixed-sex relationships. Sign your son up for a co-ed sports club or art class. During the teenage years, of course boys will choose their own friends. Perhaps the best thing adults can do at this stage is back off, and not tease or make embarrassing comments about girl friends being "girlfriends."

Adults can also remind boys not to stereotype. We can validate an individual's feelings without making sweeping comments about one sex or the other. Say something when you hear a boy make a statement like, *All the girls in my class are* X or *All of the girls at my school want to do* Y. Remind him that one girl's behavior is simply that— one girl's behavior. Stereotypes are false and potentially dangerous. After all, he would not want people to make assumptions about him based on what other boys do. We need to extend the same respect to people of all genders.

Being an expert on anti-violence, Ted had a lot to say about this issue. "We bond over conquest. And we teach our boys to do the same. And one of the most common conquests that we seek to achieve is the objectification of women and girls. The purpose of a girl is not to have a friend—it is to be the object for our conversation. So, if a boy has a platonic female friend, the implication is that he has either failed at this conquest, or he isn't interested in girls. And both are considered wrong. And this is in the air that all boys breathe—it is in their collective socialization. This explains sexual assault in the military, on college campuses—why women between the ages of sixteen and twenty-four are at the highest risk for being sexually assaulted, and why when a woman says no, boys either try harder or try to get her drunk."

To counter this air that boys breathe, we must explicitly and pointedly counter this concept. We need to tell boys, over and over, that female friends are great. That having a female friend does not mean failure—just the opposite.

Ted was also careful to note that we can't always fall back on making a comparison with a boy's female family members, for example, saying, *Would you want someone to treat your sister that way?* "I hear men all the time threaten to beat up the guy who talks to his sister, but then he goes and does it to another guy's sister. There's a huge disconnect there. And this is really what patriarchy is all about, protecting the specific women in your life instead of genuinely respecting all women. We need boys to be friends with all kinds of people to help them recognize our shared humanity."

APPROACH #6. JUST . . . TALK

If traditional masculinity is characterized as emotionally distant, quiet, and stoic—the EP40 believe in a more open and honest dialogue with boys. We should never assume that boys understand an unsaid truth, or something that seems obvious to you but has gone unspoken. Quite the opposite—we need to talk. And perhaps even more importantly, we need to listen.

Elton works hard to maintain conversations every day. We have not yet met Elton; Elton was the man in chapter 5 who said he grew up "almost homeless." He is from Illinois and identifies as Black. Elton, like many other EP40, grew up with role models who showed him what not to do. "Some people will do anything for a dollar. But not me. There are things I value more than money—like honesty and being a stand-up person. I mean, money is nice. But being a good person is more important." He met Imani in high school. He converted to Islam, and they married. At the time of our interview, their children were twenty-five and fourteen. The elder child was living at home working on a graduate degree, and the younger was in high school.

Elton has always been responsible for taking the kids to and from school—for both kids when they were younger, and now for his teenage son. (If Imani had her druthers, she would have had the kids take the bus. But Elton was adamant about providing a ride, so she went along with it.) Elton told me that those car rides offer time to just talk to his son, to hear stories from school, and listen to his son's concerns. "You have to meet kids where they are, and work to understand them the best you can. Adults do a lot of talking—but I think it is more important to listen to your kids. Really work to know them. That's when you have the chance to teach them the lessons they need." Elton knows when his son is faced with a tough decision, is stressing about a test, or has a problem with a friend. It doesn't always come out right away. But Elton knows that if he is there, every day, it eventually comes out.

Some routines occur less frequently, but are no less important. In chapter 6 we learned how Hector pushes back on gender norms when visiting his in-laws. He explained that having direct conversations with his son is an important follow-up to all of those visits with extended family. Hector does not assume anything; he pointedly initiates conversations to process experiences and make sure he and his son maintain an open line of communication and dialogue. "I know our family seems foreign to him because he sees the world very differently than they do. . . . When we visit family, it almost always ends in a car conversation on the way home. We explicitly call out [things that were done or said] during the visit to help him see norms that we do not adhere to. We ask him questions and give him the space to process his experiences. Those car conversations are really important."

Other conversations are not embedded in routines at all; they are special, stand-alone moments. Martin did not grow up talking to men in his family, and this is something he is changing in his life now. Martin was the boy deemed the man of the house at age twelve; although his father was gone, he did have other male role models in his life. Sadly, those men did not give Martin what he wanted. "Men did not provide what I needed growing up. When I turned eighteen, do you know what they did? They all got together and took me to a strip club and blew a bunch of money they didn't have on booze and women." He took a long pause, as if allowing me the time to digest the many implications of what he just told me. "Let me tell you, that is not what a young man needs from his family. Not at all."

Martin is now trying to rewrite some family traditions. He can't stop his cousins or nephews from going to a strip club, but he doesn't have to join. Instead, he recently invited a few of his teenage nephews and cousins out to dinner. He left his own kids at home, so he could focus his attention on the young men. "We went for pizza and just sat and talked. I asked them about how things were going in school, and we talked about some of the challenges they are facing. I offered my help where I could. I asked them what their next steps were—after high school graduation. I told them explicitly, 'Whatever you need, I am here for you.' *This* is what we need from older men. We need guidance and love and patience and help. This is what I want to be for the next generation."

Sarah believes that quality communication is, of course, important, but she agrees you can't always schedule those amazing moments. "If there isn't sufficient quantity, how can we possibly hope for sufficient quality?" Spending more time talking with your kids, like Elton does, increases the likelihood of quality moments.

Gary was careful to point out that we don't want to perpetuate this idea that a boy needs a male role model to be a real man; that is a stereotype we're trying to break. "But we do live in a gendered world, and most often, boys don't see men as emotionally available as they see women. And we need as many men as possible to break that mold (uncles, friends, cousins, fathers, neighbors) to show boys that we can be emotionally expressive, and we can be vulnerable and show our full humanity. And yes, that happens through role modeling. But it also happens through dialogue: asking questions of each other and providing honest answers."

Gary also made an important point about *how* fathers talk to their kids. Talking is a great start—but it is *what* men talk about that can be transformative. "We interviewed boys and their parents on the East Coast and the West Coast from a variety of political backgrounds. Again and again, we heard how boys go to their mothers when they feel vulnerable or about emotional issues, while dads, they told us, are for doing and playing. Even as we work to push against outdated ideas of manhood, we continue to separate the world that way—that moms provide emotional support and dads not so much. That's why it's so important that boys see their fathers, as well, as nurturing, able to express emotions, so boys feel they, too, can develop their full emotional repertoire."

TURNING LESSONS INTO ACTIONS

Aside from the five approaches listed above, I want to ensure all the lessons from the EP40 are captured. Their origin stories, motivations, and strategies can all translate into actions that we can use with young people. Again, the following lessons may be particularly important for boys in order to counter gendered social norms. But I believe these suggestions are helpful in working with children of all genders. Instead of teaching our kids how to operate in the Female Role or the Male Role, the following advice can help us better prepare all children for a more gender-equitable life.

EP40 ADVICE FOR RAISING THE NEXT GENERATION

Expose Kids to a Range of Possibilities	Travel to another place is fantastic, but not necessary. You can also visit a library or museum, or have regular video calls with friends in another state.
Teach Self-Sufficiency	Take a lesson from the single parents: there is great value in teaching kids the importance of taking care of themselves. Take time to teach kids how to do physical tasks, and teach them how to be a cognitive laborer.
Bridge to Gender	If the child in your life isn't responding to conversations about gender, start with an issue that resonates with them, for example, racism, xenophobia, ableism, or ageism. Help them see the link between all forms of oppression and injustice.
Value Caregiving	Help create opportunities for the kids in your life to be caregivers. Give kids positive feedback when they take on caregiving roles, and tell them directly how important caregiving is to your family and your community. Normalize boys and men in caregiving roles.
Fix or Listen?	When a child comes to you with an issue, it is OK to clarify—*Are you asking me to fix this, or are you asking me to listen?* More often you might find that they just want you to listen. This is less pressure—you don't have to think about solutions. You can just listen and be the support they need
Make the Most of Teachable Moments	No one would ever wish their child to be othered, but if it does happen, use it as a teachable moment. Talk to the child about how being othered makes them feel, and how they can use that empathy to show others kindness in the future.
Discuss Negative Role Models	Do not pretend toxic behavior does not exist. If kids see this behavior, talk directly about it and the consequences. Ask them how that behavior makes them feel and where it might come from, and then help them explore alternative options.
Reinvent Old Stereotypes	Adapt the EP40's broad definition of "providing for the family." Talk about how all parents can provide for the family financially, and all parents can provide for the family by doing caregiving and household work.

Assign Domains	Make sure you don't assign chores based on gender, and when kids are old enough, try assigning them an appropriate "domain" so they learn to take responsibility for both the physical tasks and the cognitive labor involved, for example, keeping one room tidy or cooking dinner once a week.
Model Vulnerability	The more kids witness vulnerability, the more they'll be able to make themselves vulnerable to others.
Call out Gender Stereotypes	We've talked about correcting mistakes that your child makes, but also draw their attention to gender stereotypes around them. When a cartoon princess has a head twice as big as her waist, when a sitcom falls back on the buffoon-dad trope, or when a song lyric describes gender-based violence—say something. Explain why you disagree, and ask your kids to share their feelings with you.
Don't Ignore the Intersection of Race and Gender	Talk to your kids about the connection between race and gender, and be honest about the fact that gender norms are compounded for people of color.
Encourage Passions	Encourage every child to follow their interests and passions, especially if they go against gender norms. If necessary, help your child navigate around peer pressure or bullying. No child should be dissuaded from following their passion because of their gender.
Give Consistent Praise	Be careful not to dole out unearned praise to boys. Praise all children evenly.
Set High Household Standards	Don't build a glass ceiling above the boys in your life. Do not assume they cannot or should not do something because of their gender identity. Set your expectations high for children of all genders, and hold them all accountable.
Reinforce the Message	Repetition matters. Make use of as many of these themes as possible. It also helps if the messages come from a range of people, not just parents.

BIRTHDAY PARTIES

I would be remiss if I completed this chapter about the next generation without writing about birthday parties. Although I am not labeling this as a specific approach, it is something that came up in many of my EP40 and EP+ interviews.

Birthday parties are a huge part of the little-kid calendar. Weekend parties are routine in our household, and they always seem to be a hot topic of conversation. Birthdays for little kids are notoriously gendered, and they reaffirm the stereotypes we're working hard to combat. So, though each of us may host only one or two parties a year, collectively this is a social institution that deserves some attention.

Retail outlets don't make it easy on parents. Our local party store has two aisles of birthday party accessories, one clearly coded for boys and one clearly coded for girls. The colors and branding are so severe that when my son initially wanted a Peppa Pig birthday party, he mysteriously changed his mind when we walked into the store and discovered all the Peppa paraphernalia was in the "pink aisle."

Any parent who is trying to get through their errand list on the weekend and dashes into the party store for accessories is highly likely to fall into a gender trap, simply because there is no other option. This means that, unfortunately, throwing a gender-neutral party can actually take more work—which is a lot to ask of an already busy parent. To help, I collected a few simple (and not terribly time-consuming) suggestions for rewriting gender norms at little-kid birthday parties:

- Depending on how much control you have of the invitation list, try to include both boys and girls at the party. Parties can get gendered very quickly when the guests are all male or all female.
- If invitations are sent by email, send the email to all parents and guardians—not just the person in the Female Role. Put social events on everyone's radar.

- Feel free to choose a mixed-sex party theme based on your child's interests, without worrying about a theme being masculine or feminine. I was actually thrilled when my son was invited to a Rainbow Unicorn party last year—his classmate unapologetically filled her party with pastels and glitter, and he loved every minute.

- If you want to choose a more neutral theme that appeals to everyone (this might be more important with older kids), stick with primary colors and choose a theme that is not coded male or female, for example, animals, sea creatures, travel, miniature golf, space, Harry Potter, glow-in-the-dark, etc.

- During free play, you might see evidence of the male/female divide that naturally happens on the school playground. Try to bring everyone together by offering a balance of high-energy games (tag, dancing) and low-energy games (coloring, puzzles) to suit the interests of everyone present.

- Use mixed groups for teams or games.

- Try your best not to feed into gender stereotypes by saying things like, *Oh, you girls are so polite* or *You boys need to go run and burn off some steam.* This is especially important for single-sex parties.

- My biggest pet peeve: do not provide different goody bags for boys and girls. Please give out the same treats to everyone. Either include a mix of male-coded and female-coded items for all, or intentionally stick to gender-neutral items like crayons, candy, or Silly Putty. Once, my daughter left a party with a coupon for a free ice-cream cone at our local scoop shop, which I thought was a brilliant idea: not gender coded, and it didn't fill our house with more junk.

TWO MORE IDEAS—INSPIRED BY THE EP40

I have started two experiments in my own home, with my own kids, based on the information I collected from the EP40 and EP+.

1. NOTICING TIME: The concept of household Noticer came up time and time again. People frustrated with their relationship noted that their partner did not notice what needed to be done in the house. People happy with their relationship noted that both people in the relationship were Noticers. I started to wonder how to teach this concept to my kids.

Assigned chores are great. But chores are specific and routine; kids learn to complete their chore list without much thought. And chores do not necessarily teach kids to notice what else needs to be done in the home. So, I started something we have come to call *Noticing Time*.

Every day (OK, honestly, if I remember a few days a week, I am thrilled), I set my phone alarm for twenty minutes and tell my kids it is Noticing Time. All they have to do is walk around the house and do anything they see needs doing. I specifically do not give them instructions or a task list, and I don't really mind what they choose. Anything that they accomplish is one less thing Evan or I have to do.

At first, this experiment was comical. At ages six and nine they would stand in the middle of our wreck of a family room and shrug. "Mo-om! The house is fine! What am I supposed to do?" But after several weeks, they started to notice the empty cups on the side table, the wrappers under the couch, the toys in the yard, the various items accumulated on the stairs, and the mystery fork next to the TV. They started to notice the places that got messy quickly—like their bathroom sink—and they returned to those places as go-to jobs. Over time, they have simply become better at "seeing" what has to be done in the house.

Full disclosure—they often choose not to see the mess; sadly, they still seem to have a high threshold for clutter. But at least they are now capable of turning on their Noticer lens when asked. After several months of Noticing Time, they rarely ask for help on what to do. When I set my timer, they might complain, but they can always find something that needs doing. And every now and then they are even proud of their noticing accomplishments.

I believe this could work in a range of situations, not just for parents or stepparents. Anyone with kids in their life could initiate Noticing Time: grandparents, caregivers, teachers, aunts, uncles, and friends. I think this would be great for a day care. And even if you do not role model household equality, this activity is something any adult could do with the kids in their life to help prepare them to share the cognitive labor.

2. EMOTIONS LIST: After my interview with Mike, I wanted to encourage empathy and be more intentional about the way I teach my kids to articulate emotions. Despite the literature, I didn't think my daughter was any better at explaining her feelings than my son, and this worried me. So, one afternoon I sat down with a marker and a piece of card stock and wrote a list of thirty emotions. I avoided sad, happy, and angry, and instead tried to find words rarely used in the little-kid lexicon: humiliated, melancholy, proud, excluded, giddy, and misunderstood.

Most days, the *Emotions List* lives on the refrigerator door unnoticed. But every few weeks, when the kids exhibit more extreme emotions for one reason or another, we have found the list to be helpful. In these instances, my husband or I will pull the list down and go through the vocabulary words one by one. The kids tell us which ones apply to their mood and which do not. They can usually identify at least a few words that resonate that day, which allows us to follow up and ask, *Why did you choose that word? What happened today that made you feel that way?* And every now and then, we think of a new word to add to the list. Our Emotions List is growing with them, helping us all identify and use more nuanced vocabulary to describe feelings.

I can see how someone might think this kind of list is cumbersome—more trouble than it is worth. But I have actually found the opposite—it actually makes parenting easier. I don't have to start from scratch every time my kids get upset. The list is an easy go-to tool that allows our family to pinpoint a variety of emotions rather quickly. It helps my kids identify their feelings and explain the situations behind those feelings. Perhaps the best outcome is that I am slowly noticing the Emotions List is also helping them understand what *others* might be going through. Just like Mike explained, the ability to empathize with others starts with the acknowledgment of one's own feelings.

Months after our interview, I wrote Mike to tell him how he inspired my Emotions List. I was thrilled when he validated the exercise and added some further thoughts. "The most important piece here is understanding where the emotion came from and why. That can be difficult to put together even for adults, so learning it at a young age is important. For siblings, you can bring kids into each other's processes to help them be on both sides of the conversation. This helps them have compassion for other people's emotions. [In the end, any way we can help them] learn how to identify, express, and manage emotions; these are skills which are critical for healthy relationships of all kinds."

Clearly, Noticing Time and my Emotions List are not scientific studies, and they may or may not have a lasting impact. (Ask me in ten years, and I'll let you know how it turned out.) I also do not necessarily recommend these for all families; everyone needs to choose what works best for them. But I wanted to share some examples of how I am turning the EP40's recommendations into practice in my own home. If you come up with a new kid-related gender activity based on the EP40's advice, I'd love to hear about it.

NOTES

Before you move on to part 3, use this space to make some personal notes from chapters 5–8. Jot down the stories from the EP40 and EP+ that resonated with you. What intentions do you have for the children in your life? ____

_____

_____

_____

_____

_____

_____

_____

_____

_____

_____

_____

PART THREE

LIVING GENDER EQUALITY

9

A MORE EQUAL SELF

As promised in the introduction, part 3 is focused on actions we can take to support household gender equality. I have tried to weave action ideas and stories throughout this book so you did not have to wait until now to think about how to apply this information. But these last two chapters will focus entirely on deciding which changes you personally are going to make in your daily life. Because chapter 8 was devoted to the next generation, this section focuses more on adult relationships.

Before already highly gender-aware readers dismiss this section, I want to remind you that our understanding of gender continues to evolve. The way I thought about gender in 2000 and 2020 are very different. I have to remind myself that the way I will think about gender in 2040 and 2060 will be different than today, but I can't get there if I don't allow myself the space to evolve. I ask readers to also allow themselves the space to grow and evolve, to be open to the fact that none of us is perfect—and everyone has the capacity to improve.

Let's begin with internal actions: your own thoughts, beliefs, and words. The way you think about an issue, and the way you choose to communicate your thoughts, will influence how you engage with others. To begin, I would like you to complete four social change mini-actions. All of these mini-actions are practical steps, designed to help readers transition from learning to doing.

As you complete the following mini-actions, remember the various levels of interaction in our lives. There's our own personal self, our immediate household, our family and friends, our work space(s), and our greater community.

The first four are fairly straightforward, and easy to define. But "community" is going to look quite different to each reader. Some of our communities are small: a neighborhood, an alumni group, a yoga studio, or a bowling league. Some of our communities are large: a city, a faith community, a university community, an ethnic group, or a state. Some people even define community at a national—or even international—level. Some people belong to two communities, and some people belong to twenty.

Take a moment to identify your communities. Then, weave as many as you can into your mini-actions on the following pages. Please note, there is no expectation of rewriting gender norms in *all* of these spaces, *all* the time. I work in gender for a living, and I have my limits, too. Everything in life ebbs and flows; sometimes you focus on yourself, sometimes you focus on your own partnership, sometimes you focus on grandkids, and sometimes you take a break completely. Life offers us different opportunities for engagement at different times. I simply ask that you be aware of the range of possibilities here, so you'll be ready when the right opportunity comes along.

FOUR SOCIAL CHANGE MINI-ACTIONS

1. CHOOSING YOUR ROLE MODELS

We often think about our role models as people we knew growing up: our parents, family members, community leaders, and teachers. According to the EP40, some of those childhood role models were amazing, and some of them were—well, less than amazing. There are people whom we looked up to as kids, and we still look up to them today. There are also people who used to be our role models, but as adults we realize we don't want to emulate their behavior after all. Now that you want to be more intentional, it may be time to consider adding some new role models to your life.

It can be easy to set aside a negative role model; someone who has demonstrated violence, bigotry, or toxic masculinity is probably a no-brainer. But what about someone you still love? Someone you still admire? A woman I interviewed years ago (we'll call her Angela) told me how she struggled to live up to her mother, a woman whom she adored, even revered. Angela's mom was an immigrant who came to the United States with little education and little money. Despite the language barrier, economic disadvantage, and structural racism, she worked hard, did the vast majority of the housework and child-rearing, and saved to put her kids through college. Angela couldn't remember her mom complaining—even once. To Angela, this was what motherhood was supposed to be; her mother role modeled what she was supposed to be when she was a mom.

But now that Angela was a mom, she frequently felt that she was failing. She didn't face the same economic or educational challenges as her mother, but she was still struggling to balance her career and her family within her own neo-traditional home. Angela felt guilty when she complained because her mother never did. She felt inadequate when she broke down because her mother was always so strong. Based on our conversation, I would guess she was in the Coping category from chapter 7.

In this circumstance, I wonder if Angela (and all the other Angelas out there) should stop thinking of her mother as a role model. These moms could continue to be a rock, a support, a friend, a confidant, and a cheerleader. But if Angela doesn't feel like she can live up to her mom's heroism (and let's be honest, no one should have to live up to that level of heroism), then maybe the role models she's looking for are a bit more attuned to the challenges of raising children in the twenty-first century. There might be other role models from whom Angela can seek guidance or insights. I know it can be hard to leave some role models aside, especially those people we care about. But it can also be freeing to choose people who set a more realistic example for us.

Thankfully, as adults, we have access to a huge range of people to choose from. We have extended families, teachers, friends, colleagues, coaches, community members, experts . . . the possibilities are limitless. We can choose role models whom we know personally, or people whom we do not know personally.

For example, I consider my friend Rachel a role model. Her kids are much older than mine; when my son was in diapers, her boys were finishing college. But I looked at the close relationship she had with her grown sons, and as I held my newborn I thought, *I want that, too! Someday, this is the kind of relationship that I want with my son.* So, I adopted Rachel as a role model. I watch how she interacts with her adult boys—the way she continues to nurture those relationships, while also giving her sons their freedom. Rachel's role modeling helps me make decisions at the little-kid stage that will (hopefully) prepare me for decisions at the big-kid stage.

Take a few moments to think through the following two reflection questions. If you like, write down your answers. Remember— role models don't *need* to know they're role models. Of course, you're welcome to demonstrate vulnerability and tell them. They might be flattered. But if you think that information would strain your relationship, then just keep this information to yourself. To be honest, I didn't even tell Rachel she was a role model for me until I wrote this book.

Which role models are you ready to shed? Don't think of this as rejection—you might still value these people very much. But perhaps, at this point in your life, you are just not going to think of them as a role model.

Who are the people you want to adopt as role models? Think about people who role model healthy household dynamics and strong partnerships, or people who role model the kind of parent you strive to be.

MINI-ACTION 1: CHOOSING MY OWN ROLE MODELS

_____

_____

_____

_____

_____

2. BEING A ROLE MODEL TO OTHERS

Just as you look to others—people look to you! Whether you like it or not, you are probably a role model to someone, and that comes with a fair amount of influence and responsibility. If you are a teacher, coach, or parent, then it is quite likely you are closely scrutinized (perhaps more than you wish). But everyone role models behavior to those around them. Just as you want to be purposeful in who you look to as a role model, you want to be purposeful in what behavior you role model to others.

Where do you have influence? Take a moment to think about who might look to you (consciously or subconsciously) as a role model. It could be a family member, friend, student, colleague, neighbor, and/or person in your faith community.

Don't worry—there's no contract here. You don't need to formalize this relationship. You don't even need to share this information with others. The purpose of completing this mini-action is to help us be more intentional with our words and our actions when we're around a person who may look up to us.

MINI-ACTION 2: CHOOSING TO BE A ROLE MODEL TO OTHERS

3. IDENTIFYING ALLIES

As we have discussed throughout this book, altering social norms is *hard*. We live and work in an environment built on generations of cultural and institutional patriarchy. Not everyone you know is going to care about gender inequity. Hopefully, every reader has at least a few people in their life who are gender allies. Some might be able to rattle off twenty allies, and others may struggle to identify two. But all you need is a starting place; even one ally is enough.

Let's start with people. Take a moment to think about specific people in your life who share your value of gender equality and will likely be interested in a conversation about this topic—people who will listen to you and respect your opinion. There might be some obvious choices, like an outspoken aunt or colleague. But don't forget the unusual suspects who might not be vocal about gender, but whom you suspect care about these topics. Who in your life shares your interest in gender equality, and who will help you live your own gender values? Most of us will have at least a few of these people in our life already. We don't need to see them every day—or even live in the same place. If they are a text, call, or email away—that works.

It is also good to look for allies in spaces—both physical spaces and virtual spaces. Where do you feel you can talk about issues around gender equality? It might be a Zoom group of high school friends, a book group, or a volunteer organization. It might be at home with your partner and kids. It could be a space you go to most days, or a space you only go to once or twice a year.

Take a moment to write the name(s) of your allies and your friendly spaces in the box on the next page.

MINI-ACTION 3:
IDENTIFYING ALLIES I CAN TRUST

GENDER ALLIES: People I can trust:

_____

_____

_____

Spaces I can trust:

_____

_____

_____

If you can't think of many people or spaces—this is good information to have, too. This means you might want to think about creating this for yourself. Not immediately, of course. This is more of an "information to keep in the back of your mind" sort of thing.

One way to find supportive spaces is to join one that already exists. Remember Remy? He was the man who left his regular Thursday night happy hour after his high school friends harassed their server. He instead started volunteering at a garage on Thursday nights, fixing headlights for people who could not afford the bill. Although he was motivated to join this group because of altruistic reasons, he now looks forward to those Thursday nights—not only so he can help people who need a headlight fixed, but so he can hang out with new friends. I haven't asked Remy outright, but I would guess that he would consider this group of volunteer mechanics to be a safe space to bring up gender questions.

If your schedule is packed, try joining a virtual group. For dad-readers, you might try one of the online subgroups at Fathering Together. (I am an enthusiastic fan of the Dads for Gender Equity subgroup.) This international organization is devoted to connecting dads with one another, both geographically and by interest. Knowing that dads are busy, Fathering Together encourages members to join online events and chats whenever they have the time.

If you don't want to join an existing group, you can always create your own. This is not easy to do and certainly won't happen overnight. My friend Jennifer started a gender group with work colleagues back in 2014. She said she wanted a place to learn about gender topics related to her profession—but without the competition and posturing that has a way of sneaking into professional working groups. She began by inviting about a dozen colleagues (from inside and outside her organization) to lunch on the third Thursday of every month. Little by little, the group organically changed and grew; some members would leave, and new members would join. When the pandemic hit, the group moved to Zoom, and now they have a hybrid approach—most meetings on Zoom with a few in-person events a year.

The Third Thursday Gender Circle is still going strong. The listserv has grown to over one hundred names, and between ten and thirty people come any given month depending on the topic. Jennifer is also proud that one of the founding members started a gender breakfast group when she moved to California, and they now have over 150 members. So, what started as a small group of colleagues getting together for a chat has turned into 250+ people regularly talking about gender.

This book, or any gender-themed book (see more options in the additional resources section), could be a way to form a group. Reach out to some friends and ask if they're interested in piloting a book group. It might take off and become something more permanent, or it might stop with one conversation. Either way, you've helped move the social needle a little bit further. And every bit helps.

4. IDENTIFYING TRIGGERS

I define "triggers" as people who support a sexual division of labor, or people who undermine women's rights. These people are not likely to support you in being gender aware, and they are not likely to help you rewrite gender norms. In fact, they might even needle you for fun, thinking it is amusing when they get under your skin. We don't need to spend too much time on negative influences in your life, but I think it is good to have these people on your radar.

I used to have a trigger that I saw nearly every day at school pickup; her kids went to school with my kids, and we frequently bumped into each other in the parking lot. She was aware of my profession, what I write about, and what my views are on gender. Clearly, she disagreed. Not every day, but often enough, she would try to get a rise out of me. She would be telling a story and add, "Oh, you know how girls are; they are so emotional. Don't you agree, Kate? You say you know a lot about girls." I tried every tactic I know: I argued back; I tried to engage her in a thoughtful discussion; I smiled and changed the subject; and once, I even just rolled my eyes and walked away. No matter what I did, she did not stop.

I like to identify who these people are in my life for my own mental health. This way, when I am having a particularly hard day, or if I am feeling especially angry about a gender-related current event, I know to avoid interactions with these people—or at the very least, steer conversations with them into innocuous territory. I know that no good will come from a heated debate, and blowing a fuse or breaking down into tears would only make me feel worse in the long run. Knowing who my triggers are helps me set healthy boundaries.

Take a few moments to identify your own triggers.

MINI-ACTION 4: IDENTIFYING MY TRIGGERS

_____

_____

_____

_____

_____

CHOOSING THE RIGHT WORDS

I encourage you to return to your mini-actions every so often. As we move between houses and jobs, meet new friends and shed others, our circles change. It might be nice to flip back to this section every year or so and update your thoughts based on your current life and current friends.

For now, let's move on to talk about the words you choose to use. Do you ever catch yourself using words that accidentally reinforced traditional gender norms? How can you alter your vocabulary to be more supportive of equal partnership? I am sure there have been many things you have read in this book that have validated the words you already use, but hopefully, you've also read things that make you realize you could be doing better. (Let's be honest; we could all do better—myself very much included.)

I am including my personal Top 5 most gendered statements that I think we should all agree to avoid. Each one of these only reinforces the gender binary and harmful gender norms. It is imperative that we each vow not to use these in the future, and try our best to say something when we hear others use these tropes. I fully appreciate that power dynamics often dictate who can say something and when. An employee may be nervous about saying something to the boss; a new member of a group may be nervous about speaking out against an older member. But the less we collectively repeat these gendered phrases, the better.

Are there any statements you regularly hear that you wish people would stop using? Make a note here.

TOP 5 GENDERED STATEMENTS TO AVOID

1. *Boys will be boys.* This is almost always used to excuse bad behavior. This phrase can be used to reference little things for small boys (like getting clothes dirty) and big things for older boys (like making inappropriate advances toward women). Don't build the glass ceiling above his head—show him you think enough of him that you are setting expectations high.

2. *I have three kids—two children and a husband.* I am sorry to report I still hear this trope over and over. Comparing grown men to children is patronizing to men and perpetuates benevolent sexism.

3. *If you want it done right, ask a woman.* I admit that this sounds complimentary, but it only perpetuates the expectation that women

will carry the cognitive load, and excuses men from assuming their share of the work—not to mention the fact that this statement undermines the capacity of men.

4. *Girls are so . . .* or *Boys are so . . .* However this sentence ends, it makes a broad assumption that undermines individual agency. There are very few ways you can end this statement and ensure it is factually accurate. Is a teenage girl mean? Does a small boy turn every toy he owns into a weapon? Link those statements to that child's name, instead of making false, sweeping stereotypes.

5. *"Men are from Mars and women are from Venus."* All humans are from planet Earth, and it is only because we are socialized differently that we are led to believe we have different capabilities. Excuses like this one only perpetuate harmful gender stereotypes, and allow no room for growth or change.

6. _____

7. _____

8. _____

Some words just need to be tweaked to move us from gender default to gender aware. Below are several statements that I hear with some frequency. As currently used, they make harmful assumptions about the Female Role and the Male Role. With a few changes, they can help us rewrite harmful norms and actually be more supportive of equal partnerships. As you read through the following examples, put a star next to the ones you would feel comfortable using. I'll also leave some blank spaces at the end, so you can rewrite some of the phrases that you hear in your family or community.

IF YOU SAY THIS . . .	IT IS HARMFUL BECAUSE . . .	MAYBE SWITCH TO THIS . . .
1 *I was lucky enough to stay home with my kids when they were young.*	It probably wasn't luck, it was privilege. And saying this suggests that the "better" option is to stay home.	*The gender norms for my generation were different than they are now. There are many more options for people now than there were when I raised my kids.*
2 *Are you going to go back to work after the baby is born?*	We need to stop putting the onus on women alone. Rarely do people ask men if they plan to return to work after a baby.	*How are you and your partner going to balance work and childcare when the baby comes?*
3 *Men were different in my day. You're lucky to have such a great husband.*	This validates past behavior and leads to unearned praise.	*I am glad things are changing. I realize in hindsight that we have set the bar way too low for men.*
4 *What do you expect? He's just a man. They're basically useless.*	I understand that this is a joke, but I hear it way too often for it to be funny anymore. These comments release men of all responsibility, and put a greater burden on women.	*He let you down, and I am sorry for that. I am sure that was hard for you. He could do better, and he didn't.*
5 *It is so hard to be a working mom.*	We need to shift away from talking about motherhood and fatherhood as separate entities. We need to normalize the work that every parent puts into raising kids.	*It is so hard to be a working parent. There's a lot to juggle between job and home.*
6 *Frank isn't coming— again. His wife has him whipped.*	Wanting to be an equal partner doesn't mean you're "whipped" by your overbearing wife. It means you made the decision to take responsibility for your household.	*Frank isn't coming—he's got family stuff. That's cool—maybe he'll come in the future.*

7	*Moms* and *Dads*	Overusing these words can reinforce gendered expectations. Stop and ask yourself, *Is it really necessary to separate the two in this context?*	Use the word *parent* whenever you can. Try to bridge the cultural gap between *motherhood* and *fatherhood*.
8	*Girls* and *Boys*	Saying *boys* and *girls* only reaffirms our gender binary, and at that age, there really are very few biological differences that need to be noted. When you find yourself using the words *boy* or *girl,* stop and ask yourself—*Is it really necessary in this context?* This is probably especially important for educators, who are frequently at the helm of a large group of kids.	Use the words *kid, child, children,* or *friends* whenever you can. One study with preschool students concluded that something as simple as using the term *kids* to address the class promotes greater communication and more positive attitudes of the opposite sex.[1]
9			
10			

Who knows? Maybe others will start using your word choice, too. And when you hear someone exhibit gender awareness with their words, say so. I often borrow words and phrases, especially from Gen Z, who are growing up far more gender aware than I did. I try to tell people, *I like the way you said that* or *Thank you for phrasing it that way.* You never know—maybe your positive reinforcement will encourage them to use it again in the future.

10
A MORE EQUAL COMMUNITY

Choosing your own words is the first step. The true test is deciding how to use these words when you are with a friend, in a group, at the mall, or at work. When we hear gendered language, we often find ourselves in the uncomfortable position of having to make a split-second choice—to say something or not?

I am the first person to admit that it is not always best to correct a gender mistake. These conversations might not work for your triggers, for example. You may not feel comfortable correcting someone in a position of power and authority for fear of retaliation. There might be people in your life who are struggling with trauma or loss, in which case gender feedback would simply not be appropriate. Only you can weigh each situation and determine if this is the right moment or if this is the right person to offer feedback.

I find it is usually more effective to use a softer approach. If someone makes a sexist or gendered statement that you disagree with, try saying something like, *Actually, I don't agree with that.* Sometimes, that is all that is necessary; the speaker will rephrase. Remember that statistic from chapter 1: about 80 percent of Americans believe in the value of gender equality. When softly called out, many people will want to rephrase.

For the times when you do get a bit of pushback, it is nice to have a few tools to help you navigate those conversations. Here are some tried-and-true facilitator phrases to help you handle those awkward moments. Remember, when using any of these, try to correct the norm or the comment—and not the person. Accusing someone of misogyny and vilifying the individual is unlikely to get you the results you are after.

1. Offer an alternative perspective. This method avoids direct criticism of others by simply explaining what you do believe.
2. Give an example or story to illustrate your point. It could be a story from your own life, from the EP40, or another source. Contextualizing the situation can often be helpful.
3. Explain how the statement made you feel, or why their words made you feel uncomfortable. Then offer a possible alternative for them to use in the future.

The following is an example of what these phrases look like in an actual conversation. Imagine that you're at a work social event, chatting with a colleague who has a similar job title to your own. (In other words, you each have equal power in the workplace.) He makes the comment, "I make more money than my wife. So naturally, she is going to do more at home to compensate for that."

EXAMPLE LANGUAGE

1. Offer an alternative perspective.	*Actually, did you know that we have data that shows the opposite? Men married to women use that excuse a lot, but in the instances when men earn less than their wives, they don't do any more work in the home.*

2. Give an example or story.	*I read this book recently, and a quote from one of the guys interviewed really stuck out to me. He said that men shouldn't be limited to providing for their family in terms of finances or material goods, and that providing can be any kind of caregiving. I liked that idea—I hope that in the future men aren't restricted to paid work—that they can provide for their family in any number of ways.*
3. Explain how the statement made you feel.	*I'm going to be honest with you, that comment doesn't sit well with me. We know that there is a pay gap in our country, and women don't earn as much as men because of structural inequality. So, if all men used that same excuse, all women would be saddled with the domestic labor, which would prevent them from excelling at work, and we would just continue this cycle. And that makes me feel—well, depressed. We need to think about this in a big-picture kind of way.*

EVERYDAY WAYS TO BE GENDER AWARE

I am presenting ten scenarios that offer ideas on how we can better live our gender values every day. All of these scenarios stem from real stories that I heard while researching this book.

I do not propose that these are groundbreaking ideas—quite the opposite. I include the following scenarios precisely because they are typical day-to-day exchanges. You know those times when you search your home for an hour, only to find your keys sitting on the kitchen counter? Sometimes the answer is hidden in plain sight. I use these scenarios to illustrate exactly how our mundane encounters can be an impetus for change.

Of course, it would be impossible to think through all the possible scenarios where we can support household gender equality in our lives. I have only selected ten. The key message here is to look for opportunities to engage everywhere, and think outside of the box. For too long, we have focused the conversation about household balance between two people within the home. Each of us likely has more influence with more people than we realize.

As you read through them, decide which scenarios sound familiar or are more likely to happen in your communities. Check the ones that resonate with you most.

☐ SCENARIO 1. THE NEW MOM: Nancy is barely keeping it together. She is the mother of a three-year-old and a six-month-old. She works two part-time jobs to bring in the income she and her husband need to make ends meet. Although her supervisors tell her they are supportive of young families, she finds that, in reality, they are not very flexible with her schedule. She is constantly struggling to find childcare, get to work on time, and keep the house in order. Over the holidays, however, she finds herself at a family party. The kids are being passed around to various family members, and Nancy finds a rare moment to relax and catch up with her younger cousins, who are all single. They rave about how great she looks, how cute the baby is, and they ask, "How do you do it all? You make it look so easy!" Nancy takes a deep breath, and then tells everyone the truth.

IMMEDIATE OPPORTUNITY: Like menopause and miscarriage, cognitive household labor is not something we commonly talk about with young adults. But this need not be a taboo topic. We need to stop selling the "superwoman" story, be brave enough to be vulnerable, and be honest about how hard work and kids can be. The cousins probably can't do anything to help Nancy, but maybe Nancy can share some things that will eventually help her cousins.

BIG-PICTURE OPPORTUNITY: Be open and honest with others about how hard it is to balance work and parenting, and hold all parents accountable to the same standards, regardless of gender identity. Don't protect younger generations from our reality—just the opposite. We need them to see now what they can do to avoid a repeat situation.

☐ SCENARIO 2. VISITING NEPHEWS: An aunt has her nephews (ages three and five) over for their first-ever sleepover, giving the boys' parents a much-needed break. After dinner, they all pile on the couch to watch an animated movie. After a while, it becomes clear to the aunt that the father character in this movie is portrayed in a stereotypical buffoon role. Halfway through the movie, they decide to take a break to make popcorn and lemonade.

IMMEDIATE OPPORTUNITY: We live in a gendered world, and the only way we can teach kids to be gender aware is to help them "see" harmful gender norms, otherwise they'll come to accept these norms as fact and not cultural constructions. In this situation, the kids are little, so there is no need for big words or a long explanation. But while the popcorn is popping, the aunt has an opportunity for a teachable moment. She can remind her nephews that this is a pretend movie, and it isn't how they are expected to be as adults.

BIG-PICTURE OPPORTUNITY: I do not think it is ever too early to start pointing out gender socialization to kids. Even toddlers can understand simple, age-appropriate messages. Around small kids, and around big kids, we all have the opportunity to point out harmful gender norms. In her book *Boys and Sex,* Peggy Ornstein writes, "Back when my daughter was tiny, for example, I would point to

Disney heroines whose eyes were larger than their wrists. Are your eyes bigger than your wrists? And look at her waist! Where do you think she keeps her uterus, in her purse? Honestly, I doubt I would have done that with a son. Yet boys grow up in the same distorted, commodified, misogynist culture as girls." Ornstein's point is an important one; kids of all genders need help seeing overly feminized norms, and kids of all genders need help seeing hypermasculine norms.

⊜

☐ SCENARIO 3. SPEAKING UP: Eddie had gone to church with his dad every Sunday morning since he could remember. The pastor and congregation were part of his community, and by the time Eddie was a teenager, he had very positive associations with the church. One Sunday, however, there was a guest pastor who used the pulpit to talk about the evils of homosexuality. Eddie was confused. He knew his parents didn't have a problem with anyone's sexual orientation, but it was strange to hear these words coming from the front of the church—from a man who had so much power and influence.

IMMEDIATE OPPORTUNITY: It is one thing to teach our kids not to be bullies, but quite another to stand up to the bullies of the world. Nevertheless, that is exactly what Eddie's dad did. After the service, Eddie's dad explained that they needed to talk to the pastor, and he took his son to the courtyard where everyone had gathered for coffee. There, in front of the crowd, Eddie's dad told the preacher what he thought of the sermon, and that he should be ashamed for using the pulpit to preach hate. To this day, decades later, Eddie remembers this event; he remembers feeling proud of his dad for standing up for something he believed in. Eddie was glad his dad didn't have a private word with that pastor; that wouldn't have had the same effect. He was glad his father spoke his mind in a public space where everyone could hear. This experience gave Eddie the confidence to do the same in the future.

BIG-PICTURE OPPORTUNITY: The best way to teach our kids to stand up to bullies is to do it ourselves. In this situation, it was Eddie's father who spoke up. But anyone else in that congregation had the same opportunity to say something.

☐ SCENARIO 4. CHECKOUT LINE: Jerome was running errands with his daughter, Jasmine, who was four years old. At the checkout line of a big-box store, Jasmine was talking loudly about what she liked in the store and what she didn't like. She told her dad what she wanted for dinner, and that was followed by a list of foods she did not like. She talked about the weather being hot, and how she couldn't wait to get home and strip down and have a cold drink. When Jerome finally reached the till, the checkout lady rolled her eyes at him and said, "Looks like you have a real bossy one on your hands. Better watch that or she'll be a nightmare as a teenager."

IMMEDIATE OPPORTUNITY: It continues to amaze me that perfect strangers think that they are entitled to voice their opinion about someone else's child. Of course, it happens all the time. In this case, Jerome replied, "Would you have made that comment if I had a son with me?" Not surprisingly, the checkout woman didn't know what to say. Jerome, trying to smooth over the situation and ease her embarrassment, added, "It's OK. We just don't use the word *bossy* in our house. I like women who have strong opinions."

BIG-PICTURE OPPORTUNITY: When a stranger makes a gendered comment, we literally have an instant to decide if we're going to say something in response or keep quiet. (I admit, I tend to clam up in the moment, and then I think of a great retort hours later.) If you do want to say something, which I think is fine given the fact that this other person was comfortable making a comment in the first place, a good place to start is to ask a question. Revealing how gendered the comment was by flipping it is a safe tactic. *Would you have said that to a boy/girl/man/woman?* At least it makes people think, and makes it clear you don't agree with them.

☐ SCENARIO 5. JUST BETWEEN US GIRLS: Lilly's neighborhood is gearing up for a big summer block party, and she is co-organizing the kids' games section with Brad, a guy who lives down the street. Brad, however, did not come to the last two planning meetings, nor is he replying to group emails. After about a month of silence, the organizer of the event called Lilly. She explained, "Brad is just so busy; you know, his job is very taxing. But I think the two of us can figure this out—just between us girls—and have the details worked out in no time."

IMMEDIATE OPPORTUNITY: I find this situation interesting because, even though Lilly and Brad are not romantic partners, the typical neo-traditional split that we see in the household seems to be happening in a community setting. Perhaps Brad feels like he can ghost the planning meeting and group emails because he assumes Lilly will pick up the slack? And the organizer, though probably just wanting to finish her list and move on, is likely himpathizing with Brad. She has no problem asking another woman to do more work, and does not think to call Brad and reprimand him for slacking off.

No doubt, if Lilly played along, she could get this project done more quickly. But she thinks, *My paid job is just as "taxing" as Brad's. Why does he get to shirk his duty and I don't?* So, she clearly explains that both she and Brad have heavy work responsibilities, but they both willingly volunteered for this position, and they should both see it through. Either he resigns, or he pulls his own weight. Lilly is not going to allow Brad to receive accolades for community planning without doing any of the work.

BIG-PICTURE OPPORTUNITY: Household roles don't always stay in the household; they often transition into work and community situations. We need to be as intentional about setting boundaries outside the home as we do inside the home, and support others trying to do the same.

☐ SCENARIO **6.** CABIN TALK: Diego loved his weeks at summer camp more than any other time of the year. He loved the activities, the fire rings at night, and the freedom from all the day-to-day rules that existed in school. At night, in the dark of the cabin, the boys would sit around for hours and talk. They'd talk about sports, camp, school, and family—and this summer they also started talking a lot about girls. Lately, these conversations were getting a little vulgar, but the raunchier the comment the bigger the laughs, so Diego thought it was all harmless. One night, before bed, he made some graphic comments about a female camper's body and what he'd like to do to her. The other boys howled.

IMMEDIATE OPPORTUNITY: Although this may not directly relate to partnership, the way men and boys *talk* about women directly links to how they treat women. Are females smart, capable, respectable humans? Or are they sexual objects for male enjoyment? Fortunately, on this particular night, Diego's counselor happened to be listening. As soon as he heard Diego's comment, he flipped on the lights and confronted the group. He told the boys he was disappointed to hear them talk like that; their words were not appropriate. He asked them, "How do you think that girl would feel if she heard you talking this way? How would you feel if someone talked that way about you?" The counselor explained that he never spoke about women that way—and never would. That one conversation turned into a teachable moment that Diego would never forget. Decades later, he still remembers that night, and says he hasn't talked about a woman in the same way since.

BIG-PICTURE OPPORTUNITY: If you overhear a human talking about another human in a degrading way, say something, especially those of you in positions of influence. Men who are around boys probably have far more chances to do this than the rest of us. This puts great responsibility in the hands of fathers, uncles, coaches, teachers, and camp counselors.

☐ SCENARIO 7. PROVIDING: Carla has two grown daughters, both of whom are married and have families of their own. A few years back, her eldest daughter quit her job to be a stay-at-home mom. Carla was happy for her and supported her decision. Recently, her younger daughter made a similar decision, but it is her husband (Carla's son-in-law) who will become a stay-at-home dad. While having lunch with her friends, Carla gave everyone this update while rolling her eyes. "I think he just wants more time to play with his woodworking in the basement. He's just being lazy. I hope this phase doesn't last long and he goes back to work soon."

IMMEDIATE OPPORTUNITY: All the people sitting at that table have an opportunity to push back on Carla's comment. It doesn't have to be done in a mean way; someone just needs to point out that if we are going to move the needle on gender equality, then we need to be willing to rewrite rules for men as well as rules for women. Someone could remind Carla that she was pleased for her daughter years ago when she left the workforce to focus on family, and ask why she feels differently now. It would be extra helpful if someone explained, *I'm proud of your son for doing this. It can't be easy for men to be stay-at-homes, so I think we should all do as much to support him and your daughter as possible. I think they're setting a great example.*

BIG-PICTURE OPPORTUNITY: We all accidentally make gendered mistakes by setting different expectations for people of different genders. But without reminders from our friends, how do we expect to grow? These comments are not innocent—they can cause harm. So, say something.

☐ SCENARIO 8. FITTING ROOMS: Hiro was out on a Saturday afternoon shopping with his girlfriend. When she took an armful of clothes to try on in the fitting room, Hiro found a couch nearby and sat down. Just as he was about to pull his phone out of his pocket, another guy sitting close by spoke up. "You wasting a Saturday here, too? Man, I hate this. But I guess we gotta pay our dues, right?"

IMMEDIATE OPPORTUNITY: Hiro didn't want to throw his girlfriend under the bus. He loves her, and making a joke at her expense felt wrong. But he didn't want to be offensive to this guy either. So, he just smiled and said, "I don't mind actually. She does so much for me and for us—it is literally the least I can do."

BIG-PICTURE OPPORTUNITY: It is no secret that men often bond at the expense of women or use their partner to get a laugh. But going along with these tropes, even when they appear outwardly harmless, just reinforces the old "ball and chain" stereotypes. So, when a friend or, as in this case, a stranger makes a comment, don't take the bait. Reframe the conversation right back to equal partnership—in which you both do things for each other. Maybe that guy Hiro met at the dressing room will think twice before making a comment in the future.

☐ SCENARIO **9.** MATERNAL GATEKEEPING: A bunch of friends got together on a Sunday afternoon. Everyone was excited that Douglas and Ryan brought their infant daughter with them. Douglas is the oldest of six kids and grew up taking care of others; Ryan is an only child and has very little experience with kids or babies. During brunch it became obvious that Douglas, who had taken parental leave and was currently staying home with the baby, was very dismissive of Ryan's help. He was constantly making jokes about Ryan's lack of knowledge about babies, retelling a story about Ryan putting a diaper on backward, and repeatedly criticized Ryan for holding the baby the "wrong" way.

IMMEDIATE OPPORTUNITY: Everyone at this gathering has the opportunity to step in and have a quiet word with Douglas. Maybe start with some questions: *Do you really think Ryan is an incapable father? Do you think maybe your comments are hurting his feelings?* Explain what maternal gatekeeping is and what the consequences can be. Sure, Douglas has more experience with kids. It is great that he can bring that expertise to the relationship. But maybe he could encourage Ryan instead of tear him down. A close friend might even suggest that Douglas find time every week to leave Ryan alone with the baby, so each of them has the time and space to create their own relationship with her.

BIG-PICTURE OPPORTUNITY: Maternal gatekeeping is more common than we realize, and it happens all the time—in big direct ways and in small passive ways. We have to work to not only recognize it, but change our language so we don't alienate men from being full and present fathers. Parenting is not a zero-sum game; both parents can be present without taking power away from the other.

☐ SCENARIO **10.** ALLOWING VULNERABILITY: Two parents host a large yard party for the Fourth of July. They literally invite everyone they know: school friends, neighborhood friends, and family. Conner is one of the attendees. While his kids run off to play in the bouncy castle, Conner hits the food table and is happy when he sees some familiar faces—neighborhood guys he regularly sees at the playground. During the usual round of pleasantries, someone asks Conner, "Hey man, how are you? I haven't seen you around much lately." Conner surprises himself (and others) by opening up. He tells the other dads that he hasn't been getting a lot of sleep, and his temper is shorter than he wishes. This morning he came down on his son pretty hard, and he's feeling really guilty about it. He admits he is struggling to balance work and kids, and he worries that he's an awful parent.

IMMEDIATE OPPORTUNITY: It would be easy for Conner's circle to make a joke and change the topic. After all, it can be uncomfortable for a man to show this level of vulnerability in a public place like a party. The opportunity here is for the other guys to be supportive. Assure him by saying something like, *Sure, we all feel this way. I totally get that.* With a kind response, Conner might find the friends he desperately needs right now. If dismissed, Conner might not open up again with others in the future. Even if the group makes a joke and moves on—an individual could find Conner later and follow up one-on-one. *Hey, you seemed pretty shaken up back there. Tell me what's going on.*

BIG-PICTURE OPPORTUNITY: We all need to remember the connection between vulnerability, empathy, and kindness, and work to overcome these discomforts to be the support that our friends and neighbors need.

In these moments or others, I also want you to be prepared to receive feedback. Once you open up conversations around gender, people might be quick to point out their own views and/or your own gender mistakes. This happens to me a lot; although I might feel defensive inside, I try not to react in a defensive way. Remember that listening to feedback does not mean you have to act on it. Saying something like, *I've heard that point before* or *Thanks for telling me your perspective* may appease the other person without compromising your own values.

Sometimes, I have to admit, people do catch me making a mistake, which may very well happen to you, too. In these moments I try to remember the EP40's advice of correcting mistakes, but not belaboring them. I will admit my blunder openly, apologize, and then move on. *Yeesh, that is a little embarrassing, I'll have to work on not doing that again in the future. Thanks for saying something.*

SOCIAL CHANGE IN THE WORKPLACE

Before I end this book, I want to bring the conversation back to the "work" aspect of gender equality at home. A dual-working household means that the two partners are also workers. We spend a great deal of time with our colleagues, which means they have the ability to influence us, and we may have the ability to influence them. We also have to work within the parameters of employers and employment situations, which greatly impact what we can (and cannot) do in the home.

Seventy percent of America's top-earning men have a stay-at-home partner.[1] What does that tell us? It means that, for those who have made it into the highest echelons of professional achievement, it helps to have a full-time domestic partner that allows them to focus their time and energy on their job. And it means that much of the leadership in our country, and the people making decisions about workplace policies, are people who have never had the experience of balancing two careers and a household.

I wanted to close this book with a brief discussion about the actions we can take to support *workers,* to enable them to do their paid job and be full and equal partners. Whether one's job is in a factory, a school, a business, a mall, a government office, or a farm—what can we do to support all workers being full participants inside the home? This book focused on social change that can happen in our personal lives, but we cannot hope for gender equality at home if we don't give people the systemic support in their place of work.

To help me answer this question, I spoke to Livia Lam, senior vice president at S360. Livia has a long history of writing workers' rights policy for both think tanks and legislators. She suggested that the answer to my question can be summarized with the concept of *job quality*. "If we start with the concept of job quality, then we begin with an intention to ensure some standards, and an acknowledgment that there is a gap. If we are held accountable to this standard, and agree that jobs should be [beneficial to equal partnerships], then we can think about the principles that embody job quality. If you are working, you have a right to job quality. And then from there, policies implement those principles."

Way back at the introduction of this book, I talked about living our gender values. I then filled the last nine chapters with ways that we could translate our values into behavior. What Livia suggested is essentially the same thing, but from the perspective of the worker. If we agree that we value gender equality in the home, and we acknowledge that the working environment greatly impacts that household balance, what structural standards should we require in the workplace in order to protect the home? Livia suggested the following five categories.

1. RESPECT: Workers should feel as though they are respected in their place of work and that their contributions are important to their employer. Respect is shown by treating people with dignity. Respect is also shown by paying workers a fair wage for their labor and eliminating pay gaps between men and women, between cisgender and trans or nonbinary people, and between white people and people of color.

2. BENEFITS: All workers should have a minimum package of benefits that allows them vacation days and health benefits. All workers need sick leave to care for themselves or a loved one on a short-term basis, as well as access to longer-term paid family leave if they need to care for a new baby, an aging parent, or a seriously ill partner.

3. SAFETY: All workers should feel safe at their place of employ-

ment. For those operating machinery, this means that protections are in place to keep them as safe as possible. If an accident occurs, they have the peace of mind that they will be cared for. Safety is also important for women, people with disabilities, trans individuals, and nonbinary people who often suffer workplace harassment, which can include emotional, sexual, and physical attacks.

4. VOICE: All workers should feel that they have the ability to voice a grievance at work without fear of punishment. This can range from a worker reporting racism or sexism in the workplace to the human resources department, to voicing a concern about a safety procedure or a work environment.

5. CAREER MOBILITY: All workers should have access to some kind of career mobility. This could range from access to a promotional ladder, to movement into a supervisory position, to a wage increase. But knowing that one's hard work will be repaid with upward mobility in one way or another is important for all workers.

Supporting the above package would indeed be a way for us to collectively live our value of equal partnership by ensuring that both workers in a partnership had access to the resources needed to provide (both materially and emotionally) for the home. Livia suggested that by starting with the question, *What does the community need?* you flip the problem on its head and can figure out what policy solutions are needed. "If you see that the Black unemployment rate is twice that of the white unemployment rate, in a good economy, then you know your policies are flawed. Start with what that community needs, and work backwards."

Imagine how many issues in the home would be solved if both partners had access to the same set of workplace provisions. We would then have households where no one had fear of losing their job for speaking up against sexual harassment, where everyone could take a day off work to care for a sick child, where everyone made enough money working forty-hour weeks that they had enough free time to care for their household and community.

Michelle Travis, a law professor at the University of San Francisco School of Law and the author of *Dads for Daughters: How Fathers Can Give Their Daughters a Better, Brighter, Fairer Future,* told me that the law will not be our full solution to household inequality, but it must be part of the solution. Supporting laws and policies that lend protections to the above five areas is important. We need to support these issues when they are up for debate in our own organizations and industries, as well as in the voting booth when we cast our ballot for government representatives. Michelle also encourages readers to vote all the way down the ballot, as workers' rights decisions are often local.

Job quality supports the health and safely of the individual worker—which supports the health and safely of that worker's home, which they may very well share with another worker. So, when you think about actions you can take to support equality in the home, consider what you can also influence in the workplace. Sure, readers in leadership roles can work on structural changes to make sure their company or organizational policies give employees the time they need to be full caregiving participants in their home. But *every* working reader can participate in some simple social changes that help improve day-to-day job quality and promote equality at home.

- Remember the argument for "leaving loudly" in chapter 4? Male readers can help normalize caregiving by being open about taking a parent to the doctor or a child to a dentist appointment.
- For those workplaces that offer parental leave, we need to create a culture of support that encourages all employees

311

(including men) to take advantage of that benefit. This is a critical point that cannot be emphasized enough. For too long, we've had an "on the books but not in practice" attitude to caregiving leave.

- Share your personal story with your colleagues. If you are of a previous generation that didn't allow for extended leave, then be vocal about how harmful that policy was for your generation. If you enjoyed parental leave, tell others how important and foundational that time was for your own equal partnership. Talk about this with leadership, your union, your human resources department, or any other decision-making body that has the authority to effect change.

During the pandemic, I co-facilitated an online, global women's leadership program. We met once a week for six months, and like any video conferencing group, we got to know each other's shoulders and faces, but we never saw each other's bodies.

About midway through the six-month program, one participant from Cameroon turned on her camera at the beginning of the session to reveal that she was sitting in a hospital room. We were all shocked and concerned! But then she held up a beautiful baby to the camera and said, with a big smile, "Oh no—I'm not sick! I'm here because I gave birth yesterday!" While we all cheered and clapped, another participant commented, "It is just like being a man! You can work right up to birth and no one knows you are even expecting!" We all laughed.

I can't stop thinking about the truth behind those words. A non-birthing parent can work right up to the end of a pregnancy; if they prefer, they never have to tell colleagues there is a baby on the way. Though most people choose to share the happy news, one could absolutely keep that information hidden. There is power and privilege in choices—deciding when, if, and to whom one divulges information. However, birthing parents have no choice but to display their growing belly to their colleagues. They are also forced to maintain job performance while negotiating back pain, swollen ankles, fatigue, nausea, and anxiety—just to name a few challenges.

What can we do to level the playing field, so to speak? I think it is great to encourage all expecting parents (not just those carrying the baby) to attend the seemingly countless prenatal checkups together. We even have research showing that fathers' participation in prenatal visits improves the health of babies, if that helps convince your human resources department.[2]

If your workplace has a tradition around baby showers, I suggest you give these for *all* expecting parents, and not just women. (See chapter 4 for examples.) Send the message that this person's life is going to change when that baby is born, that they have a lot of new responsibilities, and that you are there to support them in any way you can.

In addition to events, I think there are changes we can make in everyday interactions. We can simply initiate meaningful conversation with our colleagues: at the water cooler, in the lunch room, at the bus stop. Sometimes, simply opening up the space for a deeper, more meaningful dialogue is enough. I know some people will feel very uncomfortable with this tactic, and might even see it as intrusive. But remember, pregnant people get these questions *all the time*. What is the harm in asking the same questions of all parents? We won't know what could be until we give it a try. I have written some suggested conversation starters below.

Here's a word of advice—that I give to myself as much as I give to others. We all like to share our own experiences and our own stories, especially those of us who are parents. What is more fun than reminiscing about our babies and birth stories? But if you intentionally choose to ask an expecting parent one or more of the following questions, try to hold back your own thoughts. Let them speak. Listen to them. Remember that this exercise is about them and not you.

TEN WORKPLACE QUESTIONS FOR NEW PARENTS AND PARENTS-TO-BE OF ALL GENDERS

1. What about being a parent are you most excited about?
2. What about being a parent are you most anxious or worried about?
3. What kind of parent are you hoping to be?
4. What is your family's caregiving plan for the new baby?
5. Have you made any changes to your home to prepare for the baby—a nursery, or a bassinet in your room? (Everyone likes sharing details about welcoming a baby home. Don't assume this is only appropriate for women.)
6. What is the best baby gift you have received so far? Why do you like it so much?
7. Have you read any baby or parenting books that have been interesting? What have you learned?
8. Have you spoken to the human resources department about your options for parental leave? Do you feel like you have all the information you need, or do you still have questions?
9. Are you nervous about taking so much time off work? Do you and your supervisor have a good "reentry" plan for you when you come back after parental leave?

> 10. Is there anything I can do to support you during the next few
>   months? (If they can't think of anything in the moment—extend an
>   open invitation. Encourage them to come talk to you at any time if
>   they need an empathetic ear.)

MOVING FORWARD

And here we are—nearly at the end. You will soon finish this book. And then what? What are you going to do next? How will you use this information in your own life? What are you going to act on? Who are you going to talk to? What language will you stop using or start using?

You have already answered most of these questions. Your "aha" moments are recorded throughout the chapters, ready to be translated into your own life.

1. Flip back to review the notes you made at the ends of part 1 and part 2.
2. Review your work on the mini-actions in chapter 9.
3. Review the phrases you put a star next to in chapter 9.
4. Review the scenarios you circled in chapter 10.

All that is left now is a bit of organization. Take a few minutes to write down your top ideas in each of the five categories in the table below. Please be realistic; be kind to yourself and choose actions and language that you know you can handle at this point in your life. You can always challenge yourself further in the future. For now, start with a plan you know you can handle. When you are done, and if you feel comfortable, share these ideas with another person. Maybe a friend, your partner, or one of your identified gender allies. Sometimes the sheer act of voicing intentions out loud makes them become real and helps us see them through to completion.

LIVING MY GENDER VALUES

Myself. What have you learned about yourself? Maybe you are more gender aware than you thought, or less gender aware. What goals do you have for yourself? Which words do you want to stop using, and which words do you want to start using?

_____

_____

_____

_____

My Household. Maybe you need to step up more, or step back more. Maybe you need to initiate some conversations or change some of the words you use with your kids. If you are single, maybe this doesn't apply to you now, but it may be something to consider in the future. How can you communicate household expectations to a future partner?

_____

_____

_____

_____

My Workspace. What can you do to support gender equality at work? Do you have the power to make structural changes that support all workers? How can you better support your colleagues?

My Friends and Family. What kind of role model do you want to be, and to whom? How will you encourage others to get out of gender default? Do you want to push back on any gender-norm assumptions in your family or circle of friends? How can you support young couples and families in your life?

My Community. Which of your communities do you want to influence? What kind of role model do you want to be? How will you reinforce gender-aware behavior? Do you want to learn more about a policy initiative in your town/state and become a supporter or advocate?

THANK YOU AND GOOD LUCK

Thank you for making it to the end with me. I am grateful for your interest in household gender equality and for the time you have invested in this topic already. I hope this book leaves you with heightened expectations for yourself and for others. Don't ever think, *It is too late* or *Small change won't matter anyway.* Just the opposite is true: it is never too late, and we should always do what we can, when we can, because every little bit helps. Remember that social change is a marathon, not a sprint. Pace yourself. Mistakes and missed opportunities are going to happen, so be forgiving of yourself and others.

Can I make just one last suggestion? Send a reminder to yourself to come back to *Equal Partners* in about eighteen months. It is worth the time to look through your notes, take the Gender Checkup again, and update your mini-actions. New people come in and out of our lives, and perspectives change with new life experiences. You might find that what resonated with you during this first read may be very different from what piques your interest in the future. You may think of new ideas that you did not contemplate today. This is especially true during life's big milestones: meeting a new partner; moving; adding a baby, grandbaby, or stepchild to your family. But shifts in perspective can happen in the everyday acts of working, living, and parenting.

As you close the cover on this book and move on to another, I hope some of the stories stay with you. I hope you remember James, Martin, Dave, Jalecia, Dylan, or Lydia. I hope you start to "see" gender socialization more regularly in your daily lives, and thereby "see" more opportunities to role model parity.

As I said at the beginning, this is an all-hands-on-deck moment. Our household gender inequality is not an issue that someone else is going to solve for us. This is our collective problem, and we each have the power to do something about it. We're far from helpless, and we don't need to wait for policy solutions to save us from ourselves. We can do this, and we'll all be better off the sooner we start.

ACKNOWLEDGMENTS

I feel profound gratitude for my agent, Amanda Annis, who was a champion of *Equal Partners* from the start. Amanda is expert, writer, coach, cheerleader, and confidante all rolled into one extraordinary individual. Her calming, reassuring voice was always the perfect balance to my roller coaster of nerves. I will be forever grateful that I mustered the nerve to approach her AWP panel and introduce myself. (And many thanks to Bethany Rydmark and Natalia Birgisson, who helped me with the mustering. Without you two, I might never have left my chair.) Additional thanks to Nicole Robson at Trident Media for helping me express myself in less than 280 characters.

I am grateful to St. Martin's Press for taking a chance on this project, and for the opportunity to work with Anna deVries. Her thoughtful feedback and wise suggestions made this book so much better than I thought was possible. Thanks to Alex Brown for lightning-speed responses throughout the process; to Ginny Perrin for insightful production editing; to Denise Larrabee for meticulous copy editing; to Jonathan Bush for a beautiful cover design; to Nicola Ferguson for transforming a boring Word document into this book. I very much appreciate the support and creativity from Martin Quinn in marketing, Sophia Lauriello in publicity, and Laura Clark, the associate publisher of nonfiction. And one last giant "thank you" to the entire St. Martin's Press team; I appreciate each and every individual who helped bring this book to life.

ACKNOWLEDGMENTS

I am grateful to every expert, author, academic, focus-group participant, and journalist who answered my emails and made time to talk to me. I am *extra* grateful to the EP40 and EP+, who shared very personal information with a complete stranger. Each interview was inspiring, enlightening, and just—fun. I especially appreciate those who made the time to talk to me during the pandemic lockdowns while balancing work, childcare, and virtual learning. This book would not exist without each of you.

I am forever indebted to two friends: Amber Johnson and Caitlin Jenkins. Amber was enthusiastic from day one, read numerous drafts, gave honest feedback, and celebrated each milestone with me. Caitlin was always willing to talk about the nuances of this topic, edited my newsletter posts, and lovingly formatted all my citations. I am thankful for my early readers, those who introduced me to the EP40, and those generous people who always made time, including Ketayoun, Ashley, JCF, Joe & Emily, Samiha, Keegan, Patti, Amy, Chloe, Karen, Mollie, Allie, Pam, Golrokh, Cynthia & David, Sophie, Mark, Allison, Victoria, Brian, Reshma, Crystal, Jessica, and Jonathan.

I thank my parents for their unconditional and unending support, and for role modeling counter-stereotypes before I knew what those words meant. I am grateful for all the weekends my mom had to work, and all the weeknights my dad cooked dinner. I thank my brother, Dan, for teaching me about empathy, caregiving, and care receiving.

People often ask how one finds time to write a book when raising little kids. But it was precisely because of my family that I could write this book. Beatrice and James were so patient throughout this process, and always willing to lighten my mood with a laugh or a board game. Hey, guys—when this is over, we'll celebrate by eating ice cream for dinner. And donuts for dessert.

ACKNOWLEDGMENTS

And most of all, I never would have finished this book without Evan's unrelenting encouragement and support. He spent endless hours hashing out new ideas with me (oftentimes at very inopportune moments), read draft after draft, took the kids out of the house when I had an interview or needed writing time, agreed to include our personal stories in this book, and believed in me when I most doubted myself.

SELECT GENDER GLOSSARY

Cisgender: When a person identifies with the gender that was assigned to them at birth.

Female-Identifying: A person who identifies with being a woman, regardless of what gender was assigned to them at birth.

Female Role: The person in a relationship who performs the household tasks that are socially dictated as female-coded work. Anyone can fall into the Female Role, regardless of their gender identity. (My term)

Heteronormative/Heteronormativity: The assumption that all people are either male or female, and all people identify with the sex assigned to them at birth.

Male-Identifying: A person who identifies with being a man, regardless of what gender was assigned to them at birth.

Male Role: The person in a relationship who performs the household tasks that are socially dictated as male-coded work. Anyone can fall into the Male Role, regardless of their gender identity. (My term)

Neo-traditional: A term used by academics to describe the most common modern family makeup. A dual-working couple, with the Female Role taking on the additional burden of managing all household work.

Nonbinary: A broad term for people whose gender identity cannot be confined to the male/female binary. Nonbinary people may identify as both male and female; neither male nor female; or believe their gender is fluid.

Transgender: A broad term to describe people who are not cisgender. This term can include trans men, trans women, trans nonbinary, and cross-dressing people.

Queer: A broad term to describe people who do not identify as cisgender or heterosexual.

ADDITIONAL RESOURCES

Chapter 1: Darcy Lockman's *All the Rage: Mothers, Fathers, and the Myth of Equal Partnership* documents America's cultural past, explaining how we ended up in our current household situation.

Chapter 2: If you're interested in how feminist theory intersects with how men and boys are socialized, I highly suggest *The Will to Change* by bell hooks.

For more on the nuture-versus-nature conversation, I enjoyed reading Gina Rippon's *Gender and the Brain*. Her message is loud and clear: there is no such thing as a male brain or a female brain, but gendered social norms will—over time—produce a gendered brain.

Chapter 3: If you are a woman in a relationship with a man who is unwilling to discuss or change his behavior, I suggest you check out Mom's Hierarchy of Needs. Leslie Forde created and facilitates this online group and resource for women. She created this resource for other moms when she felt herself heading toward burnout. https://momshierarchyofneeds.com/

Brené Brown is the leading expert on working through and rejecting shame. Her books and website are fantastic resources for those who would like further help on this topic. I suggest starting with *The Gifts of Imperfection* or *I Thought It Was Just Me (But It Isn't.)*

Chapter 4: Eve Rodsky's *Fair Play: A Game-Changing Solution for When You Have Too Much to Do (and More Life to Live)* offers help to couples reallocating household tasks, including cognitive labor.

New America's Better Life Lab has a free, practical online collection of experiments for families to try in order to promote gender equality in the home. https://www.newamerica.org/better-life-lab/better-life-lab-collections/better-life-lab-experiments/

Chapter 5: If you want to read more about the intersection of gender and caregiving through a touching personal story, I recommend Kate Washington's book, *Already Toast: Caregiving and Burnout in America.*

Chapter 8: For those who want to learn more about empathy, I suggest *The War for Kindness, Building Empathy in a Fractured World,* by Jamil Zaki. Thanks to Zaki's research, I learned that empathy is critical in human relations because it lies at the core of kindness. I also learned that empathy is partly genetic and partly learned.

Peggy Ornstein's books *Girls and Sex* and *Boys and Sex* are, in my opinion, must-reads for all parents. Your kids are never too young for you to read these stories; do not wait for them to be teens.

Chapter 9: If dad-readers are looking for affinity groups, try Fathering Together. This is an international, online group of dads who organize by both interest and location. I am especially fond of Dads for Gender Equity. https://www.fatheringtogether.org/register/dads-for-gender-equity/

Chapter 10: To find inspiration around job quality at your business or organization, Project Matriarchs crafted a Pledge to Care statement (free for download on their website), which encourages employers to pass caregiver-friendly policies. https://d3n8a8pro7vhmx.cloudfront.net/projectmatriarchs/pages/15/attachments/original/1627673679/Pledge_to_Care_Final_PDF.pdf?1627673679

Both Scott Behson's *The Whole-Person Workplace: Building Better Workplaces Through Work-Life, Wellness, and Employee Support* and David G. Smith and W. Brad Johnson's *Good Guys: How Men Can Be Better Allies for Women in the Workforce* offer information on workplace behavior and policy for leaders and managers.

NOTES

INTRODUCTION

1. Megan Cassella, "The Pandemic Drove Women Out of the Workforce. Will They Come Back?" *Politico*, July 22, 2021, https://www.politico.com /news/2021/07/22/coronavirus-pandemic-women-workforce-500329.

2. Jess Huang, Alexis Krivkovich, Ishanaa Rambachan, and Lareina Yee, "For Mothers in the Workplace, a Year (and Counting) Like No Other," *McKinsey and Company*, May 5, 2021, https://www.mckinsey.com/featured-insights /diversity-and-inclusion/for-mothers-in-the-workplace-a-year-and-counting -like-no-other.

3. Emily Peck, "Exclusive: Pandemic Could Cost Typical American Woman Nearly $600,000 in Lifetime Income," *Newsweek*, May 26, 2021, https://www .newsweek.com/2021/06/11/exclusive-pandemic-could-cost-typical-american -woman-nearly-600000-lifetime-income-1594655.html.

4. Arlie Russell Hochschild and Anne Machung, *The Second Shift: Working Parents and the Revolution at Home* (New York: Viking, 1989).

5. Sarah Thébaud, Sabino Kornrich, and Leah Ruppanner, "Good Housekeeping, Great Expectations: Gender and Housework Norms," *Sociological Methods and Research* 50, no. 3 (2019), doi/10.1177/0049124119852395.

1. OUR MODERN HOUSEHOLD REALITY

1. "The Rise in Dual Income Households," Pew Research Center, June 18, 2015, accessed August 27, 2021, https://www.pewresearch.org/ft_dual-income -households-1960–2012–2/.

2. "Employment Characteristics of Families 2020," U.S. Bureau of Labor

Statistics, Economic News Release, April 21, 2021, USDL-21–0695, https://www
.bls.gov/news.release/famee.nr0.htm.

3. Mylène Lachance-Grzela and Geneviève Bouchard, "Why Do Women
Do the Lion's Share of Housework? A Decade of Research," *Sex Roles* 63, no. 11
(2010): 767–780, doi.org/10.1007/s11199-010-9797-z.

4. Suzanne M. Bianchi, Liana C. Sayer, Melissa A. Milkie, and John P. Robinson, "Housework: Who Did, Does or Will Do It, and How Much Does It
Matter?" *Social Forces* 91, no. 1 (2012): 55–63, doi.org/10.1093/sf/sos120.

5. "Employment: Time Spent in Paid and Unpaid Work, by Sex," Organisation for Economic Co-operation and Development, accessed August 27, 2021,
https://stats.oecd.org/index.aspx?queryid=54757.

6. Sharon J. Bartley, Priscilla W. Blanton, and Jennifer L. Gilliard, "Husbands and Wives in Dual-Earner Marriages: Decision-Making, Gender Role
Attitudes, Division of Household Labor, and Equity," *Marriage & Family Review*
37, no. 4 (2005): 69–94, doi.org/10.1300/J002v37n04_05.

7. Scott Coltrane, "Research on Household Labor: Modeling and Mea-
suring the Social Embeddedness of Routine Family Work," *Journal of Marriage
and Family* 62, no. 4 (2000): 1208–1233, https://doi.org/10.1111/j.1741-3737.2000
.01208.x.

8. Allison Daminger, "The Cognitive Dimension of Household Labor," *American Sociological Review* 84, no. 4 (2019): 609–633, doi.org/10.1177/0003122419859007.

9. Kimberlee D'Ardenne, "Study Finds Women Who Feel Overly Responsible for Household Management and Parenting Are Less Satisfied with Their
Lives and Partnerships," *Arizona State University News*, January 22, 2019, https://
news.asu.edu/20190122-discoveries-asu-study-invisible-labor-can-negatively
-impact-well-being-mothers.

10. Mylène Lachance-Grzela, Shawna McGee, and Mylène Ross-Plourde,
"Division of Family Labor and Perceived Unfairness Among Mothers: The Role
of Mattering to Family Members," *Journal of Family Studies* 27, no. 3 (2021): 321–
335, doi.org/10.1080/13229400.2018.1564350.

11. Gary Barker, Aapta Garg, Brian Heilman, Nikki van der Gaag, and
Rachel Mehaffey, "State of the World's Fathers 2021: Structural Solutions to
Achieve Equality of Care Work," MenCare.org, accessed September 1, 2021,
https:\\210611_BLS21042_PRO_SOWF_ExeSumm.v04-web.pdf.

12. Makiko Fuwa and Philip N. Cohen, "Housework and Social Policy," *Social Science Research* 36, no. 2 (2007): 512–530, doi.org/10.1016/j.ssresearch.2006.04.005.

13. Erling Barth, Sari Pekkala Kerr, and Claudia Olivetti, "The Dynamics of Gender Earnings Differentials: Evidence from Establishment Data," *National Bureau of Economic Research*, May 2017, rev. July 2019, accessed September 1, 2021, doi.org/10.3386/w23381.

14. Justin Wolfers, "Fewer Women Run Big Companies Than Men Named John," *The New York Times*, March 2, 2015, https://www.nytimes.com/2015/03/03/upshot/fewer-women-run-big-companies-than-men-named-john.html.

15. "2020 Women on Boards Advances Goal to Gender-Balanced Corporate Boards with New Campaign Name and Vision: 50/50 Women on Boards," *Cision PR Newswire*, January 12, 2021, https://www.prnewswire.com/news-releases/2020-women-on-boards-advances-goal-to-gender-balanced-corporate-boards-with-new-campaign-name-and-vision-5050-women-on-boards-301206759.html.

16. "Too Few Women of Color on Boards: Statistics and Solutions (Quick Take)," *Catalyst: Workplaces that Work for Women*, January 31, 2020, https://www.catalyst.org/research/women-minorities-corporate-boards/.

17. "World University Rankings 2021," *Times Higher Education*, updated January 20, 2020, https://www.timeshighereducation.com/world-university-rankings/2021/world-ranking#!/page/0/length/25/sort_by/rank/sort_order/asc/cols/stats.

18. Coltrane, "Research on Household Labor."

19. Suzanne M. Bianchi, Liana C. Sayer, Melissa A. Milkie, and John P. Robinson, "Housework: Who Did, Does or Will Do It, and How Much Does It Matter?" *Social Forces* 91, no. 1 (2012): 55–63, doi.org/10.1093/sf/sos120.

20. "Engaging Men as Fathers in Gender Equality, Maternal and Child Health, Caregiving and Violence Prevention," Facilitator's Manual Produced by RWAMREC in Collaboration with Promundo-US for the MenCare+ Project in Rwanda, accessed September 1, 2021, https://promundoglobal.org/wp-content/uploads/2019/03/Male-Allyship-Study-Web.pdf.

21. Coltrane, "Research on Household Labor."

22. Joanna R. Pepin, Liana C. Sayer, and Lynne M. Casper, "Marital Status

and Mothers' Time Use: Childcare, Housework, Leisure, and Sleep," *Demography* 55, no. 1 (2018):107–133, https://doi.org/10.1007/s13524-018-0647-x.

23. Suzanne M. Bianchi, John P. Robinson, and Melissa A. Milkie, *Changing Rhythms of American Family Life* (New York: Russell Sage Foundation, 2006), http://www.jstor.org/stable/10.7758/9781610440516.

24. Claire Cain Miller, "How Same-Sex Couples Divide Chores, and What It Reveals About Modern Parenting," *The New York Times*, May 16, 2018, https://www.nytimes.com/2018/05/16/upshot/same-sex-couples-divide-chores-much-more-evenly-until-they-become-parents.html.

25. Ylva Moberg, "Does the Gender Composition in Couples Matter for the Division of Labor After Childbirth?" (working paper 2016:8, Institute for Evaluation of Labour Market and Education Policy, 2016), RePEc:hhs:ifauwp:2016_008.

26. Alyssa Schneebaum, "The Economics of Same-Sex Couple Households: Essays on Work, Wages, and Poverty" (PhD diss., University of Massachusetts Amherst, 2013), Open Access Dissertations 818, doi.org/10.7275/aan3–2p77.

27. Ellie Bothwell, "Female Leadership in Top Universities Advances for First Time since 2017," *Times Higher Education*, March 6, 2020, https://www.timeshighereducation.com/news/female-leadership-top-universities-advances-first-time-2017.

28. Coltrane, "Research on Household Labor."

2. SOCIALIZED INEQUALITY

1. Linda Thompson and Alexis J. Walker, "Gender in Families: Women and Men in Marriage, Work, and Parenthood," *Journal of Marriage and the Family* 51, no. 4 (1989): 845–871, https://doi.org/10.2307/353201.

2. Lachance-Grzela and Bouchard, "Why Do Women Do the Lion's Share of Housework?"

3. Claire Cain Miller, "A 'Generationally Perpetuated' Pattern: Daughters Do More Chores," *The New York Times*, August 8, 2018, https://www.nytimes.com/2018/08/08/upshot/chores-girls-research-social-science.html.

4. "Healthy Manhood," A Call to Men: The Next Generation of Manhood, accessed September 1, 2021, https://www.acalltomen.org/healthy-manhood/.

5. "Engaging Men as Fathers in Gender Equality, Maternal and Child Health, Caregiving and Violence Prevention."

6. Lina Eriksson, "Social Norms Theory and Development Economics" (policy research working paper no. 7450, World Bank Group, 2015), http://hdl.handle.net/10986/22863.

3. INEQUALITY WITHOUT KIDS

1. Kristen M. Shockley, Malissa A. Clark, Hope Dodd, and Eden B. King, "Work-Family Strategies During COVID-19: Examining Gender Dynamics Among Dual-Earner Couples with Young Children," *Journal of Applied Psychology* 106, no. 1 (2021): 15–28.

2. Rachel Minkin, "Most Americans Support Gender Equality, Even If They Don't Identify as Feminists," Pew Research Center, July 14, 2020, accessed September 6, 2021, https://pewrsr.ch/2OqNl93.

3. Leon Festinger, *A Theory of Cognitive Dissonance* (Palo Alto, CA: Stanford University Press, 1957).

4. Allison Daminger, "De-gendering Processes, Gendered Outcomes: How Egalitarian Couples Make Sense of Non-egalitarian Household Preferences," *American Sociological Review* 85, no. 5 (2020), doi.org/10.1177/0003122420950208.

5. Sanjiv Gupta, "Her Money, Her Time: Women's Earnings and Their Housework Hours," *Social Science Research* 35, no. 4 (2006): 975–999, doi.org/10.1016/j.ssresearch.2005.07.003.

6. Manuela Baretto and Naomi Ellemers, "The Burden of Benevolent Sexism: How It Contributes to the Maintenance of Gender Inequalities," *European Journal of Social Psychology* 35, no. 5 (2005): 633–642.

4. INEQUALITY WITH KIDS

1. Brigid Schulte, "Once the Baby Comes, Moms Do More, Dads Do Less Around the House," *The Washington Post*, May 7, 2015, https://www.washingtonpost.com/news/parenting/wp/2015/05/07/once-the-baby-comes-moms-do-more-dads-do-less-around-the-house/.

2. Sharon Lerner, "The Real War on Families: Why the U.S. Needs Paid Leave Now," *In These Times*, August 18, 2015, https://inthesetimes.com/article/the-real-war-on-families.

3. Brigid Schulte, Alieza Durana, Brian Stout, and Jonathan Moyer, "Paid Family Leave: How Much Time Is Enough?" New America: Better Life Lab, 2017, accessed September 6, 2021, https://www.newamerica.org/better-life-lab/reports/paid-family-leave-how-much-time-enough/a-timeline-of-paid-family-leave/.

4. Sarah. M. Allen and Alan J. Hawkins, "Maternal Gatekeeping: Mothers' Beliefs and Behaviors That Inhibit Greater Father Involvement in Family Work," *Journal of Marriage and Family* 61, no. 1 (1999): 199–212, doi:10.2307/353894.

5. Sarah Schoppe-Sullivan et al., "Maternal Gatekeeping, Coparenting Quality, and Fathering Behavior in Families with Infants," *Journal of Family Psychology* 22, no. 3 (2008): 389–398, doi:10.1037/0893-3200.22.3.389.

6. Bharathi J. Zvara, Sarah J. Schoppe-Sullivan, and Claire Kamp Dush, "Fathers' Involvement in Child Health Care: Associations with Prenatal Involvement, Parents' Beliefs, and Maternal Gatekeeping," *Family Relations Interdisciplinary Journal of Applied Family Science* 62, no. 4 (2013): 649–661, doi.org/10.1111/fare.12023.

5. FROM KING OF THE CASTLE TO EQUAL PARTNER

1. Jamil Zaki, *The War for Kindness: Building Empathy in a Fractured World* (New York: Crown, 2019).

6. TOWARD EQUAL PARTNERSHIP

1. Jo Jones and William D. Mosher, "Fathers' Involvement with Their Children: United States, 2006–2010," *National Health Statistics Reports* 71, December 20, 2013, https://www.cdc.gov/nchs/data/nhsr/nhsr071.pdf.

NOTES

7. EMBRACING EQUAL PARTNERSHIP

1. Ellen Lamont, "If You Want a Marriage of Equals, Then Date as Equals," *The Atlantic*, February 14, 2020, https://www.theatlantic.com/ideas/archive/2020/02/if-you-want-marriage-equals-then-date-equals/606568/.

2. Susan Kelley, "Hands-On, Intensive Parenting Is Best, Most Parents Say," *Cornell Chronicle*, January 15, 2019, https://news.cornell.edu/stories/2019/01/hands-intensive-parenting-best-most-parents-say.

3. Coltrane, "Research on Household Labor."

9. A MORE EQUAL SELF

1. Lacey J. Hilliard and Lynn S. Liben, "Differing Levels of Gender Salience in Preschool Classrooms: Effects on Children's Gender Attitudes and Intergroup Bias," *Child Development* 81, no. 6 (2010): 1787–1798, doi: 10.1111/j.1467-8624.2010.01510.x.

10. A MORE EQUAL COMMUNITY

1. Jill E. Yavorsky, Lisa A. Keister, Yue Qian, and Michael Nau, "Women in the One Percent: Gender Dynamics in Top Income Positions," *American Sociological Review* 84, no. 1 (2019), doi.org/10.1177/0003122418820702.

2. Sarah J. Scoppe-Sullivan, Kevin Shafer, Eric L. Olofson, and Claire M. Kamp-Dush, "Fathers' Parenting and Coparenting Behavior in Dual-Earner Families: Contributions of Traditional Masculinity, Father Nurturing Role Beliefs, and Maternal Gate Closing," *Psychology of Men & Masculinities* 22, no. 3 (2021): 538–550, doi.org/10.1037/men0000336.

INDEX